A
C
gr
Ormskirk Grammar School and Liverpool University. He recently took early retirement from teaching in order to write full-time but he has had a varied career, having worked for the BBC, IPC Business Press and as a marketing consultant before entering teaching. He loves travel and has spent part of the year abroad for the past twenty years, usually in France or Italy, since he is reasonably competent in both languages. He is deeply interested in the history and culture of Italy and has been the editor of a magazine dealing with Italian postal history for the past 17 years, a service for which he has gained international recognition. He is very fond of Venice, a fondness which even survived the fact that his first visit to the city was at the head of a party of 22 teenage schoolchildren.

Acknowledgments

For an inexhaustible supply of information about the city and the services offered to the visitor I am indebted to Cesare Battisti of the Azienda di Promozione Turistica of Venice. Useful additional information was provided by staff in the CIT Venice office. Nor must I forget a wealth of advice given by my friends in the Italy and Colonies Study Circle; in particular, Bruno Crevatto-Selvaggi who pointed the way to some of the lesser-known aspects of Venice.

For looking after me during my own visits to Venice I am indebted to the management and staff of the Hotel San Moisè and the Special Bookings department of Citalia, especially Grace. I was also assisted in my researches, especially in the leg work involved in covering the museums, galleries and churches, by my colleague, and tame art expert, Paul Bagshaw.

A Request

The authors and publisher have tried to ensure that this guide is as accurate and up-to-date as possible. Inevitably things change, hotels and restaurants open and close and prices go up. If you notice any changes that should be included in the next edition of this book, please write to Colin Pilkington c/o the publisher (address on title page). A free copy of the new edition will be sent to persons making a significant contribution.

Lascelles City Guides

VENICE

Colin Pilkington

Roger Lascelles, Cartographic and Travel Publisher
47 York Road, Brentford, Middlesex TW8 OQP. Tel: 081-847 0935

Publication Data

Title	Venice
Typefaces	Times and Helvetica
Photographs	Colin Pilkington and Don Ruprecht
Printing	Martin's of Berwick Ltd
ISBN	0 903909 95 2
Edition	1992
Publisher	Roger Lascelles
	47 York Road, Brentford, Middlesex, TW8 0QP
Producer	Snap! Books
	129 Leighton Gardens, London NW10 3PS
Copyright	Colin Pilkington (Text)
	Colin Pilkington and Don Ruprecht (Photographs)

Distribution

Africa:	South Africa	– Faradawn, Box 17161, Hillbrow 2038
Americas:	Canada	– International Travel Maps and Books, PO Box 2290, Vancouver BC V6B 3W5
	U.S.A.	– Available through major booksellers with good foreign travel sections
Asia:	India	– English Book Store, 17-L Connaught Circus, PO Box 328, New Delhi 110 001
Australasia:	Australia	– Rex Publications, 15 Huntingdon Street, Crows Nest, N.S.W.
Europe:	Belgium	– Brussels – Peuples et Continents
	Germany	– Available through major booksellers with good foreign travel sections
	GB/Ireland	– Available through all booksellers with good foreign travel sections
	Italy	– Libreria dell 'Automobile, Milano
	Netherlands	– Nilsson & Lamm BV, Weesp
	Denmark	– Copenhagen – Arnold Busck, G.E.C. Gad, Boghallen
	Finland	– Helsinki – Akateeminen Kirjakauppa
	Norway	– Oslo – Arne Gimnes/J. G. Tanum
	Sweden	– Stockholm/Esselte, Akademi Bokhandel, Fritzes, Hedengrens Gothenburg/Gumperts, Esselte Lund/ Gleerupska
	Switzerland	– Basel/Bider: Berne/Atlas; Geneve/ Artou; Lausanne/Artou; Zurich/Travel Bookshop

Contents

Introduction

Introduction

You can visit Rome, Florence or Naples and tell your friends, 'I went to Italy'. But, if you visit Venice you say, 'I went to Venice'. Because Venice is not really Italy: it is nowhere but Venice, gloriously unique.

Henry James said that Venice is the easiest city in the world 'to visit without going there'. Venice has been written about, sung about, painted, drawn, photographed and filmed so often that it seems as if we should know every stone in its buildings and every ripple on its canals.

Yet, for all that it seems familiar, there are aspects of Venice that you can only experience at first hand. There are massive skies over the lagoon and a strange quality of light that comes partly from those skies, and partly from its reflections in the water. And, while everyone knows about the canals and the old buildings, it is still a considerable surprise to experience a modern city without motor vehicles and skyscraper blocks. Faced with this thousand-year accumulation of art, architecture and history you may well be forgiven for wondering where to start. The aim of this book is to help you to make that start and to discover this fascinating city for yourself.

Obviously the place to start is with the monuments and sights described in this book. But I also hope to encourage you, as a visitor to Venice, to look for yourself and make your own casual discovery. It may be an obscure painting in a little-visited church; or an idyllically peaceful, secluded square overlooked by the crowds; or simply the best pizza you have ever tasted. Whatever it is, rest assured that you will find it, because the most signal fact about Venice is that, however well you think you may know it, the city always has the power to surprise. To visit Venice is never an anti-climax. No matter how great the anticipation; the reality always exceeds the expectation.

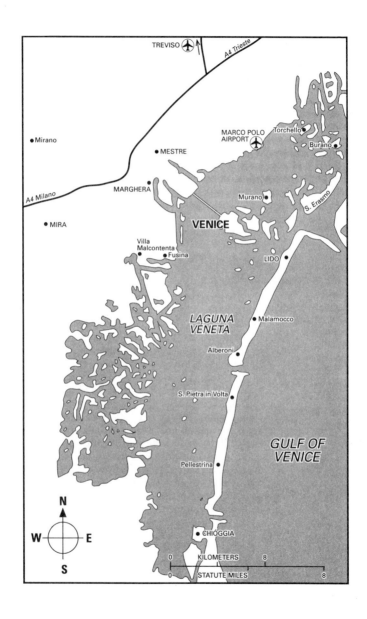

ONE

Venice and the Venetians

The first pedestrianised city

All over the world cities are attempting to cope with the motor car and vehicular traffic. To town planners trying to deal with the problem Venice must seem like the impossible dream. Certainly, the lack of motorised traffic is the first thing to strike the visitor to Venice. The noise is different, the air is scented differently, even the pace of movement about the city is different. Elsewhere in the world they are having to recreate historic streets or villages, so that a visitor can envisage how our ancestors lived. In Venice there is no need to wonder what the past was like because, in Venice more than anywhere, the past is what you see around you. It would be possible to take one of Canaletto's drawings of St Mark's Square in the 18th century and send it home as a picture postcard because the view is virtually unaltered today. In nowhere more than Venice is a visitor more aware of the unique history and geography of a city.

The Lagoon

The great rivers of Northern Italy pour their waters into the Adriatic Sea, carrying with them mud and silt brought down from the Alps. Trapped in the land-locked cul-de-sac of the sea, the silt is carried backwards and forwards on currents and tides until it is finally deposited as a coastal strip that is neither land nor water, which extends northwards from Ravenna, around the head of the Adriatic, almost as far as Trieste. It is a strange country of low-lying, marshy islands and shallow lagoons with a beauty of its own, albeit a sad and desolate beauty. In this unpromising environment arose one of the great cities of the world.

St. Mark's Square, from an eighteenth century engraving of a Canaletto drawing.

Origins

When Goths and Vandals burst into the Roman Empire in the 5th century the lagoon country seemed to be the ideal place where refugees from Roman cities around the coast could hide in safety from the invaders. A Venetian legend says that the city was founded at twelve noon on Friday, March 25th, 421 AD, when three consuls from Padua established a settlement on the islands of the Rialto. Reality is nowhere near so precise. The islands of the lagoon were at first no more than a temporary haven, the refugees returning to their cities when the barbarians had passed by. Increasingly, however, the refugees tended to stay, especially after the fury of Attila and the Huns swept through the region in 452.

The need to use boats in the watery world of the lagoons turned the refugees into proficient seamen. When Byzantine forces attempted to recapture Italy in 539 they raised a naval fleet from ships belonging to the lagoon-dwellers, then known as the Venetii. This was when the first two churches were built on the Rialto, in the vicinity of the present-day St Mark's Square.

Next came the Lombards, most ferocious of the barbarian

tribes, before whom there was a permanent evacuation of the mainland cities; their entire populations transferring to various islands in the lagoon. This was a loose association of independent communities, forever quarrelling among themselves, but they elected a common leader whom they called *dux*. In the Venetian dialect this Latin word for ' leader' was pronounced *Doge*.

The foundation of Venice as we know it came when the Franks under King Pepin arrived in the lagoons in the year 810, to demand their submission to the Western Emperor. The inhabitants chose to confront him at their chief settlement of Malamocco, while the women and children were sent for safety to the islands of the Rialto, centrally situated and far more easily defended. That ease of defence meant that, when Pepin retired in defeat, the people of the lagoon chose to move from their scattered settlements to the Rialto.

In 811 a treaty between the Western and Eastern Empires agreed that the Venetian settlements belonged to the Byzantine Empire, an agreement which gave the Venetians those trading concessions throughout the Eastern Mediterranean that were the foundation of the city's wealth. Moreover, by looking to the East, Venice avoided the political troubles that plagued the rest of Italy throughout the Middle Ages.

In the late 820s two merchants sailed into Venice with a priceless cargo; the body of St Mark the Evangelist, already patron saint of the Patriarch of Grado and the Lagoon. The official story was that the body had been smuggled out of Alexandria in order to save it from desecration by the Saracen rulers of Egypt, but it is far more likely to have been a straightforward theft. Whatever the truth, the effect on Venice was immediate. Mark replaced Theodore as patron saint of the city and a chapel was built to house the saint's body. Located between the Doge's Palace and the Church of St Theodore the chapel was destined to become the Doge's Chapel but would also grow into the Basilica of St Mark. The winged lion which represented the Evangelist would become the badge of the city-state.

The Venetian Empire

It was an age of expansion. Venice signed a commercial treaty with the Saracens to obtain trading benefits throughout the Eastern Mediterranean. The rest of the Christian world condemned them for trading with the infidel but, good Catholics though they were, the Venetians never let religion get in the way of business. Venice also began to acquire towns and ports along the Dalmatian Coast, initially because foundations for buildings on the Rialto required timber piles that were driven into the mud, and later timber and stone for the buildings themselves, all commodities that were in short supply on the islands of the lagoon. Wealth began to flood into the city, especially after 1094 when the Doge decreed that every merchant returning from the East must bring back at least one work of art to decorate the Basilica of St Mark.

Recognition of Venice's standing in the world came in 1177 when the city was chosen as the setting for the reconciliation between the Western Emperor, Frederick Barbarossa, and Pope Alexander III. The pomp and pageantry that Venice laid on for this meeting firmly established the city as one of the powers of Europe and the Doge as an equal of popes and emperors.

Beyond pious statements and expressions of goodwill, Venice played little part in the early Crusades as they were doing too much good business with the Saracens of the Levant to go to war with them. Venetian activity was restricted to competing with Genoa and Pisa for trading privileges in the Frankish Kingdom of Jerusalem. Venice's greatest opportunity and most inglorious act came, after the fall of Jerusalem, with the Fourth Crusade.

In 1201 the crusaders contracted with Venice for transportation to Egypt. The Doge, Enrico Dandolo, blind and an octogenarian but a consummate negotiator, agreed an exorbitant fee with the crusaders, plus a monopoly of trading rights for Venice in whatever territories were conquered by the crusaders. However, when the Crusade turned up in Venice there was only one third of the expected numbers and they could not afford the agreed fee. Dandolo offered them concessionary rates in return for help in regaining the port of Zara from the Hungarians. This they agreed to and carried out. Dandolo then went on to suggest that the crusaders could further assist in restoring by force a pretender to the Byzantine throne. This led to the siege, storm and subsequent sack of Constantinople in April 1204, one of the greatest acts of wanton destruction in history, the crusaders burning or smashing everything in their way. The Venetians had no part in the destruction. They were systematically plundering the city, shipping innumerable works of art back to Venice, including the most famous plunder — the four bronze horses from the Hippodrome which for so long decorated the facade of St Mark's.

The Venetians' main spoils from the Fourth Crusade were, in the famous phrase, *one quarter and half of one quarter of the Empire*. The Venetian Empire spread from the Adriatic to the Black Sea and included colonies in Corfu, Crete and the Morea. Its influence spread beyond as, in 1292, Marco Polo returned from the Court of Kublai Khan, forging trade links that stretched from Venice to China.

The Dreaded Council of Ten

The Council of Ten as a state security body was founded as a temporary measure in 1310 but remained in existence for the rest of the life of the Republic. It was amazingly efficient. There were no major uprisings in Venice as there were elsewhere in Italy and the Republic existed for a thousand years without the tyranny of one-man or one-family rule. The reputation of the Council was fearful. It was commonly believed that a denunciation slipped into one of the *bocca di leone* boxes would result in the disappearance and elimination of the one denounced. There were rumours of midnight arrests, blood-stained torture chambers, corpses in weighted sacks dropped into the Lagoon at dead of night. To the liberal-minded 18th century the spectre of the Council of Ten with a network of spies throughout Europe represented the same object of fear and hate as the Gestapo or KGB assumed in the 20th century. And yet it was largely mythical. There were so many safeguards in the complicated Venetian constitution that the Ten did not have half the powers they were supposed to have. There were almost as many prosecutions for false and malicious denunciations as there were actions taken as the result of denunciations, the worst torture inflicted in the torture chamber was suspending prisoners under interrogation by their wrists and when Napoleon's soldiers burst into the prisons to free the political prisoners they found only criminals. The fact was that the reputation of the Council of Ten was little more than a brilliant public relations exercise. They very seldom needed to do anything; the fear engendered by their reputation was enough to deter anyone from contemplating action against the state.

Decline

The decline of Venice began at the very moment of her greatest triumph. The commercial dominance of Venice that resulted from the Fall of Constantinople led to bitter wars with her chief trading rival, Genoa. For a time Genoa seemed to come out on top, when her forces occupied Chioggia and her ships penetrated the Lagoon, but the war ended in stalemate and it was Genoa who went under. The financial drain of the wars, however, had seriously weakened Venice.

The wars with Genoa had turned the eyes of Venice westwards and, during the 14th century, the city turned increasingly to the west. The ambitions of Gian Galeazzo Visconti for a united Northern Italy under Milanese control led to Venetian fears for the security of her food supplies and trade routes and, in a policy of expansion, Venetian rule was extended over increasing areas of the *Terra Firma*, as they called the mainland of Italy. Treviso, Padua, Vicenza and Verona; one by one the cities of the Veneto came under the control of the Venetian Republic. By the end of the 15th century Venice controlled half of Lombardy as well as the Veneto. Yet this apparent growth in power carried with it the seeds of decay because, while up to that time Venice had belonged more to the Levant than to Italy, the city was now fatally entwined in Italian politics. The power, wealth and what was seen as the arrogance of Venice provoked the envy and hostility of the other Italian states and, what was worse, attracted the attention of powers from beyond the Alps. At its worst this hatred and enmity led to the League of Cambrai in the early 16th century when Venice stood alone against an alliance that included the Pope, France, Spain and the Empire as well as all the other Italian states. Secure in her Lagoon Venice survived but this constant threat further depleted the once overflowing Venetian coffers.

Most serious of all was the Turkish threat. When Mehmet took Constantinople and ended the Byzantine Empire it was the beginning of the end for Venice. It took 200 years and there were glorious reversals like the Battle of Lepanto, the Siege of Candia and the 25-year reoccupation of the Morea, but these were mere interruptions in an inevitable decline. Crete, the Aegean, the Morea and Cyprus all fell to the Turks, even Corfu and Dalmatia were threatened. By the end of the 17th century most of the Venetian Empire had gone.

As political power waned, so did the commercial. The expensive monopoly that Venice maintained over trade with the East led the maritime nations to seek their own supplies. Portugal discovered the Cape route to India and the Spice Islands. Spain, with the help of the Genoese Christopher Columbus, discovered the Americas. The reliance of western Europe upon Venice for the silks and spices they craved was broken for ever. At the same time Venetian superiority in ship-building was undermined. The strength of Venice had always been the narrow-beamed galley. But to the west of Venice the maritime nations were developing wide-beamed sailing ships that could either carry large cargoes as merchant vessels, or mount increasing numbers of cannon as warships. The days of the Most Serene Republic's maritime supremacy had also gone.

Decadence

It seems an exaggeration to say that nothing happened in the 18th century but, as far as Venice is concerned, very little did. Once a major European power, Venice now became aggressively neutral, a policy sustained by highly skilled diplomacy. Through the wars of the Spanish and Austrian Successions and the Seven Years War Venice remained neutral and aloof.

Venice had found instead its future as a tourist city. It was the age of the Grand Tour and there was no one with pretensions to culture in Northern Europe who did not visit Venice at one time or another. There are more paintings by Canaletto in England than anywhere else because a whole generation of young aristocrats brought back a picture of Venice as a souvenir of their tour; stately homes in Northern Europe were built according to the ideas developed by Palladio, and painters, writers and musicians took home the inspiration they had found in the city.

There were less cultured pleasures in casinos, gambling hells, masked balls and sexual adventures; this was, after all, the age of Casanova. The Carnival reached new heights at this period to last the best part of six months, and many otherwise sober individuals lost their inhibitions behind the anonymity of carnival masks. There was also a more sinister side as Venetian diplomacy gave them a reputation for deviousness and cunning. The city's security watchdog, the Council of Ten, did not discourage exaggerated rumours of denunciations, midnight arrests, deep dungeons and devilish tortures.

Hedonistic but vaguely sinister, debauched and devious, it was a very different Venice from the expansionist, merchant-venturer city-state of the Middle Ages that faced Napoleon in his invasion of Italy in 1797. With the French Army massed menacingly on the shores of the Lagoon, and faced with an ultimatum from General Bonaparte, the Grand Council met and voted itself out of existence. The last Doge removed his ceremonial cap and the Most Serene Republic ceased to exist.

To the United Kingdom of Italy

Napoleon gave Venice to Austria but took it back in 1805 as part of his Kingdom of Italy and it remained French until 1815, with the city looted to the benefit of French art collections. The Congress of Vienna after the fall of Bonaparte gave Venice back to the Austrians; the city and its province became part of the Kingdom of Lombardy-Venetia within the Austro-Hungarian Empire.

The Austrians were hated and Venice was the scene of one of the most successful rebellions against Austria during the 1848 'Year of Revolutions', when Daniel Manin led the citizens into declaring a reborn Republic of Venice which lasted from March 1848 to August 1849. It was under the Austrians, however, that Venice was first joined to the mainland; they built the causeway that carries the railway into the island city. In other respects, however, Austria contributed to the ruin of Venice because they built up their own port of Trieste as the Empire's main outlet onto the Mediterranean. Deprived of purpose the city lapsed into poverty and during the 19th century most of Venice's treasures were sold off by churches and patrician families.

It was 1866 before Venice could break free from Austria to join the newly united Kingdom of Italy. For a long time the new political order made little difference to Venice which remained impoverished. But the importance of maritime communications to a unified country, that is largely mountainous in the interior, led to a modest revival of Venice as a port and ship-building centre. The end of the 19th century, however, saw the establishment of tourism as the city's main industry. This was the era of the great hotels such as the Danieli and the development of the Lido as the first sea-bathing resort on the Mediterranean.

Invaders from the East

The latest problem for Venice is an influx of day-trippers from East Germany, Hungary and Czechoslovakia. As the Iron Curtain collapsed the inhabitants of Eastern Europe rushed to see the fabled city they had all heard of but not been allowed to visit for 40 years. In June 1990 the number of coaches arriving in Venice from Eastern Europe was a mind-boggling 1,200 a day. With each coach carrying about 50 passengers, that was a daily influx of 60,000 people. To make matters worse the East Europeans do not have much money to spare and, once they have scraped together the fare to Venice, they have nothing to spend in the cafes, restaurants and shops of the city. To the dismay of Venetians, they have seen Venice become desperately over-crowded without any compensatory financial benefit to the economy of the city.

The New Venice

Venice was one of the first cities in Italy to adopt Fascism and it was well-rewarded by the regime after it took power in 1922. The vision of a revival of Venice came from Count Giuseppe Volpi who began to develop the city's potential after the First World War and who was able to promote the interests of Venice through his own prominence in the Fascist Party; he was Mussolini's Minister of Finance in the early 30s. The towns of Marghera and Mestre across the Lagoon were developed as a new port, industrial complex and residential area. A road bridge was built alongside the railway to link the historic centre with its expanding suburbs. This growth continued with ever-increasing pace after the Second World War, not always with the best of results for Venice. The historic centre of Venice has become a city almost one hundred percent devoted to the care and entertainment of the visitor and tourist. Twenty million people visit the city every year and provide its life-blood, while native Venetians have dropped to no more than 80,000 according to the last census.

The Venetian Character

Venetians are more withdrawn, brusquer and less outgoing than most Italians. To southerners the Venetian is cold, arrogant and secretive but, living in a society with a secret police like the Council of Ten, taught the Venetians the value of guarding their tongues and avoiding commitment. Even today they remain largely taciturn and non-commital. In many ways the symbol of Venice is the mask that was and is worn at Carnival time because most Venetians, now as in the past, can only lose their inhibitions and be truly themselves when shielded behind the mask. The centuries of commercial activity have made the Venetians good at business and careful with money. They are fond of outward show and, just as they decorated their city and buildings and developed glass-blowing into a *rococo* art form, they lavish great care on their personal adornment; Venetians are very smart and fashion conscious. The character of the Venetian people is very like that of their churches: highly decorative and showy on the outside, shadowy and secretive within.

Festivals

All that history and a Venetian talent for pomp and pageantry has created a series of festivals and events throughout the year which both bolsters civic pride and entertains the visitors.

First, chronologically and in importance, is **Carnival**. The word is Venetian in origin and derives from *Carne Vale* (Farewell to Meat). It is, like *Mardi Gras* celebrations elsewhere, a last fling of merrymaking before the fast of Lent. Historically it began on St Stephen's Day (December 26) and lasted until Shrove Tuesday but, at its height in the 18th century, it expanded to fill half the year. It was celebrated by a mixture of religious and civic ceremonies together with popular entertainments such as dancing in the streets and bull-catching in the *campi*. The culmination was on the final Thursday of Carnival (*Giovedì Grasso*) when an orchestra played in an ornate pavilion set up in the Piazzetta while rival groups competed at building human pyramids and dancing the *Moresca* — a sort of Morris Dance. At the end of the evening the bandstand exploded in a set-piece firework display. On the following Tuesday there was a Ball in the Piazza and other squares, festivities that ended abruptly at midnight with the onset of Ash Wednesday.

After the fall of the Republic, Carnival declined until it was nearly forgotten. In the late 70s it was spontaneously revived by the young of Venice and surrounding cities such as Padua and Vicenza. After three years it was officially recognised by the city authorities who now organise events for Carnival and have turned it into a major tourist attraction. Many people don the traditional cloak, tricorne hat and white half-masks while the many exhibitionists have special costumes and masks made at great cost so that a feature of the scene are extravagances of fantasy and transvestism. The modern festivities last for the ten days prior to Lent and culminate on Shrove Tuesday with a masked ball for the *glitterati* and dancing in the Piazza S. Marco for everyone.

April 25th is **St Mark's Day**, a public holiday marked by religious ceremonies and processions. In Venice it has a similar function to St Valentine's Day elsewhere, as it is the day when men traditionally present a rosebud to the ladies they most admire. The day also marks the start of the rowing and regatta season in Venice. In the Basilica of St Mark the *Pala d'Oro* is exposed on the high altar (it can also be seen at Christmas and Easter).

Ascension Day (or **Festa della Sensa** in Venetian dialect) sees one of the oldest traditions in Venice's history. In the year 1000 a Venetian fleet had defeated the pirates who infested the Adriatic and had imposed Venetian control over much of the Dalmatian coast. It was decreed that on every Ascension Day, anniversary of the fleet's departure, the Doge and dignitaries of Venice would sail out to the mouth of the Lagoon off the Lido and hold a ship-board service of thanksgiving. Towards the end of the twelfth century (legend says it was as a result of Pope Alexander's visit in 1177) the ceremony expanded to include the ceremony of a gold ring thrown into the sea. Thus began the *Sposalizio del Mar* (Marriage to the Sea) which grew ever more splendid, as did the state-galley *Bucintoro*, until it all came to an end with the fall of the Republic. Today there is a watered down version of the ceremony with the Mayor, the

Patriarch and other notables making the crossing to the Lido in what passes nowadays as the official barge. The service of commemoration is held, as it always was held, in the church of S. Nicolò on the Lido.

Also on a Sunday in late May is the **Vogalunga**, the 'Long Row', which is a non-competitive rowing marathon open to all comers. The course runs from St Mark's Basin to Burano by way of the eastern end of the city and returns through the Cannaregio Canal and the Grand Canal to end at the Punta della Dogana; a distance of 32 kilometres. Over 5,000 rowers take part in about 1,500 boats of all shapes and sizes. Departure is at 9.30 and the last rowers get back at about 15.00, although the leaders will be back from 11.00 onwards.

On July 21st, 1577, the authorities in Venice finally dared to announce that the Plague, which had lasted two years and had claimed the lives of over 50,000 Venetians, was over. In thanksgiving for their deliverance the people of Venice raised the Church of the Redeemer on Giudecca, one of Palladio's greatest works. In further commemoration of the end of the Plague the Feast of the **Redentore** was initiated on the third Sunday of July. It is still celebrated with a bridge of boats built across the Giudecca Canal from Zattere into the very door of the church. On the preceding Saturday evening all the boats in Venice, hung with lights, gather in St Mark's Basin, from which all motor-boats are banned after 21.00. People eat and drink on board their boats and from them watch the firework display over Giudecca. The night is completed by all the boats making their way out to the Lido to wait for the dawn.

The first Sunday in September has, since 1920, been the official date of the **Regata Storica.** The main feature is a rowing race requiring considerable strength and stamina which arouses a great deal of partisan support among the spectators. Before the race there is an impressive procession, along the whole length of the Grand Canal, of modern replicas of historic Venetian craft, including the *Bucintoro,* the boats crewed by men and women in period costume, the procession accompanied by music.

In 1631 the Plague returned in force to Venice and nearly 50,000 people died in little more than a year. They now decided to build a church to plead for intercession against the pestilence. The foundation stone of S. Maria della Salute was laid on April 1, 1631, although the church was not completed until 1687. Before that, in November, 1631, the plague had been declared over and, in celebration, the Doge and Signoria led a procession from the Piazza, past S. Moisè, to a bridge of boats built across the Grand Canal to the site of the new church. That procession and thanksgiving service, complete to the bridge of boats, is repeated every year on the 21st November as the **Feast of the Salute**.

Those are only the main and most spectacular festivities. There are many others during the course of the year, particularly boat-races, on the islands of the Lagoon as well as in Venice itself. Check with the Information Office or consult *Un Ospite di Venezia* for details of those with varying dates.

Venice in Peril — Problems of the Modern City

Venice was one of the first cities to attract the environmentalists and those concerned with pollution and conservation. Halfway between land and sea Venice has always been on the see-saw of the balance of nature. In the 1960s it became obvious that the see-saw was becoming unbalanced. The *acqua alta* — a high tide produced by a combination of low pressure, spring tides and the sirocco winds — has always been a problem in spring and autumn but, in 1966 and 1967 the waters twice rose two metres above their normal level and it became obvious that Venice was in danger.

The problem was largely due to 20th-century developments. Ever larger ships entering the Lagoon had led to the dredging of deep-water channels while the growth of Mestre and Marghera had changed the outfall of the Brenta and other rivers. The delicate balance of tides and currents which kept Venice above the waters was being upset. What is more, the industrial complex at Marghera was polluting both the waters and the air of the Lagoon. Artesian wells drawing water from the rock beneath the Lagoon to meet the needs of industry were undermining the land and Venice was sinking. The petrified wooden foundations and marble damp courses of Venetian buildings were sound enough but the lowering of the city, the recurrent *acqua alta* floods and the wake of speeding motor-boats on the canals was allowing salt and polluted water to get into the brickwork of the buildings above the damp course, causing the fabric to crumble and decay.

Even at the busiest times it is always possible to find a quiet corner and a nearly deserted canal.

Worst affected have been the many beautiful frescoes. Behind the frescoes the brick and plaster is crumbling away while their outer surfaces are blackened and pitted by air pollution. The United Nations organisation UNESCO recognised the problem and declared that the salvation of Venice was a world problem. No fewer than 14 countries responded with assistance, co-ordinated after 1971 as 'Venice in Peril', backed up by massive support from Italian government and regional bodies, despite the mysteries of Italian bureaucracy.

Some success has been measured. Construction of aqueducts to carry water to Marghera in 1973 have stopped the sinking of the city and indeed the level has risen by two centimetres in the past twenty years. A consortium has been working since 1988 to clean up the waters of the Lagoon and the sale of phosphate-based detergents has been banned. Work has begun on steel caissons that will form tidal barriers across the three entrances to the Lagoon to prevent flooding, although opinion is divided as to whether this will help or will cause even greater difficulties. The need to keep the flood waters out has to be balanced against the very real need for the scouring and cleansing actions of the tides. Air pollution has been reduced, although it remains formidable and many famous facades such as those in St Mark's Square remain terribly blackened. The future well-being of Venice is now a more hopeful prospect, although much remains to be done.

Restoration of works of art has continued apace through contributions of 30 different organisations world-wide. Frescoes, paintings, mosaics, statues, stained glass and the fabric of the buildings themselves have all been renovated. In some cases works of art are in better condition today than they have been for many years. In the sightseeing sections of this guide you will find repeated mentions of the restoration work that has been done and is continuing. If you are interested in the current situation as regards the restoration effort — particularly if you would like to help — you could contact the *Amici dei Musei* at **UNESCO**'s office in the Piazza San Marco (5209 988) or the **Venice Committee/World Monuments Fund**, Chiesa della Pietà (5237 614)/San Polo 2454 (5224 229).

Un bocolo

Long ago, so the story goes, a young Venetian soldier lay dying after a battle with the Turks. As his sight dimmed his eyes lighted on a bush of white roses and, in memory of his love in far-off Venice, he plucked a white rose-bud and kissed it to bid her farewell. Some time after his death, by some undefined miracle, the rose-bud found its way to Venice and the hands of the young lady beloved of the dead soldier. But now the white rose-bud had turned to deepest red, stained by the young man's blood. From that day on the tradition has grown on St Mark's Day, April 25th, that the young men of Venice should present their lady-loves with a red rose-bud, *un bocolo*.

An elaborate decorative doorway on the Villino Canonica.

TWO

Planning and Preparation

When to go

There is no closed season in Venice, although some of the smaller hotels do shut between November and March. Officially, the high season in Venice, Marghera and Mestre runs from the first weekend in April to the first weekend in November. Two periods that are also treated as high season are Christmas, from December 21st to January 6th, and Carnival which occupies the ten days prior to Lent, usually the middle two weeks of February. The Lido and resorts along the coast from Punta Sabbioni to Cavallino have a much shorter high season; from July 1st to August 31st.

July and August are peak months anywhere and the heart of Venice becomes almost impossibly overcrowded. If crowds are anathema to you but you have to visit Venice during the high season, remember that the crowds are usually packed into an area between St Mark's and the Rialto. Even at the height of the season it is possible to escape the crush by moving just a few steps from the main thoroughfares.

Climatically the Northern Adriatic is closer to Central Europe than the Mediterranean, which can mean cold winters and hot summers. Some winter days are beautiful with a clear frosty air that offers crystal sharp views across the lagoon and the snow-covered Dolomites can be seen from vantage points in the city. At other times a romantic mist softens the hard outlines of the buildings. On the other hand, if you are unlucky, it can be simply cold, wet and foggy. For details of monthly temperature and rainfall figures see page 131.

Recently a consortium of hotels, business and tourist organisations known as **Promove** (San Marco 2233) was formed to promote the concept of *Venezia d'Inverno* (Venice in Winter). There are 35 participating hotels offering a variety of inducements to winter visitors. For those booking winter holidays through a number of tour operators, such as Thomas Cook, there is a booklet of tickets available giving the winter visitor discounts on meals and drinks, and either free access or reduced entry charges to museums and concerts. For those willing and able to risk the less certain weather there are definite economic benefits to be gained from visiting Venice in the low season.

Summer is extremely hot and humid, although there is usually a gentle breeze off the sea to temper the heat, in the streets open to the lagoon. Most hotels have air-conditioning which is operational from June 1st to September 30th but, although this is included in the price for all hotels of four stars or more, the others might well impose an air-conditioning surcharge of 10% or more of the room cost.

Probably the ideal times to visit Venice are either in May or June when the temperature is 20–25°C or from mid-September to late October, which is the driest time. During these periods the weather is pleasant, the crowds are not excessive and prices, while higher than in the low season, are below their high season peak.

How to get there

By Air

For British travellers **British Airways** and **Alitalia** both operate daily flights between London Heathrow and Venice Marco Polo Airport. The standard APEX fare, in 1991, is between £231 and £269 depending on the season. There are also direct scheduled flights linking Venice with Brussels, Dusseldorf, Frankfurt, Lyons, Munich, Nice, Paris, Stuttgart, Vienna and Zurich (via Lugano). There is no direct air link with the Republic of Ireland but there are connecting flights from Dublin through London. From countries outside Europe it is necessary to fly to Rome and connect with an internal flight; although there is a daily flight from New York to Venice via Milan Malpensa. Within Italy there is a daily flight between Venice and Naples/Palermo; 2 daily flights to and from Milan; and 9 daily flights between Venice and Rome.

There are no direct flights to Venice from provincial British airports. You can change planes at either Heathrow or Paris but APEX fares are not available and return tickets are up to £200 more expensive. You can fly to Milan from Manchester or Glasgow and continue from there by rail. The APEX air fare Manchester-Milan, in 1991, is £245–£281 with a further £30 for the 1st class rail journey. Both air and rail tickets can be booked in the U.K.

During the high season (between May and the end of September) many tour operators have spare capacity on their charter flights and offer a limited number of cheap places to independent travellers. These charter flights seldom use Venice Marco Polo, however; the normal charter airport is Treviso. Cheap flights are available from:

Italy Sky Shuttle (formerly Pilgrim Air) [081 748 1333 or 061 798 8228] Daily flights between Gatwick and Treviso, from £99 return, low season; £149 return high season (to Marco Polo as well as Treviso).

Citalia [081 686 5533] offer flight only deals, with discounts on scheduled **Alitalia** and **BA** services between Heathrow and Venice, and cheap deals on charter flights between Gatwick and Treviso. £210 scheduled return, £174 charter return, high season.

Skybus Holidays Ltd 24A, Earls Court Rd, London SW5 0TA (071 373 6055) offer **Italy Skybus** returns from Gatwick or Luton, £159 and £179 high season only.

Most charter flights arriving at Treviso will connect with Venice by special coaches or there are regular bus or rail connections with Venice; it is a journey of only 30 kilometres.

Air/Coach

The best bargain and the cheapest way to travel to Venice, for those to whom time is not a problem, is offered by **Italy Sky Shuttle** and **Italy Skybus**, in conjunction with **Eurolines**. Under this deal you fly out to Venice from Luton or Gatwick and return by coach. Fares range from £54 to £75, low season; £85 to £107 between May and October. You must spend at least 6 nights (and not more than 12 nights) in Venice. Your return cannot be pre-booked but must be arranged in Venice, not more than 48 hours before you propose to leave. Return by 2nd class rail to Milan or Turin and coach from there to London, the journey takes 24 hours.

By Rail

There is not much to be gained by the British visitor in travelling the whole distance by rail, unless he or she has a phobia about flying. There is no direct link and, apart from the ferry crossing, the passenger has to change stations in Paris. Including a *couchette* the cost is much the same as a charter air fare (an ordinary return fare in 1991 was about £150). The principal connecting train service leaves London Victoria at about 9.00 to connect with a late afternoon departure from Paris, arriving in Venice at around 9.00 the following day.

Rail connections with other European countries are better and more practical. Direct Intercity or Eurocity trains, many with *Wagon-Lits* sections, link Venice with Berne, Geneva, Innsbruck, Lausanne, Munich, Paris, Vienna and Zurich. No doubt the possibilities for the British traveller will improve when the Channel Tunnel links Britain into the European rail network.

Enquiries and bookings can be made through the **British Rail European Travel Centre** at Victoria Station (071 834 2345). Anyone who can prove that they are under the age of 26 can obtain an **InterRail** pass, which cost £175 in 1991, and which gives unlimited free rail travel in Europe for the period of one month, together with discounts of 30% or more on cross-Channel ferries. In May 1991 a new pass became available for British travellers of any age over 26 — **InterRail 26** at £175 for 2 weeks and £235 for a month. For visitors normally resident outside Europe there is a **EurRail** pass available for about $500 which provides much the same facilities.

One way to arrive in Venice by rail is by flying to Milan and continuing from there by train as already suggested for passengers travelling from British provincial airports. Since it is so remarkably inexpensive in Italy, rail travel is also recommended for travellers who are dividing their time between Venice and another Italian city. Enquiries and bookings for Italian Railways can be made through the **British Rail European Travel Centre** or through **E.N.I.T.** (Italian National Tourist Office), **Thomas Cook** or **Citalia** (addresses and telephone numbers listed pp. 135–6). In Britain there is a booking agency specialising in European railways who can handle seat reservations and train supplements (which is more than British Rail can). This is **Washeels**, 121 Wilton Rd, London SW1, 071 634 7066.

Many of the Intercity or Eurocity trains are 1st class only or demand a hefty surcharge on 2nd class tickets. In 1991 the return 1st class from Milan to Venice was £30 paid in Britain with a L10,000 surcharge on one of the named Eurocity trains, payable to the conductor on the train. In the season it is advisable to book seats, which can be done up to two hours before departure. Journey time from Milan to Venice is three and a quarter hours and, although most of the journey is boring, the arrival is magical.

The Orient Express

There is of course one way to travel to Venice that is unique and which combines romance, nostalgia and unashamed luxury. That is aboard the **Venice-Simplon Orient-Express.** The train runs from the end of February to mid-November with two services per week from London to Venice and return, via Paris, Zurich and Innsbruck. Outward journeys are on Thursday and Sunday, with return journeys on Wednesday and Saturday. In the high season two Thursday departures and two Saturday returns each month are not available because on those dates the train goes to Vienna and Budapest instead of Venice. Travel is by Pullman Coaches in England and Wagon-Lits on the Continent. Prices include a shared two-berth cabin and table d'hôte meals. In 1991 the cost one way was £850 and return was £1,235. Departure was at 11.00 from London (Victoria) and arrival in Venice (Santa Lucia) was at 18.48 the following day. Return was at 10.40 from Venice with arrival in London at 17.47 the following day.

By Car

There is really no good reason for anyone to take their car as a means of getting to Venice. It is difficult and expensive to park the vehicle during your stay and, of course, you will not be able to use a car while in Venice. On the other hand there may be those wishing to include a visit to Venice in a more general car tour of Italy and Europe.

Approaching Venice from the west on the A4 you should leave the motorway at the Marghera (or Mestre Ovest) exit, signposted VENEZIA. This gives directly onto the Via della Libertà which in turn becomes the Ponte della Libertà, the causeway across the Lagoon. The causeway leads straight into the Piazzale Roma or to the various car parks (see page 41).

Signs on the causeway relay information as to how full the car parks are.

In the high season, and sometimes during Carnival, it is worth considering leaving your car on the mainland. There are a number of car parks in Mestre, such as S. Giuliano (signposted), from which you can catch the bus or train into Venice. Another alternative on leaving the A4 is to take the Chioggia/Ravenna road south. In about 5 kilometres you will reach the Brenta Canal near the **Villa Malcontenta** (Ca' Foscari). Turn left and continue for another 5 kilometres to **Fusina** where there is a large car park, run by the **A.C.I.**, which has a regular water-bus connection with Venice during the high season by means of the no. 16 service to Zattere.

In the Mestre area it is also worth exploring the airport where there is free, but unguarded, parking space available. You can then use the airport services to get into Venice. Alternatively the motorist can cross the causeway to Tronchetto, where it is possible to take the car ferry for the Lido, where there are also car parks. The car ferry is service no. 17 and connects Venice not only with the Lido but with Punta Sabbioni. This service is sign-posted on the causeway and there is a special information office on the right-hand side of the road as you leave Mestre.

By Coach
The cheapest and most uncomfortable way to get to Venice is by coach. **Eurolines** at Victoria Coach Station (071 730 0202) run a coach to Milan every Sunday (and Tuesday in high season), from where Venice can be reached either by Italian coach (**Sadem Eurolines**) or by rail. The coach journey to Milan takes 23 hours and you can add on at least another 4 for the journey to Venice, together with what can be a considerable wait in Milan for your connection. Travel by this means is only for those with stamina. In fact, a return fare by coach will not save you much on the air/coach services described above.

Package Deals
It is well-worth considering a transport + accommodation package since a wide range of companies offer a complete package at slightly less than you would pay in making your own arrangements. In most cases the package offers scheduled air services, bed and breakfast accommodation in regular hotels

plus such extras as water-launch transfers between airport and hotel.

All major tour operators as well as a number of smaller specialist companies offer a range of holidays in Venice within their 'City' or 'Short Break' programmes. Some of these programmes run for 12 months of the year but are rather more common in the low season. Normal lengths of stay are 3, 5 or 7 nights. A degree of shopping around is recommended to find the deal which suits you best but some of the major operators are listed pp. 135–6. Typical costs for 3 nights in a 3-star hotel with scheduled flights are £200–£250 in low season, £350–£400 in high season; for 7 nights, £300–£370 in low season and £550–£600 in high season.

One useful option offered by many of the tour operators is travel to or from Venice by the Orient-Express with the other half of the return journey completed by air. Costs are of course dependent on the class of hotel used but it is possible to have three nights in a 3 star hotel for around £1,000, or less than the train-only return fare. It is incidentally cheaper to fly out and return by the Orient-Express rather than make the outward journey by train. The explanation for this is that you get a lunch going from London to Venice, where the return journey provides a mere brunch!

If you like the idea of having your travel and accommodation booked and paid for before departure but you do not like any of the arrangements on offer, or you wish to travel by train, or you want to combine Venice with another Italian city, then it is possible to have an individual package tailor-made by **Citalia Special Bookings** (081 688 9989).

Money

Budgeting

Venice is an expensive city, although a diversion off the well-trodden tourist routes can halve prices in eating, drinking or shopping. Over and above the cost of accommodation, you can expect **an average outlay** of about **£25** or **L50,000** per day. This assumes you spend L25,000 for an evening meal with wine, L7,500 on a 'pizza and drink' lunch, L5000 on a couple of drinks during the day, L3,600 on transport and L9,000 on entrance charges.

Currency

The Italian unit of currency is the Lira (plural Lire). A rough conversion rate is L2,100–L2,300 to the pound, or just over L1,000 to the dollar.

Bank notes issued are to the value of 1,000, 2,000, 5,000, 10,000, 50,000 and 100,000 lire; coins for 50, 100, 200 and 500 lire. There is a limit on the amount of currency that can be taken into Italy of L400,000. It is advisable to carry a reasonable amount of currency with you for your immediate needs as you will get a better rate of exchange at home than you will in Venice.

The most common abbreviation for lira is L., although the £ sign is still used (which can upset the British visitor who sees a commonplace article priced at thousands of £s). Banks and other institutions use the abbreviation Lit. (for *lire italiane*) to distinguish the Italian lira from the pound sterling — Lst. (*lira di sterlina*). Many shops and businesses express their prices without the final three zeros, or with a dash in their place, so that L14.- means 14,000 lire. They are also likely to express this in speech so that 14,500 is said to be *quattordici, cinque* (fourteen, five).

How to take your money

The most obvious way to take your money is in the form of Travellers' Cheques. To avoid surcharges, take lira cheques which ensure that you get the amount stated regardless of the rate of exchange at the time. Most holders of current bank accounts can obtain a **Eurocheque** card and cheque book in return for a small annual fee of about £8. The Eurocheque is drawable on your bank account in the normal way except that the amount is made out in the local currency. There is a £100 limit on each cheque but there is nothing to stop you issuing more than one cheque for a single transaction. Most banks and many shops and hotels in Venice accept Eurocheques; just look for the red, white and blue logo. The vast majority of cash dispensers in Venice operate on Eurocheque cards, and this is a convenient way of obtaining cash at any time but unfortunately, as I found by personal experience, not all banks (only National Westminster and Midland in the U.K.) offer a PIN number to enable you to use this service.

Credit or charge cards are more widely accepted in Italy than they used to be and most of the larger hotels, smarter shops and restaurants will accept the four main cards: Visa (known as Bank Americard), Mastercard (most often known as Eurocard), American Express and Diner's Club. It is not easy to find cash dispensers for these cards but Visa cards are acceptable at the **Banca d'America e d'Italia** and Amex cards can use the dispenser at the **American Express** office — both in the Calle Larga XXII Marzo.

Beginning to make their appearance — currently at the railway station and the airport — are machines known as 'Bancomats' which convert foreign currency notes into lire. You feed in your pound or dollar notes, press a couple of buttons and the machine dispenses the lira equivalent. Exchange rates tend to be poor.

Documentation

Passports and Visas

All citizens of the European Community are free to stay in Italy indefinitely so long as they are in possession of a valid passport. For U.K. visitors this passport can be the British Visitor's Passport, although this is valid for only one year. Citizens of some Commonwealth countries such as Australia and New Zealand can also enter Italy on no more than a valid passport,

---

The Missing Coins

Nowadays the supply of coins in Italy is sufficient for the country's needs but it was not always like that. Only a few years ago there was a real crisis as it was realised that only about one tenth of the coins that had been minted were in circulation. The trouble was the peasant mentality which did not trust banks and preferred to keep its wealth under the bed. The same mentality did not trust bank notes but preferred coins; all coins that came into their possession were popped into bags and secreted away. At that time there were millions of ten lire coins in existence but none were ever seen. The expedients that were adopted by shops, post offices or motorway tollbooths who needed to give L10 in change ranged from L10 postage stamps in little plastic envelopes to hard-boiled sweets. The crisis has now passed but there is a nostalgic regret for the days when you would tender a L100 for a L90 postage stamp and receive back the stamp and a strawberry-flavoured toffee.

although such stays are limited to three months. Visitors holding any other passports are advised to check with their embassy or consulate as to visa requirements.

All foreign visitors are required to register with the police within three days of arrival in Italy. In a hotel, hostel or managed camp site this will be done for you. Reception will take your passport when you check in and return it an hour or so later, having registered it with the police. If you are in self-catering accommodation or staying with friends it is your own responsibility to register. This should be done at the **Questura** of the Municipal Police which is on the Fondamenta di S. Lorenzo. (*Ufficio Passaporti* — Tel. 5203 044). The same office should be informed immediately if your passport is lost or stolen.

Police have the right to ask to see your papers at any time so, theoretically, you should always carry your passport with you.

Insurance and Health Matters

Most package tour operators will automatically arrange in-surance for you but the independent traveller should cover themselves against such things as cancellation charges, loss or damage to luggage plus full medical cover. Any insurance broker should be able to advise on the many holiday and travel policies available. A recent Consumer Association report said that the best cover, in relation to premium paid, was provided by the **General Accident** company of Perth in Scotland.

EC citizens can obtain free medical treatment from an Italian doctor on production of form E111, obtainable in Britain from the Department of Health and valid for three years. Any medicines or prescribed drugs can be obtained at 10% of cost. The chemist in Italy (*farmacia*) has a greater status than is usually granted to his British counterpart and for minor ailments is the first port of call rather than the doctor. If you are under regular medication it is as well to have your drug packet or bottle with you since it may have a different name in Italy. Even with form E111 it is advisable to take out your own medical insurance since some treatments, the dentist for example, are not available from the Italian health service.

If you have anything stolen while in Italy it is necessary for insurance purposes to report its loss to the police, either to the **Questura** or to the **Carabinieri**.

Motoring

Foreigners are permitted to drive in Italy on their national driving licence provided that it is accompanied by an Italian translation. In the U.K. these translations are available on demand from the **A.A., R.A.C., E.N.I.T.** or **Citalia** (motoring department). Even if your licence is in the standard EC format (pink), it is still advisable to have a translation since not all of Italy's traffic police have heard of the new regulations. Under EC regulations your car insurance is valid in Italy for compulsory third party cover only. If you wish to retain your comprehensive cover you must request a foreign extension policy (Green Card) from your insurers.

In Italy a wing mirror on the offside of the car (nearside to British drivers) is mandatory.

A common sight: washing strung across the alleyway.

Clothing

In deciding what clothes to pack it is worth remembering that Venice can be extremely cold in winter and exceedingly hot in summer and choose accordingly. The dilemma is at its greatest in the summer when the need to keep cool and the feeling that you are on holiday encourages casual dress. There is no law against this but visitors should remember that they are in a city and not on a beach. Their own self-pride should remind them that Italians of both sexes are extremely fashion-conscious and almost aggressively smart and well-groomed; casual dressing should not be sloppy dressing.

For women a number of cool dresses, skirts or trousers and tops in natural fibres are ideal. For men the standard summer wear seems to be short-sleeved and open-necked shirts with slacks rather than shorts. In the evening a touch of formality can be achieved by a long-sleeved shirt worn with a tie; even in the more prestigious establishments a jacket is not obligatory, with the exception of the Casino where you will not get in without one.

Remember that many of the sights you will be visiting in Venice are churches and there is a strict dress etiquette which in the height of the season is often enforced by a church 'policeman' standing in the church porch to turn away the unsuitably dressed. What causes most disapproval is the sight of too much bare flesh. Shorts are frowned on if worn by either sex and, while the days when it was thought obligatory for women to cover their heads are gone, there is still disapproval of bare upper arms and shoulders. A woman is advised to take lightweight scarf or silk square with her so that she can drape this over her shoulders when entering a religious building.

Maps and Literature

Much useful literature can be obtained from the Italian State Tourist Office before departure but the most useful publication *Un Ospite in Venezia* (A Guest in Venice), which will be mentioned later, is best obtained after your arrival.

A good plan of the city is essential. Street plans can be obtained from the information office, and there are plenty of simple maps, but Venice is a rabbit's warren of little streets and for serious wandering a plan which includes every alley-way and all *vaporetto* landing stages is a must. Recommended are the street plans produced by **Hallwag** or **Litografia Artistica Cartografica**, both available outside Italy. The former is slightly clearer having a 1:5,500 scale but the latter, on the scale of 1:6,000, includes the all-important sestiere boundaries, indicates pictorially the location of all the major monuments and tourist sights and is particularly good in its large-scale coverage of the Northern Lagoon. Clearest of all is the map produced by the **Touring Club Italiano** which is on the scale 1:5,000 and comes in a plastic folder with a separate index. However, it is unwieldy and difficult to obtain outside Italy.

Visitors might like to do some background reading before visiting Venice. For the fullest, wittiest and most elegant account of Venice's history, it is hard to beat *A History of Venice* by John Julius Norwich (Penguin-Allan Lane). Equally good, at less length, is *The Venetian Empire* by Jan Morris (available as a Penguin paperback). By the same writer in an earlier incarnation is *Venice* by James Morris (Faber) which has almost reached classic status although the style is considered too contrived by some. Over a century old but still said to be the finest guide to the art and architecture of Venice is *The Stones of Venice* by John Ruskin, out of print for many years but recently re-issued with a foreword by Jan Morris. One of the most exhaustive guide-books ever written about a city is *Venice and its Lagoon* by Guido Lorenzetti, a massive volume and quite useless as a pocket companion. However, if you fall in love with the place and want to know all there is to know about it, this is the book to get: but you are unlikely to be able to obtain a copy outside Venice itself, where editions in both Italian and English are to be found at the better bookshops.

Many novels have been set in Venice and any writer of romantic or thriller fiction seems to feel it obligatory to set at least one of their works in Venice. In a more serious vein five of the best novels with a Venetian setting are:

Across the River and into the Trees: Ernest Hemingway
The Aspern Papers: Henry James
Death in Venice: Thomas Mann
The Desire and Pursuit of the Whole: Frederick Rolfe (Baron Corvo)
Stone Virgin: Barry Unsworth

Massed gondolas at rest for the night on the Bacino Orseolo.

THREE

Arrival, Departure and Getting Around

By air

Marco Polo Airport is situated at Tesséra, on the SS14 Venice-Trieste road, north-east of the lagoon causeway, 12km from Venice by road and 10km by boat. As Italy's third busiest airport it has daily links with all major Italian and European centres and, via Milan, with New York.

On arrival the international traveller passes through passport control into baggage collection. There is ample space while awaiting your luggage and toilets are provided. You then proceed through Customs into the Arrivals Hall. Passengers on domestic flights have their own baggage collection area before also proceeding into the Arrivals Hall.

In the arrivals area can be found offices for both tourist and hotel information, a bank and exchange bureau, left luggage, car-hire firms, ticket offices for both bus and water transport, as well as telephones and toilets. At the end of the Arrivals Hall the doors straight ahead lead out onto the landing stage for motor-boat transport to Venice. The doors on the right lead out onto the front of the terminal building where the buses and motor-taxis are to be found.

The main airport bank is the *Cassa di Risparmio di Venezia*. Counter service is from 8.15 to 18.15, every day except Sunday. There is a 24 hour cash dispenser which takes Eurocheque cards and a machine for changing bank-notes. The *Banco di Roma* also has a counter service at the airport, but not a cash dispenser. You can also change money, as well as make travel arrangements, at the *Bucintoro* Travel Agency which has an airport branch office in the Arrivals Hall.

The restaurant for the airport, *Lo Zodiaco*, is 200 metres from the terminal building. It is open every day. One of the facilities they offer is booking your boat passage to Venice while you eat. But beware! This is the water-taxi service and will cost you a lot more than the motor-boat.

Arrivals are at the eastern end of the terminal building, departures access is by the four doors in the middle of the building. In the reception area the check-in desks are opposite the doors, with international departures to the right and domestic to the left. The reception area also has telephones and toilets, bank and exchange bureau, ticket counter and a newspaper stand. Those passing through passport control into the International Departures Lounge will find the usual services such as a bar, duty-free shop and boutique.

Airport-Venice Connections

Bus: There are two bus services. The normal **Actv** service bus, route no. 5, runs between the airport and the Piazzale Roma from 4.10 until 1.10 the following morning. Between 7.10 and 20.10 the service is half-hourly, at 10 and 40 minutes after the hour. This is the cheapest service but it is a stopping bus and therefore the slowest, taking something over half an hour.

The **ATVO** company runs a direct bus service between the airport and the Air Terminal building in the Piazzale Roma. The departure times for the ATVO buses are linked with the expected arrival times of flights, so you are likely to find a bus waiting on your arrival. The service from Venice to the airport leaves the Piazzale Roma one hour before the flight departure time. Remember to buy your ticket in the Arrivals Hall or at the Piazzale Roma office; you can pay on the bus but it will cost more. In 1991 the cost was L4,000 per person and the journey time was 20 minutes.

Boat: The motor-boat connection is run by the Cooperativa San Marco and the boats run from the landing stage, outside the doors of the airport's Arrival Hall, to the S. Marco landing stage. Departures are timed to coincide with flights and in 1991 cost L13,000 per person. For the journey from the airport, book your ticket at the desk in the Arrivals Hall. To book your return trip to the airport contact the Coop S. Marco office in the Calle dei Fabbri, or telephone 5235 775.

Taxi: The motor-car taxi service can take you from the airport to the Piazzale Roma or vice versa. In 1991 the cost was L25,000 and the taxi can take up to four people. Suitcases may be subject to charge. The water-taxi service is luxurious but pricey. In 1991 the cost for a motor-launch taxi from the airport to a destination in the historic centre was L72,000. There is a water-taxi stand at the airport (5415 084).

By car

Assuming that you have decided not to leave your car on the mainland (see page 29) you will find, on crossing the causeway, that you are offered a choice. Straight ahead, the road leads into the Piazzale Roma while a slip road right leads to Tronchetto and the Lido car-ferry. Although parking is available in the Piazzale Roma it is normally so difficult that you are advised not to make the attempt but to proceed directly to Tronchetto. This is an artificial island reached by way of the commercial port and constitutes the largest car park in Europe, if not the world.

As you cross over onto Tronchetto the large parking area on your right is reserved for Venice residents. The entrance to the car park proper is midway down the main island, beyond the Line 8 landing stages. There is a large multi-storey garage and four spacious open-air car parks. There is a small area set apart for the clients of certain Venice hotels, as well as a coach park. Parking charges in 1991 were L5000 for the first 3 hours, either covered or open. The next 9 hours cost L10,000 in the garage or L8,000 in the open. Successive 12-hour periods are charged at L12,000 or L10,000 for covered or open parking respectively (parts of 12 hours are charged as for the full 12 hours). The daily rate is therefore L27,000 for the first day in the garage and L24,000 for each following day; or it is·L22,000 for the first day in the open and L20,000 for each successive day. Minibuses, motor-caravans or campers are charged L15,000 per 12 hours. There is no free parking.

Both garage and parking lots are automatically controlled. You receive a ticket on arrival which you retain until departure, when you present it at the cash-desk and pay before collecting your car. You have a limited time after having paid to collect the car and leave the parking area.

There are a number of services available on Tronchetto. There is a filling station on the road out, just past the Line 1 landing stage, and a service station in the base of the garage. There is a bar in the garage building and a snack-bar next door to the filling station. The information office is adjacent to the hotel clients' car park. Other services grouped around the garage building include telephones,. toilets, bank and exchange facilities, the 'Gran Canal' travel agency and a police station.

For onward transportation there are two water-bus landing stages — the one nearest the entrance is for the Line 1 service to the Lido via the Grand Canal and St Mark's. In the summer this landing stage also serves the Line 5 (barrato) service to Murano. The second landing stage in front of the garage is used by the Line 8 service for S. Zaccaria via Giudecca and, in summer, the Line 34 route to the Lido, following the same route as Line 1 but with fewer stops.

The car-ferry for the Lido, Line 17, leaves from beyond the Line 8 landing stage towards the end of the island. The service departs every 50 minutes.

There is a water-taxi stand by the Line 8 landing stage.

By road

Immediately after the causeway was opened in 1933 the Piazzale Roma was developed as the road terminal in Venice. At the same time the first garages were built. The post-war boom in car ownership and tourism rapidly stretched the capacity of Piazzale Roma to breaking-point; hence the development of Tronchetto. Piazzale Roma is situated at the extreme north-west of the islands and is a large rectangle running north-west to south-east, its northern side follows the line of the Grand Canal, while the eastern edge is bounded by the Rio Nuovo. It is not the most picturesque of arrival points, the area of the Piazzale is crowded with vehicles and services, and often subject to road works and rebuilding.

Dominating the Piazzale is the **Autorimessa Municipale** — the Municipal Garage. This is almost exclusively occupied by Venice residents and the few places remaining are rapidly snapped up. The second largest garage in the Piazzale, and the largest private venture, is the **Garage S. Marco**. This is on the south-western side of the Piazzale, behind the Autorimessa, in the Campo S. Andrea. The garage charges a 24 hour daily rate dependent on the size of car. The charges in 1991 were L24,000 for a small car such as a Fiesta; L32,000 for a medium car such as an Escort; and L36,000 for a car of Sierra size or above. There is also a L2,000 supplement for arrivals and departures before 6.30 or after 22.00. There are other garages but these are mainly for short-term parking, not necessarily offering a 24 hour service and extremely expensive.

In the Campo S. Andrea, behind the Autorimessa, there is supervised open-air parking run by the A.C.I. but this is essentially for short-term parking with charges around L7,500 for 3 hours; preference and discount is given to A.C.I. members. There is still a small section where cars can be parked on the Piazzale for free — it is down in the southernmost corner — but waiting is limited to 30 minutes, after which unattended vehicles are towed away to Mestre.

The main central space is given over to the bus station and taxi stands. Buses and coaches leave here for the airport, Mestre and many other destinations in mainland Venice or the Veneto. The Actv bus services have a large booking hall, enquiry service and information office along the north side of the Piazzale, between the bus stops and the water-bus landing stages on the Grand Canal. Many Actv tickets are interchangeable between the motor-buses and water-buses.

There are toilets in the Autorimessa, and others in the angle between the Rio Nuovo and the Campazzo Tre Ponti, in the southern corner of the Piazzale. Down in this southernmost corner is a branch of the *Cassa di Risparmio* offering banking and exchange facilities. In this part of the Piazzale, and also around the Autorimessa and the Actv offices, there are a number of bars, snack-bars and trattorie. Both the urban police and Carabinieri have stations on the Piazzale and there is an office of the SIP telephone service.

From the Piazzale many locations are within walking distance. If you are inconvenienced by luggage there is porters' stand in the Piazzale. They will charge L8,350 for 1 or 2 pieces of luggage to any point in central Venice. They can be reached on 5203 070.

To travel by water-bus, obtain your ticket at the Actv ticket office and continue through onto the side of the Grand Canal. The closest landing stage on the right is for Lines 2, 5 and the seasonal 34. The further landing stage to the left is for Line 1. Fuller details of the water-bus services are given later in this chapter. Between the two landing stages is the water-taxi stand, and a gondola stand near the bridge over the Rio Nuovo.

By rail
Although the railway reached Venice in 1846 the present station was opened only in 1955. It is a busy station with a network of suburban and regional services within the Veneto as well as national and international train services. Within Italy

the main routes from Venice run west for Milan and Turin, south for Bologna, Florence and Rome and east for Trieste. International connections are with Basle, Belgrade, Berne, Geneva, Innsbruck, Lausanne, Munich, Paris, Vienna, Zagreb and Zurich.

In the arrivals part of the station are toilets, including an *albergo diurno*, 1st and 2nd class waiting rooms, newspaper stands and a 24-hour left-luggage office. Passing through into the station concourse there is another news-stand, a gift-shop and information offices both for the F.S. (railways) and for Venice, together with a hotel reservation service. Also in the concourse are computer-screen information machines operating in several languages. If you are arriving off a major train you can expect to be pestered by touts from hotels along the Lista di Spagna.

Across the front of the concourse, between the main entry/exit doors is the bank, run by the *Banca Nazionale delle Communicazioni*, which provides counter services, an exchange bureau and a bancomat cash dispenser. At opposite ends of the concourse are, to the left as one enters, booking offices for tickets, seats and supplements for special trains; and, to the right, the station buffet which offers a bar and snack bar (pay at the cash-desk, collect food and drink from the respective bars and consume standing up), a self-service restaurant, and a sit-down, waiter-service section for the café-bar. The buffet is very good and reasonable.

The station itself is like any railway station in the world but, as you leave the concourse, you exit onto a plateau set above the banks of the Grand Canal. Facing you across the water is the domed S. Simeon Piccolo Church, while to the left lies the Scalzi Church and Bridge and the first *palazzo*-lined curve of the Grand Canal. It is probably the most magical station forecourt in the world.

There is a porters' stand on the plateau in front of the station, if you wish to walk to your hotel. For transport, descend the steps to the waterside. There are three water-bus landing stages. Furthest to the right is for Line 1, to the immediate left for Line 2 and the seasonal 34, beyond the Scalzi Bridge is that for Line 5. There are also water-taxi and gondola stands and a *traghetto* (gondola-ferry) to the opposite bank of the canal.

When returning to the station for departure remember that

the water-bus stop you want is **Ferrovia**. That is also the name you will find on directional street signs.

Orientation in the city

Let us begin by looking at the basic lay-out of Venice's historic centre. In the centre of the lagoon, connected to the mainland by a causeway 4 kilometres long, are 118 islands divided by around a hundred canals. These islands bunch together to form an egg-shaped group, four and a half kilometres long from west to east and two and a half deep from north to south. Two deep-water canals run through this group of islands. The first and widest, running more or less straight from west to east, is the Giudecca Canal, dividing the main group of islands from the islands of Sacca Fisola, Giudecca and San Giorgio Maggiore. The second major canal runs north to south through the main group of islands in two wide bends like an inverted 'S', so winding that it takes four kilometres to cover a distance that is only one and a half kilometres as the crow flies. This is the Grand Canal which effectively divides central Venice into two. At its southern end the Grand Canal joins the Giudecca Canal to form the Basin of St. Mark's. At the northern end of the Grand Canal are the railway station, the Piazzale Roma and the industrialised area around the Stazione Marittima and commercial port.

In 1171, in order to finance a war against the Byzantine Empire the Venetian government raised a forced loan from its people. In order to make collection of the money easier Venice was divided into six districts — the **Sestieri** — three on each side of the Grand Canal. That structure remains today. Although the sestieri boundaries seem to have no logic they are still the basis of addresses in the city and the easiest way to describe the lay-out of the city is to describe the six districts.

The Sestieri
East of the Grand Canal lie —
San Marco: Very small in area — about 1 kilometre by 500 metres — the sestiere occupies the land projecting into the lower bend of the Grand Canal. Containing St Mark's Square and Basilica, the Doge's Palace and the Rialto Bridge, as well as the most fashionable shops, restaurants and hotels, this is the

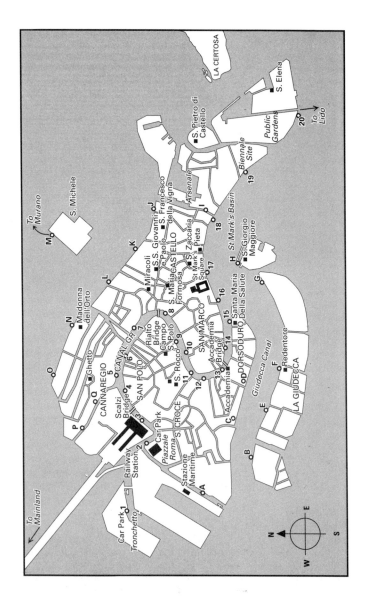

To Mainland

To Murano

S. Michele

M

To Lido

20

Public Gardens

S. Elena

LA CERTOSA

S. Pietro di Castello

Biennale Site

19

Arsenale

S. Francesco della Vigna

J

I

18

S. S. Giovanni e Paolo

S. Zaccaria

Pietà

St Mark's Basin

H

S. Giorgio Maggiore

G

Miracoli

K

S. Maria Formosa

St Mark's Square

17

16

Madonna dell'Orto

L

N

Ghetto

CANNAREGIO

O

CANAL GR.

Rialto Bridge

7

6

5

Campo S. Polo

SAN MARCO

15

Santa Maria Della Salute

CANAL GR.

P

Scalzi Bridge

4

SAN POLO

9

10

8

Accademia Bridge

14

DORSODURO

F

Redentore

Railway Station

1

2

3

S. CROCE

S. Rocco

11

12

13

Accademia

C

D

Giudecca Canal

E

LA GIUDECCA

B

Car Park Tronchetto

Piazzale Roma

Car Park

Stazione Marittime

A

N
W · E
S

Vaporetto Stops on Line 1	Vaporetto Stops on Line 5
1. Tronchetto	A. S. Marta
2. Piazzale Roma *	B. Sacca Fisolo
3. Ferrovia	C. S. Basilio
4. S. Biasio	D. Zattere
5. S. Marcuola	E. S. Eufemia
6. S. Stae	F. Redentore
7. Ca' D'Oro	G. Zitelle
8. Rialto	H. S. Giorgio Maggiore
9. S. Silvestro	I. Tana
10. Sant' Angelo	J. Celestia
11. S. Toma	K. Ospedale
12. Ca' Rezzonico	L. Fondamenta Nuove
13. Accademia	M. Cimeterio
14. S. Maria del Giglio	N. Madonna dell' Orto
15. Salute	O. S. Alvise
16. S. Marco	P. Tre Archi
17. S. Zaccaria *	Q. Guglie
18. Arsenale	
19. Giardini Pubblici	
20. S. Elena	

* stops shared with Line 5

real centre of the city and it is estimated that 90% of visitors do not venture further afield. It is therefore very crowded and the most expensive part of the city. It is nevertheless the area where you will spend most of your time in Venice, and where it is more than likely that you will stay.

Castello: So called after the castle built at the far eastern end of the Rialtine islands in the 9th century, Castello extends for more than two kilometres east of the Doge's Palace. It has many important monuments but they are dispersed. The busiest section is the Riva degli Schiavoni but north and east there are quiet residential areas. At the far eastern end of the sestiere are the public gardens, one of the quietest areas and the most neglected by visitors. Castello is the only sestiere untouched by the Grand Canal.

Cannaregio: Following the east bank of the Grand Canal from a point just beyond the Rialto this sestiere runs to the far north-west of the city and the railway station. North of the area fringing the Grand Canal are quiet, village-like districts such as the Ghetto. The northern edge is mostly built on reclaimed land, replacing the reed-beds after which the sestiere is named, and most of the city's working class live in this area. The part following the curve of the Grand Canal is bustling and highly commercialised, becoming more so the nearer you get to the railway station.

West of the Grand Canal lie —

Dorsoduro: The largest of the sestieri. As its name (meaning 'hard-back') suggests, it is the area of Venice with the firmest foundation. At its eastern end the sestiere faces San Marco across the Grand Canal, with notable monuments such as the Accademia and the Church of the Salute. In the north-eastern sector near the boundary with S. Polo the sestiere contains the university, centred on Ca' Foscari. The southern edge is formed by the Zattere, a long lagoon-side frontage along the Giudecca Canal. In the west the sestiere becomes industrialised as it runs into the dock area. With the university and artistic centres such as the Accademia and Guggenheim Collection within its boundaries Dorsoduro has a Bohemian, Left-Bank atmosphere that is very attractive.

The island of **Giudecca**, so called because it was the home of Venice's Jewish community before the founding of the Ghetto, is attached to Dorsoduro for administrative purposes.

Santa Croce: Named after a church that has since been demolished, this is a sprawling sestiere that faces Cannaregio along the Grand Canal but extends in the north-west to include the Piazzale Roma and the huge artificial islands of the Commercial Port and the Tronchetto car parks. Not really a tourist sestiere, it is more commercial and contains fewer major monuments than any other of the six.

San Polo: The smallest of the sestieri, it is squeezed between Dorsoduro and Santa Croce into the curve of the Grand Canal at the western end of the Rialto Bridge. It is the smartest of the western sestieri and a good place for shopping and interesting trattorie. The most interesting shops are along the route between the Rialto and the Frari. The Campo S. Polo is the largest square after the Piazza. It is often much quieter than other squares and acts as a haven of peace in this sector.

Getting around in Venice

There are only two ways of seeing Venice: on foot or from the water. Surprisingly enough, given the importance of the canal system in the city, you will find that you spend far more time on your feet than you do in a boat. Only the most expensive forms of transport can penetrate the network of small canals that run through the city, while the public transport boats are restricted to the Grand Canal and the outer circle of Venetian islands. For most sightseeing purposes the only option available is to walk.

This is no bad thing. There is an intimacy about seeing a city from walking its streets that you cannot get from the seat of a car or coach and a lack of traffic makes this even more true for Venice. Until you have experienced a city without motor traffic you cannot know how much easier and pleasanter that makes it to walk in. Furthermore, the distances are not great, it would take you less than an hour to walk from one end of the city to the other and the city centre is very well signposted.

There are six key points in the city. They are **S. Marco** (meaning St Mark's Square), **Rialto**, **Accademia**, **Piazzale Roma**, **Ferrovia** (meaning the railway station) and the **Ospedale di SS. Giovanni e Paolo** (meaning the main hospital next door to the church of that name). If you have a clear picture in your mind as to where these six places are and how they relate to each other you will have no difficulty in navigating about the city, as all the main thoroughfares are well signposted, mostly with black arrows on bright yellow signs fixed to the walls of buildings, indicating the route to be followed to reach one of these six points. (Except for the hospital of SS. Giov. e Paolo, signs for which are in blue and white.) Even if you get momentarily lost, easy enough in the maze of alleyways, you will soon emerge onto a main thoroughfare where you can re-orientate yourself thanks to the directional signs.

Within the areas bounded by the main thoroughfares the main sights are signposted. Be warned that it is not always the most obvious monument that is signposted. I have already mentioned that, in order to see the Church of SS. Giovanni e Paolo, you should follow signs for the hospital next door. In the same way, in S. Polo, it is not the Frari Church which appears on the signposts but the adjacent Scuole di S. Rocco. For getting to your actual destination you should always carry a large-scale street plan as suggested on page 37. One problem here can be that the name on your map is not necessarily the name which appears on the street signs, since your map will be written in Italian while the street signs are in Venetian dialect.

It sounds irritating but in fact contributes to the fascination of the city. Do not worry if you get lost: Venice is too small for you to be lost for too long. The accidental discoveries of hidden canals and quiet squares are part of the city's charm.

Two other useful signposts you will see are for **Vaporetto** and **Traghetto**. These indicate the way to the nearest water-bus stop or gondola ferry point respectively.

The Public Transport System

The public transport system in Venice is operated by the *Azienda del Consorzio Trasporti Veneziano*, known as the **Actv**. Within the Lagoon they operate a number of water-bus and ferry services as well as municipal bus services on the mainland. Currently the whole basis of the Actv is under review by the Commune and Province of Venezia and it looks as though deregulation, with competing services allowed, is likely to result. Agreement on the need for reform was reached between commune and province in early March 1991 but bureaucracy is slow in Italy and the existing services are likely to remain as described below for some time. They are remarkably efficient and very good value. Ferries and other services to the islands will be discussed later. For now, let us look at water-bus services in and around the historic centre.

Water Buses
Water buses fall into two types. There is the **Vaporetto** (which means 'little steamship') and there is the **Motoscafo** (which means 'motor vessel'). Obviously it is a long time since any vessel was steam-powered but *vaporetti* remains the name for the larger, lumbering stopping-bus services along the main routes; the *motoscafi* are smaller, faster craft, making fewer stops. When they follow roughly the same route the *motoscafi* are quicker but more expensive than the *vaporetti* and they are not accessible for the disabled. The main *vaporetto* routes are:

Line 1 (known as the *Accelerato*)
Tronchetto — Piazzale Roma — Ferrovia — S. Marcuola — S. Biasio — S. Stae — Ca' d'Oro — Rialto — S. Silvestro — S. Angelo — S. Tomà — Ca' Rezzonico — Accademia — S. Maria del Giglio — S.Marco — S. Zaccaria — Arsenale — Giardini — S. Elena — Lido (S. Maria Elisabetta).

Every 10 minutes from 7.00 to 23.00, with a less frequent service during the night. Tickets — L2,200.

Line 5 (Circular)

Murano — Fondamenta Nuove — Madonna dell'Orto — S. Alvise — Tre Archi — Guglie — Ferrovia — Piazzale Roma — S. Marta — Sacca Fisola — Zattere — S. Eufamia — Redentore — Zitelle — S. Giorgio Maggiore — S. Zaccaria — Tana — Celestia — Ospedale — Fond. Nuove — Cimitero — Murano. The route described goes anti-clockwise and is known as *circolare sinistra*; there is also a clockwise route known as the *circolare destra*.

Every 15 minutes in each direction from 6.30 to 21.00. A less frequent service through the night is only available on the *circolare sinistra*. Tickets — L2,200.

Line 8

Tronchetto — Sacca Fisola — Giudecca (Traghetto) — Zattere (Traghetto) — Zitelle — S. Giorgio — S. Zaccaria.

Every 15 minutes from 7.00 to 20.15 and at hourly intervals during the night. Tickets — L2,200.

Line 9 (Traghetto)

Ferry service Zattere — Giudecca and return. Every 15 minutes. Tickets — L1,500.

Line 34 — Summer only.

S. Marco — Redentore — Sacca Fisola — Tronchetto B — Piazzale Roma — Ferrovia — S. Marcuola — Rialto — S. Tomà — S. Samuele — Accademia — S. Marco — S. Zaccaria — Giardini — Lido.

Every 10 minutes. Tickets L2,200.

The main *motoscafo* routes are:

Line 2 (Diretto)

Rialto — Ferrovia — Piazzale Roma *Via Rio Nuovo* S. Samuele — Accademia — S. Marco — S. Zaccaria — S. Elena — Lido.

Every 10 minutes from 6.30 to 20.30. Every 20 minutes to midnight. Hourly overnight. *Note that this is the fastest way to get from the railway station or Piazzale Roma to the St Mark's area but, by cutting through the Rio Nuovo, about three-quarters of the Grand Canal is missed out.* Tickets L3,300.

Line 5 (barrato) Summer only
Tronchetto — Murano via P. Roma and Ferrovia and S. Zaccaria — Murano via S. Elena.
Every 30 minutes. Tickets L2,200.

Line 28 (Casino) Summer only
Piazzale Roma — S. Zaccaria — Lido (Casino)
Every 30 minutes when Casino is open.

All the routes detailed above also travel in the reverse direction. Tickets are one price no matter how much of the route you follow. Some of the landing stages permit a *traghetto* crossing between two adjacent landing stages for L1,500 (see tariff at ticket office for availability). Children over 1 metre tall and suitcases over 50 cm in length must also have a ticket. Tickets must be obtained before boarding the boat, either at the landing stage ticket office or at the many *tabacchi* and other shops showing the Actv sign. Many of the smaller landing stages do not have ticket offices and, unless you have bought a ticket from a shop you must board the boat without a ticket, in which case a L500 supplement is payable. Each landing stage has a small box with a slit into which the ticket is inserted to be punched with the date and time; the ticket becomes valid only when it is so punched (the purpose and location of this machine is not clearly indicated; watch the regulars to see what to do. Also note that some ticket offices such as that at S. Marco, issue paper tickets which will not fit the validating machines but which are printed with date and time instead). Although no one may ask to see your ticket, spot checks are made and someone found without a validated ticket can be fined on the spot.

Although the fares and times quoted were correct at the time of writing they are liable to vary and you should always check with the timetables and tariffs which are prominently displayed at every landing stage.

Two special tourist tickets are available. The 1-day ticket, in pink, gives unlimited travel on Actv water and motor buses for 24 hours from validation, at a cost of L10,000. The 3-day ticket, in blue, gives similar unlimited travel for 72 hours from validation, at a cost of L17,000. The tickets are, however, not valid on Lines 2 and 28, nor on out-of-town motor-buses. For the under-26s a 3-day ticket is available for L13,000 on production of a *Carta Giovani* (see 'Youth Pass' on page 141).

Tourist tickets are available from most landing stage ticket offices, Actv offices and the APT (Tourist Information offices).

If you feel you might well be making a number of visits to Venice within a 3-year period it is worth considering the **Carta Venezia**. This is not a season ticket but its possession allows you to buy tickets on all Actv services (road and water) at less than half price. It can be obtained for L10,000 from the Actv head office at the Corte dell'Albero near the S. Angelo water-bus stop. You must go there in person and you will need your passport and a passport-sized photograph to obtain it. It is valid for three years from the day of issue.

Privately owned transport

Water Taxis

Water taxis are beautiful and luxurious boats and they have the advantage over the water buses of being able to penetrate the smaller canals so that they can get you close to your destination. But they are very expensive with a fixed charge of L24,000 for up to 4 people, on a journey of not more than 7 minutes. There is a meter charge of L420 per 15 seconds and further surcharges for night calls, extra passengers etc.

Taxi stands are available at the railway station, Piazzale Roma, Rialto, St Mark's, Lido and airport. Or the radio taxis can be contacted on 5232 326 or 5222 303.

Gondolas

Once the normal mode of transport in Venice, the gondola has long since ceased to serve an everyday purpose and has instead become a tourist institution. Each hiring of a gondola is an individual contract between the gondolier and customer and the price should be agreed before you step aboard. Prices are fixed by the commune but they are minimum rates. You cannot expect to pay any less; if you are not a good bargainer you could well pay much more. Do not be deterred by these cautionary remarks however; a ride in a gondola may well be expensive but it is a unique form of travel that you should experience at least once in your life.

First 50 minutes	L70,000
Each successive 25 minutes	L35,000
Night rate, between 20.00 and 8.00.	L90,000

The cost is per gondola, not per person. The maximum number a gondola may carry at one time is 5 people.

The gondola stands are at:
Bacino Orseolo, north of St Mark's Square in front of the Hotel Cavalletto; **Calle Vallaresso**, near Harry's Bar; **Riva degli Schiavoni**, in front of the Danieli; **The Molo**, at the end of the Piazzetta; **Piazzale Roma**, on the corner of Grand Canal and Rio Nuovo; **Tronchetto**; **Ferrovia**, in front of S. Simeon Piccolo; **S. Maria del Giglio**, next to Hotel Gritti Palace; **Rialto**; **S. Sofia**, Cannaregio; **S. Tomà**; **Campo S. Moisè**, next to the Hotel Grunwald.

Boat Hire

It is possible to hire boats by the day to drive or row yourself but boating in Venice is not for novices. Even the most experienced boatmen find the Grand Canal more heavily trafficked than any other piece of water they know, while the narrow canals are not easy to navigate, especially if you do not know the local traffic regulations. If you venture out into the Lagoon the complex pattern of channels and shallows is really only known to experienced locals and should not be contemplated without an extremely good chart. Do not undertake the hire of a boat lightly.

If you are determined, you might try the following, who may be willing to hire against a deposit and on production of a passport:
For rowing: **Nino (el afitabarche)** on Campo S. Boldo, not far from the Frari, will hire a *sandolino* for L8,000 a day.
For motor-boats: **Giampietro Brussa** at Cannaregio 331 (near Palazzo Labia), tel. 715787, will hire for around L15,000.

Crossing the Grand Canal

There are just three bridges across the Grand Canal. There are obviously times when you wish to cross the Canal but to get back to the nearest bridge requires a substantial detour. It would of course be possible to use the *vaporetti* which zigzag from bank to bank along the Canal but this would be uneconomic, even on a traghetto fare of L1,300. The answer is the **traghetti** services offered by the gondolas. There are seven points along the Grand Canal where the gondolas run a simple

---

The Gondola

The word 'gondola' comes from the Latin *cymbula*, meaning 'small boat'. Part of the Venetian scene since 1100 the gondola evolved over the centuries into its present form which is fixed to the pattern of 1750. That was the year that all gondolas became black, in a law passed by the government in order to stop the wasteful competition of the Venetian patricians each of whom wanted gondolas that were more colourful and more decorative than anyone else's.

Today's gondola weighs 1,000 lbs and is made of 280 separate pieces of wood, mainly larch and oak. The design is very precise and, if you look closely, is not symmetrical; the right side is narrower than the left. This is to preserve the balance of the boat as the gondolier stands at the rear to row with the single oar. At the front is the scimitar-shaped ornament known as the *Ferro*. This has six comb-like bars facing forward and one back. The six facing forwards represent the six sestieri while the single one facing back stands for Giudecca which is like a sestiere but is not.

---

cross-canal service. For many visitors this might be one affordable way to get a gondola ride; although custom dictates that you stand for the crossing. The fare for a single crossing is L400. Traghetti are:

From in front of the railway station to S. Simeon Piccolo.
From the Campo S. Marcuola to the Fondaco dei Turchi.
From near the Ca' d'Oro to the Fish Market.
From the Riva del Carbon near the Palazzo Dandolo to the Fond. del Vin, S. Silvestro.
From S. Angelo to S. Tomà.
From S. Samuele to Ca' Rezzonico.
From S. Maria del Giglio to a point between Salute and the Guggenheim Collection.

Porters

If you wish to walk but need your luggage carried there are 12 porters' stands in the city. The charges within Venice (Tronchetto excluded) are L8,350 for 1 or 2 pieces of luggage, with L2,350 for each successive item. You are also expected to tip the porter. Stands, with their phone numbers, are:

Accademia (5224 891), Bragora (5287 273), S, Zaccaria (5228 901), Ferrovia (715272), Piazzale Roma (5223 590), Rialto (5205 308), S. Geremia (715694), S. Marco — Orologio (5232 385), S. Marco — Orseolo (5200 545), S. Maria Formosa (5237 578), S. Moisè (5237 578), Calle Vallaresso (5224 412).

An indispensable companion

The Porters' Association for most of the hotels in Venice publishes a guide, monthly in winter and fortnightly in the high season, which is distributed free through the reception desks of hotels belonging to the Association, and can also be obtained from Information Offices. This is *Un Ospite di Venezia/A Guest in Venice* and is bilingual Italian/English. This is not only a full guide to what is on in the way of plays, concerts and exhibitions, but contains museum charges and opening hours, tariffs and timetables for public transport, gondolas, etc. And much more in the way of useful information. It is invaluable for up-dating times and charges quoted in this guide and you should endeavour to obtain a copy soon after your arrival.

The bustling scene of the Grand Canal looking south from Rialto.

FOUR

Accommodation

Hotels

The Italian word for hotel is *albergo* but the term *hotel* is far more frequently used. The term *pensione* is also used for simpler hotels specialising in half or full board accommodation. A simple hotel might also refer to itself as a *locanda* which strictly speaking is an inn but, in a city such as Venice, usually represents a restaurant with rooms. In these the emphasis is on the food, with rooms as an extra convenience. Just because the accommodation is cheap and simple the guest should not expect a meal in the restaurant to be the same, the opposite is often the case.

In 1988 the system of hotel classification was totally revised in Italy. Under the old system hotels had been categorised according to IV, III, II, I and De Luxe categories, with separate rating tables for hotels and *pensioni*. The reformed system did away with the separate classification for *pensioni* and they are all graded as hotels now. The classification of the new unified listing is now by stars, with one star corresponding to the old category IV and five stars representing the old De Luxe category. 5-star hotels which meet international standards can add the letter 'L' for De Luxe to their five stars. Only hotels with at least four stars are allowed to call themselves 'Grand Hotel' or 'Palace Hotel'.

Venice is well provided with hotels of every class, although the city is notable in having no fewer than five hotels entitled to the De Luxe classification, three of them ranked among the leading hotels of the world. Prices in all categories tend to be higher than the Italian average, and all hotels become fully booked very quickly. As a general rule the hotels are more expensive and more popular in San Marco, the Riva degli

Schiavoni area of Castello and along the Lista di Spagna close to the railway station. They are cheaper and more likely to have vacancies further away from these tourist centres. During the high season and Carnival it is essential to book your hotel room in advance. If you arrive in Venice without pre-booked accommodation you can save yourself a wearying and frustrating hunt by using one of the booking offices provided by the Venetian Hoteliers Association (the A.V.A.). These are located at Marco Polo Airport, the railway station, Piazzale Roma and at the Marghera exit from the A4 motor-way. These offices will find you a room as close as possible to your requirements given the availability on the day. Having made your booking you pay a deposit of L10,000. The receipt you get for this is handed to your hotel when you check in and the L10,000 will be knocked off your bill.

In common with most European hotels, those in Venice charge primarily by the room rather than the person but, if you are given a double room when you asked for a single, the hotelier is not allowed to charge more than the maximum single rate. Similarly, if a third bed is put into a double room the charge for the third person must not be more than 25% of the room cost. The range of charges for all rooms have by law to be prominently displayed at reception and the charge for a specific room must be shown in that room. 99% of hoteliers are honest but it does no harm to check that you are being charged the correct rate. Although breakfast is still theoretically an optional extra, hotels are increasingly quoting a room price that includes breakfast.

If you have any complaints about standards of service, overcharging or any other problem you should address your complaints to *Dipartimento Turismo, Giunta Regionale del Veneto*, Lista di Spagna 168, Tel. 792638.

Paying for your hotel, if it is not prepaid before departure, can sometimes cause problems. Although most hotels of three stars and over do accept credit cards they do not necessarily take all cards. Even some 4-star hotels still do not accept any cards at all. It is probably better to pay by Eurocheque.

In the list which follows hotels are grouped by sestiere. For each I give their star rating, address and telephone number (with telex and fax numbers where they exist). Costs quoted are based on the 1991 tariff and allowance should be made for inflation. The two figures quoted for room charges are for low season and high season; they represent the average cost in that hotel for a double room with private facilities (where no private facilities are available the room cost is shown in italics — where a hotel is closed in winter and does not have a separate low season tariff, just one figure is given); prices for breakfast, however, are per person. Costs for single rooms are between 15% and 20% cheaper than double rooms. The prices quoted by a hotel are inclusive of VAT, central heating and a fixed service charge but you may be asked to pay a surcharge for air-conditioning in the summer. The prices do not allow for surcharges on superior rooms, balconies or views of the Lagoon or Grand Canal. Nor do they allow for any special deals such as winter discounts that may be available. Additional information includes the location of the nearest water-bus stop, usually on route no. 1.

Most Venice hotels are listed but some have been excluded where a lack of facilities is combined with the hotel being closed except in the high season.

Hotels by Sestiere

San Marco
5-star De Luxe
Bauer Grunwald & Grand, S. Marco, Campo S. Moisè, 1459. Tel. 5207 022, Tx. 410075 Fax 5207 557: One of Venice's prestige hotels, located on the Grand Canal, just one block away from St Mark's Square, although entrance is from the Campo S. Moisè. Rooftop bar commands superb view of the Salute. The most economical of Venice's 5-star hotels. Rooms L230,000–L460,000. Breakfast L20,000. Water-bus: S. Marco.
Europa e Regina, S. Marco 2159. Tel. 5200 477. Tx. 410123. Fax 5231 533. Also on the Grand Canal virtually next door to the Bauer Grunwald. Created from five linked 18th-century buildings. The Terrazzo-Tiepolo restaurant and bar are out-doors on the canal side overlooking the Salute. Belongs to the luxury CIGA hotel chain. Rooms L262,000–L512,000. Break-fast L25,000. Water bus:S. Marco.
Gritti Palace, S. Marco 2467. Tel. 794611. Tx. 410125. Fax 5200 942. World famous for luxury and comfort and the second most expensive hotel in Venice. On the Grand Canal in a *palazzo*

once owned by Doge Andrea Gritti (1523–38). It has been patronised by the famous from Graham Greene to Ernest Hemingway and has a largely American clientele. A CIGA hotel. Rooms L393,000–L666,000. Breakfast L32,000. Water-bus:S.Maria del Giglio.

4-star

Cavaletto e Doge Orseolo, S. Marco 1107. Tel. 5200 955. Tx. 410684. Fax 5238 184. Just off St Mark's Square and overlooking the main gondola stand of the Bacino Orseolo. One of Venice's oldest hotels. Small outside terrace. Rooms L133,500–L265,000. Breakfast L20,000. Water-bus:S. Marco.

Concordia, Calle Larga S. Marco 367. Tel. 5206 866. Tx. 411069. Fax 5206 775. The only hotel in Venice directly opposite the north front of St Mark's Basilica, although you will have to pay a surcharge of up to L17,500 a night for a room with that view. Rooms L140,000–L280,000. Breakfast L12,000. Water-bus: S. Marco.

Luna Hotel Baglioni, S. Marco 1243. Tel. 5289 840. Tx 410236. Fax 5287 160. Recently refurbished with elegant public rooms and outdoor restaurant. Adjacent to St Mark's Square, on the S. Moisè side in the Calle Ascensione. Rooms L185,000–L365,000. Breakfast L30,000. Water-bus: S. Marco.

Monaco e Grand Canal, S. Marco 1325. Tel. 5200 211. Tx. 410450. Fax 5200 501. Adjacent to the San Marco water-bus landing stage and across the Calle Vallaresso from Harry's Bar, the hotel is located in an elegant 18th-century *palazzo* with a leafy central courtyard. A canopied terrace looks across the canal towards Giudecca. Regarded by many as one of the most desirable hotels in Venice and probably far better value for money than many 5-star hotels. Rooms L175,000–L345,000. Breakfast L22,000. Water-bus: S. Marco.

Saturnia & International, S. Marco 2398. Tel. 5208 377. Tx. 410355. Fax 5207 131. On the smart shopping street of Calle Larga XXII Marzo, a 14th-century building with an impressive Gothic foyer, carved timber ceilings, ornamental staircase and old well-head. Two restaurants, one with two Michelin rosettes. Rooms L230,000–L345,000. Breakfast L14,000. Water-bus: S. Marco.

Star-Hotel Splendid Suisse, Mercerie 760. Tel. 5200 755. Tx. 410590. Fax 5286 498. Situated halfway between St Mark's and Rialto on the city's most celebrated shopping street.

Completely rebuilt in last few years. Rooms L190,000–L380,000. Breakfast L25,000. Water-bus: Rialto.

3-star

Ala, S. Marco 2494. Tel. 5208 333. Tx. 410275. Fax 5206 390. Another converted *palazzo* on the Campo S. Maria del Giglio opposite the Gritti Palace. Rooms L112,000–L150,000. Breakfast L16,500. Water-bus: S. Maria del Giglio.

All'Angelo, Calle Larga S. Marco 403. Tel. 5209 299. Tx. 420676. Fax 5231 943. Close to the Concordia but without view of St Mark's. Rooms L75,000–L151,000. Breakfast L14,500. Water-bus: S. Marco/Zaccaria.

Ambassador Tre Rose, Calle dei Fabbri 905. Tel. 5222 490. Tx. 215660. Medium-sized hotel very close to the Rialto Bridge. Rooms L129,000–L151,000. Breakfast L23,000. Water-bus: Rialto.

Ateneo, S.Marco 1876. Tel. 5200 588. Tx. 420655. Fax 5228 550. Smallish hotel quite close to the Fenice Theatre. Completely restored in recent years. Rooms L86,000–L151,000. Breakfast L20,000. Water-bus: S. Maria del Giglio.

Bel Sito e Berlino, S. Marco 2517. Tel. 5223 365. Tx. 420835. Fax 5204 083. Makes a special feature of Venetian glass and mirrors in the public rooms. Rooms L94,000–L137,000. Breakfast L13,000. Water-bus: S. Maria del Giglio.

Bonvecchiati, Calle Goldoni 4488. Tel. 5285 017. Tx. 410560. Fax 5285 230. Large rooms with high ceilings. Good collection of modern art. Near the Goldoni Theatre and the Campo S. Luca. Rooms L132,000–L152,000. Breakfast L17,000. Water-bus: Rialto.

Boston, S. Marco 848. Tel. 5287 665. Tx. 420307. Quite close to the Rialto Bridge. Rooms L110,000–L150,000. Breakfast L12,500. Water-bus: Rialto.

De l'Alboro, S. Marco 3894. Tel. 5206 977. Fax 5228 404. Near to the Grand Canal close to S. Benedetto. Small hotel of 16 rooms. Rooms L115,000–L150.000. Breakfast L15,000. Water-bus: S. Angelo.

Do Pozzi, S. Marco 2373. Tel. 5207 855. Tx. 420042. Fax 5206 390. Quiet and secluded old building set back off the Calle Larga XXII Marzo, with a pretty courtyard and the two well-heads that give it its name. Runs special 'Taste of Venice' gourmet short stays in association with Raffaelle Restaurant. Rooms L100,000–L146,000. Breakfast L15,000. Water-bus: S. Marco.

Flora, S. Marco 2283a. Tel. 5205 844. Tx. 410401. Fax 5228 217. Pleasant hotel in quiet cul-de-sac off the Calle Larga XXII Marzo, with attractive garden. Air of exclusivity because it will not accept package tourists. Very popular with British visitors. Rooms L113,000–L150,000. Breakfast L15,000. Water-bus: S. Marco.

Graspo de Ua, Rialto 5094. Tel. 5205 644. Tx. 420180. Small hotel of only 20 rooms. Actually one of Venice's leading restaurants, with rooms. Rooms L90,000–L151,000. Breakfast L15.000. Water-bus:Rialto.

Kette, S. Marco 2053. Tel. 5222 730. Tx. 420653. Fax 5228 964. Quiet hotel off the *calle* running north from the Calle Larga XXII Marzo to the Fenice Theatre. Completely renovated. Interesting art collection in the public areas. Rooms L86,000–L151,000. Breakfast L19,500. Water-bus:S. Marco.

La Fenice et des Artistes, S. Marco 1936. Tel. 5232 333. Tx 411150. Fax 5203 721. Close to the theatre and with regular clientele of actors, singers and musicians. Lots of marble, elegance and comfort. Might be some noise from Taverna on ground floor. High season only. Rooms L151,500. Breakfast L15,000. Water-bus: S. Maria del Giglio.

Montecarlo, S. Marco 463. Tel. 5207 144. Tx. 411098. Fax 5207 789. In side street between St Mark's and Rialto. Buffet breakfasts and adjacent to two restaurants which offer discounts to hotel clients. High season only. Rooms L151,000. Breakfast L22,000. Water-bus: S. Marco.

Panada, Calle Specchieri 646. Tel. 5209 088. Tx. 410153. Fax 5209 619. Old family hotel in alley running between St Mark's Square and S. Zulian. Its bar, *Al Speci,* is a great favourite of locals. Rooms L115,000–L151,000. Breakfast L17,000. Water-bus: S.Marco.

Rialto, S. Marco 5149. Tel. 5209 166. Tx. 420809. Fax 5238 958. At the end of the Rialto Bridge with a gondola stand below the terrace bar. Has a restaurant, snack bar and pizzeria. Rooms L81,000–L151,000. Breakfast L20,000. Water-bus: Rialto.

San Marco, S. Marco 877. Tel. 5204 277. Tx. 420888. Fax 5204 277. Very close to St Mark's Square on the Rialto side. Rooms L129,000–L151,000. Breakfast L23,000. Water-bus: S. Marco.

San Moisè, S. Marco 2058. Tel. 5203 755. Tx. 420655. Fax 5228 550. Small hotel by the Rio dei Barcaroli, reached by alleyway from the Calle Larga XXII Marzo. Small canalside terrace. Rooms L86,000–L151,000. Breakfast L20,000. Water-bus: S. Marco.

Torino, S. Marco 2356. Tel. 5205 222. Tx. 420655. Fax 5228 227. A 15th-century building with a pretty courtyard close to the Fenice. Rooms L110,000–L151,000. Breakfast L22.000. Water-bus: S. Maria del Giglio.

2-star

Astoria, Calle Fiubera 951. Tel. 5225 381. Fax 5200 771. Between St Mark's and Rialto. Only two-thirds rooms with private facilities. Rooms L75,000–L81,000. Breakfast L10,000. Water-bus: S. Marco.

Bartolomeo, Calle dell'Orso 5494. Tel. 5235 387. Close to main post office. About half rooms with private facilities. Rooms L55,000–L81,000. Breakfast L12,500. Water-bus: Rialto.

Centauro, Campo Manin 4297A. Tel. 5225 832. Fax 5239 151. In attractive square. Almost all rooms with facilities. Rooms L59,000–L81,000. Breakfast L12,000. Water-bus: Rialto.

Città di Milano, S. Marco 590. Tel. 5227 002. Fax 5227 834. Quite close to St Mark's on Rialto side. Restaurant with rooms. Very few rooms with private facilities. Rooms L56,000–L81,000. Breakfast L12,000. Water-bus: S. Marco.

Diana, S. Marco 449. Tel. 5206 911. Fax 5238 763. In same area as the Città di Milano. Most rooms with private facilities. Rooms L41,000–L81,000. Breakfast L15,000. Water-bus: S. Marco.

Firenze, S. Marco 1490. Tel 5222 858. Tx. 410627. Close to S. Moisè Church. Less than half the rooms have private facilities. Rooms L42,000–L81,000. Breakfast L13,000. Water-bus: S. Marco.

Gallini, Calle della Verona 3673. Tel. 5236 371. Tx. 420353. Family hotel run by two brothers, close to Fenice and Campo S. Fantin. Half the rooms have private facilities. Rooms L61,000–L81,000. Breakfast L13,000. Water-bus: S. Angelo.

Gorizia a la Valigia, Calle dei Fabbri 4696A. Tel. 5223 737. Tx. 420354. Not far from Rialto. Restaurant but very few rooms with private facilities. Rooms L49,000–L77,000. Breakfast L12,000. Water-bus: Rialto.

Lisbona, Calle Larga XXII Marzo 2153. Tel. 5286 774. Small hotel with 15 rooms, all with private facilities, situated on Venice's most exclusive shopping street. Rooms L65,000–L81,000. Breakfast L13,000. Map ref. P20. Water-bus: S. Marco.

Orion, S. Marco 700A. Tel. 5223 053. Fax 5238 866. Small family-run hotel with 17 large rooms, all with private facilities bar a couple of single rooms. Recently renovated. Rooms L63,000–L81,000. Breakfast L14,500. Water-bus: S. Marco.

San Gallo, S. Marco 1093A. Tel. 5227 311. Fax 5225 702. Just 12 rooms, half with private facilities. Rooms L50,000–L81,000. Breakfast L13,500. Water-bus: S. Marco.

San Giorgio, Calle della Mandola 3781. Tel. 5235 835. Fax 5228 702. 16 rooms all with private facilities in *calle* linking Campo S. Angelo with Campo Manin. Rooms L60,000–L80,000. Breakfast L12,500. Water-bus: S. Angelo.

San Stefano, S.Marco 2957. Tel. 5200 166. Fax 5224 460. Twelve rooms all with private facilities. On the Campo S. Stefano (or Campo Morosini). Rooms L60,000–L80,000. Breakfast L15,000. Water-bus: S. Maria del Giglio.

San Zulian, S. Marco 534. Tel. 5225 872 Fax 5232 265. Between St Mark's and Rialto near church of the same name. Unpretentious with large, pretty rooms. Rooms L63,000–L81,000. Breakfast L14,500. Water-bus: S. Marco.

Serenissima, Calle Goldoni 4486. Tel. 700011. Fax 5223 292. Medium-sized hotel with majority of rooms having private facilities. Close to Goldoni Theatre. Rooms L45,000–L81,000. Breakfast L13,500. Water-bus: Rialto.

1-star

Al Gambero, Calle dei Fabbri 4687. Tel. 5224 384. Halfway between St Mark's Square and Rialto near S. Salvatore. Room L68,000. Breakfast L8,500. Water-bus: Rialto

Casa Petrarca, S. Marco 4386. Tel. 5200 430. Very friendly and welcoming but only 6 rooms, 3 with private facilities, all attractively furnished in traditional Venetian style. Rooms L70,000. Breakfast L6,500. Water-bus: S. Marco.

Locanda Fiorita, Campiello Nuovo 3457A. Tel. 5234 754. Close to the Accademia Bridge. Ten simple but pleasant rooms, about half have private facilities. Rooms L60,000–L70,000. Breakfast L9,000. Water-bus: S. Maria del Giglio.

San Salvador, S. Marco 5264. Tel. 5289 147. Small hotel between S. Salvatore and the Rialto. Only 7 rooms, most with private facilities. Essentially a restaurant with rooms. Rooms L40,000–L59,000. No breakfast served. Water-bus: Rialto.

(Opposite): The facade of the Doge's Palace overlooking the Lagoon, with the balconied window designed by the Dalle Massegne family in 1404.

Overleaf Top: The water-gate to the Arsenal, barred to all but the no. 5 water-bus.

Bottom: The bulk of S. Zanipolo rises over the rooftops. Beyond, the northern Lagoon with Murano and the cemetery island of S. Michele.

Dorsoduro & Giudecca

5-star De Luxe

Cipriani, Giudecca 10. Tel. 5207 744. Tx. 410162. Fax 5203 930. Undoubtedly one of the world's great hotels, owned by the organisation running the Orient Express. A modern building set in three acres of grounds with swimming pool and tennis courts. Transport to and from Venice by hotel's private launches. Immense luxury and everything for your needs but also the most expensive hotel in an expensive city. Rooms L390,000–L780,000. Breakfast L49,000. Water-bus: Zitelle.

3-star

Accademia Villa Maravegie, Fondamenta Bollani 1058. Tel. 5210 188. Fax 5239 152. A rambling 17th-century villa set back in large, quiet garden. Very popular with British and can be booked up a year in advance. No restaurant but they will let you eat your snacks in the garden. Rooms L100,000–L130,000. Breakfast L15,000. Water-bus: Accademia.

American, S. Vio 628. Tel. 5204 733. Tx. 410508. Fax 5204 048. On the fondamenta of the S. Vio Canal, notable for its quiet location. Recently renovated throughout. Rooms L75,000–L150,000. Breakfast L15,000. Water-bus: Accademia.

Pausania, Dorsoduro 2824. Tel. 5222 083. Tx. 420178. Converted 14th-century *palazzo* with very comfortable rooms. Rooms L76,000–L151,000. Breakfast L17,000. Water-bus: Zattere.

2-star

Agli Alboretti, Dorsoduro 884. Tel. 5230 058. Small family-run hotel with home-from-home atmosphere. Rooms simple but more than adequate. Near the Accademia. Rooms L72,000–L81,000. Breakfast L12,000. Water-bus: Accademia.

Alla Salute da Cici, Dorsoduro 222. Tel. 5235 404. Medium-sized hotel with restaurant and garden. Only two-thirds of the rooms have private facilities. Rooms L78,000. Breakfast L10,000. Water-bus: Accademia.

Casa Frollo, Giudecca 50. Tel. 5222 723. Fax 5206 203. Large villa with magnificent public rooms crowded with art and antiques. Superb views across Lagoon to St Mark's and Salute. Only half the rooms have private facilities. Closed November to March. Rooms L75,500–L81,000. Breakfast L13,000. Water-bus: Zitelle.

Messner, Dorsoduro 216. Tel. 5227 443. Fax 5227 443. Only 13 rooms because essentially a restaurant with rooms. Rooms L81,000. Breakfast L9,000. Has 1-star annexe. Water-bus: Accademia.

Seguso, Zattere 779. Tel. 5222 340. Fax 5222 340. A modest hotel with an air of faded gentility. Wonderful views across to Giudecca. Rooms L78,000–L81,000. Breakfast L16,000. Water-bus: Zattere.

Tivoli, Dorsoduro 3838. Tel. 5237 752. Close to Grand Canal and the Frari. Only half the rooms have private facilities. Rooms L50,000–L80,000. Breakfast L10,000. Water-bus: S. Tomà.

1-star

Antico Capon, Campo S. Margherita 3004. Tel. 5285 292. A restaurant with rooms (7) in student district on attractive square. Rooms L70,000. No breakfast. Water-bus: S. Tomà.

Ca' Foscari, Calle della Frescada 3888. Tel. 5225 817. Also in student area and also restaurant with rooms. Only 10 rooms, none with private facilities. Family run, with great pride in the service offered. Room *L44.000*. Breakfast L5,500. Water-bus: S. Tomà.

Casa de Stefani, Calle Traghetto San Barnabo 2786. Tel. 5223 337. For the eccentric lover of decayed grandeur. Painted ceilings and lots of cats. No breakfast served. Rooms L55,000. Water-bus: Accademia.

Montin, Fondamenta di Borgo 1147. Tel. 5227 151. The anomaly is that one of Venice's most famous and prestigious restaurants has some of the most economical accommodation. Praised by all who stay there but there are only 7 rooms and they are all booked up weeks, if not months, ahead. No private facilities. Do not expect to eat here at the same bargain prices! Rooms *L40,000–L44,000*. Breakfast L4,000. Water-bus: Zattere/Accademia.

San Polo & Santa Croce

4-star

Carlton Executive, Santa Croce 578. Tel. 718488. Tx. 410070. Fax 719061. Large and rather impersonal international-style hotel just across Grand Canal from the railway station. Closed November-April. Rooms L210,000–L290,000. Breakfast L20,000. Water-bus: Piazzale Roma.

Pulman Park Hotel, Giardino Papadopoli 245. Tel. 5285 394. Tx. 410310. Fax 5230 043. Another large international hotel overlooking wooded park opposite the railway station and adjacent to the Piazzale Roma. Rooms L238,000–L310,000. Breakfast L18,000. Water-bus: Piazzale Roma.

3-star

Al Sole Palace, Santa Croce 136. Tel. 5232 144. Tx. 410070. Fax 719061. In the centre of Santa Croce, a large hotel which only accepts half board bookings in the low season. Rooms (high season only) L151,000. Breakfast L20,000. Water-bus: Piazzale Roma/S. Tomà.

Capri, Santa Croce 595. Tel. 718988. Tx. 410070. Fax 719061. In same area as the Carlton. High season only. Rooms L100,000. Breakfast L19,000. Water-bus: Piazzale Roma.

Gardena, Santa Croce 239. Tel. 5235 549. Tx. 410070. Fax 5235 549. Smallish hotel adjacent to Piazzale Roma. High season only. Rooms L150,000. Breakfast L19,000. Water-bus: Piazzale Roma.

San Cassiano — Ca' Favretto, Santa Croce 2232. Tel. 5241 760. Tx. 420810. Fax 721033. Gothic *palazzo,* on the dark side but well-converted and comfortable. View across the Grand Canal to the Ca' d'Oro. Rooms L86,000–L151,000. Breakfast L20,000. Water-bus: S. Stae.

Santa Chiara, Santa Croce 548. Tel. 5206 955. Tx. 420690. Fax 5228 799. Small hotel adjacent to Piazzale Roma. Rooms L76,000–L151,000. Breakfast L17,000. Water-bus: Piazzale Roma.

2-star

Airone, Santa Croce 557. Tel. 5204 800. 13-room hotel, about half with private facilities. Also in vicinity of Ponte degli Scalzi. Rooms L52,000–L75,000. Breakfast L10,000. Water-bus: Riva di Biàsio.

Basilea (with 1-star annexe), Rio Manin 817. Tel. 718477. Tx. 420320. Fax 720851 Medium sized hotel overlooking the Rio Manin canal close to the Scalzi Bridge. Rooms L65,000–L81,000. Breakfast L14.000. Water-bus: Riva di Biàzio.

Canal, Santa Croce 553. Tel. 5238 480. Fax 5239 106. Smallish hotel on the Grand Canal directly opposite the railway station. Rooms L42,000–L81,000. Breakfast L13,000. Water-bus: Piazzale Roma.

Falier, Salizzada S. Pantalon 130. Tel. 5228 882. Fax 5206 554. Halfway between the Frari and Piazzale Roma. Rooms L71,000–L81,000. Breakfast L14,500. Water-bus: Piazzale Roma/S. Tomà.

Iris, S. Tomà 2910A. Tel. 5222 882. Fax 5222 882. One of the few hotels in S. Polo, close to S. Tomà Church and water-bus stop of same name. High season only. Rooms L75,000. Breakfast L5,000. Water-bus: S. Tomà.

Marconi e Milano, S. Polo 729. Tel.5222 068. Smallish hotel at the San Polo end of the Rialto Bridge, under the same management as the San Cassiano. Rooms L75,000–L81,000. Breakfast L12,000. Water-bus: Rialto.

Piazzale Roma, Santa Croce 390. Tel. 703065. 18-room hotel convenient for the car parks and bus terminal. Rooms L65,000–L81,000. Breakfast L13,000. Water-bus: Piazzale Roma.

Walter, Fondamenta Tolentini 240. Tel. 5286 204. Fax 5239 106. Across the Papadopoli Gardens from Piazzale Roma. Only 11 rooms. Rooms L42,000–L81,000. Breakfast L13,000. Water-bus: Piazzale Roma.

1-star

Antiche Figure, Santa Croce 686A. Tel. 718290. Essentially a restaurant with only 13 rooms, no private facilities. Near the Scalzi Bridge. Rooms *L35,000–L40,000*. Breakfast L6,500. Water-bus: Riva di Biàsio.

Da Bepi, Santa Croce 160. Tel. 5226 735. Not far from the Piazzale Roma. Just 10 rooms, about half with private facilities. No breakfast served. Rooms L62,000–L65,000. Water-bus: Piazzale Roma.

Dalla Mora, Santa Croce 42A. Tel. 5235 703. Near S. Pantalon. Rooms L58,000–L65,000. Breakfast L5,000. Water-bus: S. Tomà.

Marin, Santa Croce 670B. Tel. 718022. Medium-sized hotel in area of Scalzi Bridge. Rooms L45,000–L58,000. Breakfast L6,000. Water-bus: Riva di Biàsio.

Stefania, Fondamenta Tolentini 181A. Tel. 5203 757. Close to Piazzale Roma. Large rooms, some with rather unorthodox decoration. Some reports speak of uncomfortable beds. Room L58,000. No breakfast served. Water-bus: Piazzale Roma.

Sturion, S. Polo 679. Tel. 5236 243. Fax 5225 702. Quite close to the Rialto Bridge. Only 8 rooms and very popular with Italians, so often fully booked. Very old building with magnificent views of the Grand Canal. No private facilities and there are reports of high charges for shower. Rooms *L29,000–L44,000*. Breakfast L8,500. Water-bus: S. Silvestro.

Castello
5-star De Luxe
Danieli, Riva degli Schiavoni 4196. Tel. 5226 480. Tx. 410077. Fax 5200 208. Next door to the Doge's Palace with magnificent views over the Lagoon and with a beautiful Gothic courtyard-foyer with arcaded stone staircase. A hotel since 1822 it has had more than its fair share of famous visitors and is another of the world's major hotels. A rather impersonal modern annexe but a superb rooftop restaurant. A room with a view of the Lagoon can cost you a supplement of L80,000. Rooms L393,000–L583,000. Breakfast L27,400. Water-bus: Zaccaria.

4-star
Gabrielli Sandwirth, Riva degli Schiavoni 4110. Tel. 5231 580. Tx. 410228. Fax 5209 455. 15th-century *palazzo* with attractive roof terrace and rose garden. Near the Pietà. Rooms L154,000–L308,000. Breakfast L16,000. Water-bus: Arsenale.
Londra Palace, Castello 4171. Tel. 5200 533. Tx. 420681. Fax. 5225 032. Prides itself on having 100 windows facing the Lagoon but a hefty surcharge on rooms with a view. Piano bar on summer evenings. Rooms L190,000–L380,000. Breakfast L25,000. Water-bus: Zaccaria.
Metropole, Riva degli Schiavoni 4149. Tel. 5205 044. Tx.410340. Fax 5223 679. Some magnificent views over the Lagoon — at a cost. Rooms crammed with antiques and collectables. Next door to Pietà and on the site of Vivaldi's orphanage. Rooms L180,000–L316,000. Breakfast L12,000. Water-bus: Arsenale/Zaccaria.

3-star
Bisanzio, Castello 3651. Tel. 5203 100. Tx. 420099. Fax 5204 114. Set back from the Riva in a quiet side street. The owner's wife is an artist whose paintings decorate the hotel. Rooms L100,000–L151,000. Breakfast L19,000. Water-bus: Zaccaria.
Castello, Castello 4365. Tel. 5230 217. Tx. 420659. Fax 5211 023. Behind the Patriarchal Palace, near S. Giovanni in Oleo. Rooms L114,000–L151,000. Breakfast L19,500. Water-bus: Zaccaria.
Savoia & Jolanda, Castello 4187. Tel. 5206 664. Tx. 410620. Fax 5207 494. On the Riva degli Schiavoni. Attractive roof terrace restaurant with views over St Mark's Basin in summer. Rooms L76,000–L151,000. Breakfast L17,000. Water-bus: Zaccaria.
Scandinavia, Castello 5240. Tel. 5223 507. Tx. 420359. Fax 5235

232. On the Campo S. Maria Formosa. Open in high season only. Rooms L151,000. Breakfast L24,000. Water-bus: Rialto/ Zaccaria.

2-star

Alla Fava, Campo della Fava, Castello 5525. Tel. 5229 224. Fax 5237 787. Not far from the Rialto Bridge. Rooms L45,000–L81,000. Breakfast L16,000. Water-bus: Rialto.

Al Nuovo Teson, Castello 3980. Tel. 705555. Tx/Fax 5285 335. With restaurant and bar. Quite close to the Arsenal. Rooms L54,000–L81,000. Breakfast L12,000. Water-bus: Arsenale.

Atlantico, Castello 4416. Tel. 709224. Halfway between St Mark's and S. Maria Formosa. Rooms L42,000–L81,000. Breakfast L13,000. Water-bus: Zaccaria.

Bucintoro, Riva degli Schiavoni, Castello 2135. Tel. 5223 240. Fax 5235 224. A plain, simple hotel but all rooms have view of the Lagoon (the Danieli's view at 2-star prices). Next door to the Naval History Museum. Rooms L64,000–L80,000. Breakfast L12,000. Water-bus: Arsenale.

Campiello, Castello 4647. Tel. 705764. Fax 5205 798. On the Campiello del Vin between S. Zaccaria and the Riva. All rooms with private facilities. Closed in low season. Rooms L81,000. Breakfast L12,500. Water-bus: Zaccaria.

Canada, S. Lio, Castello 5659. Tel. 5229 912. Fax 5235 852. Just over the S. Lio Canal from the Rialto Bridge and Fondaco dei Tedeschi. All rooms with private facilities. Rooms L42,000–L81,000. Breakfast L13,000. Water-bus: Rialto.

Canaletto, S. Lio, Castello 5487. Tel. 5220 518. Fax 5229 023. Next door to the house belonging to the painter Canaletto the hotel was rebuilt 4 years ago. Simple but comfortable. 10% surcharge for air-conditioning. Rooms L60,000–L81,000. Breakfast L14,500. Water-bus: Rialto.

Casa Fontana, Campo S. Provolo, Castello 4701. Tel. 5220 579. Fax 5231 040. Halfway between S. Zaccaria and the Doge's Palace. High season only. Rooms L81,000. Breakfast L12,000. Water-bus: Zaccaria.

Da Bruno, Castello 5726A. Tel. 5230 452. Close to S. Maria Formosa. Rooms L60,000–L81,000. Breakfast L12,000. Water-bus: Rialto.

La Residenza, Castello 3608. Tel. 5285 315. Fax 5238 859. On the Campo S. Giovanni in Bragora near the Arsenal. Palatial public rooms but bedrooms a little shabby. Only open in high season, 10% surcharge for air-conditioning. Rooms L81,000.

Breakfast L13,000. Water-bus: Arsenale.

Lux, Castello 4541. Tel. 5235 767. Fax 5211 023. North of S. Zaccaria Church. Rooms L53,000–L69,500. Breakfast L9,500. Water-bus: Zaccaria.

Paganelli, Riva degli Schiavoni, Castello 4182. Tel. 5224 324. 5 of the 21 rooms have a view over the Lagoon, the rest are round the corner. One third of the rooms and the hotel's restaurant are in an annexe on the Campo S. Zaccaria. High season only, with 10% surcharge for air-conditioning. Rooms L81,000. Breakfast L12,000. Water-bus: Zaccaria.

Pellegrino e Commercio, Castello 4551A. Tel. 5228 814. Fax 5225 016. By the S. Provolo Canal near S. Zaccaria. All rooms with private facilities. 10% air conditioning. Rooms L40,000–L81,000. Water-bus: Zaccaria.

Trovatore, Castello 4534. Tel. 5224 611. Fax 5227 870. A very simple hotel but very close to the Doge's Palace and St Mark's Square. Rooms L41,000–L81,000. Breakfast L15,000. Water-bus: Zaccaria.

Wildner, Castello 4161. Tel. 5227 463. Tx. 218402. Fax 5285 615. On the Riva degli Schiavoni. Restaurant. Rooms L50,000–L81,000. Breakfast L15,000. Water-bus: Zaccaria.

1-star

Belvedere, Castello 1636. Tel. 5285 148. Smallish hotel, with only half a dozen rooms having private facilities. Has a restaurant and half-board terms are very little more than bed and breakfast. At the far end of the Riva near the Public Gardens. High season only. Rooms L70,000. Breakfast L6,000. Water-Bus: Giardini.

Canal, Castello 4422C. Tel. 5234 538. Only 7 rooms, 2 with private facilities. Rooms L65,000–L70,000. Breakfast L7,000. Water-bus: Zaccaria.

Caneva, Castello 5515. Tel. 5228 118. Near S. Maria Formosa. Rooms L45,000–L70,000. Breakfast L7,000. Water-bus: Rialto.

Casa Verardo, Castello 4765. Tel. 5286 127. 7 double rooms with private facilities and 2 single rooms without. Run by friendly and exuberant family. Rooms L55,000–L65,000. Water-bus: Zaccaria.

Rio, Castello 4356. Tel. 5234 810. High season only. Rooms L70,000. Breakfast L8000. Water-bus: Zaccaria.

Sant'Anna, Castello 269. Tel. 5286 466. At the very eastern end of Venice near S. Pietro di Castello. Attractive rooms in a very

The beautiful little square of Campiello S. Barbaro in Dorsoduro.
Note the typical Venetian chimney-pot on the further building.

peaceful setting. High season only. Rooms L70,000. Breakfast L6,000. Water-bus: S. Elena.

Tiepolo, Castello 4510. Tel. 5231 315. Just off the Campo SS Filippi e Giacomo. Huge rooms with antique furniture and painted ceilings. High season only. Rooms L70,000. Breakfast L8,000. Water-bus: Zaccaria.

Toscana Tofanelli, Castello 1650. Tel. 5235 722. A restaurant with rooms in a quiet location by the Public Gardens. No private facilities. Rooms *L36,000–L39,000.* Breakfast L5,000. Water-bus: Giardini.

Cannaregio

4-star

Amadeus, Lista di Spagna 227. Tel. 715300. Tx. 433322. Fax 5240 841. Fountains and a private garden, recently redecorated in 18th-century style. Two restaurants. Close to the railway station. Rooms L125,000–L250,000. Breakfast L18,000. Water-bus: Ferrovia.

Principe, Lista di Spagna 146. Tel. 715022. Tx. 410070. Fax 719061. Large hotel (152 rooms) with restaurants and bars. Rooms L210,000–L290,000. Breakfast L20,000. Water-bus: Ferrovia.

3-star

Bellini, Lista di Spagna 116A. Tel. 715095. Tx. 420374. Fax 715193. At the very start of the Lista di Spagna and therefore close to the railway station. Surprisingly few rooms with private facilities for a 3-star hotel. Rooms L80,000–L149,000. Breakfast L12,000. Water-bus: Ferrovia.

Continental, Lista di Spagna 166. Tel. 715122. Tx. 410286. Fax 5242 432. Large hotel (96 rooms) with restaurant and bar. Rooms L108,000–L151,000. Breakfast L18,500. Water-bus: Ferrovia.

Corso, Lista di Spagna 119. Tel. 716422. Tx. 410286. Medium-sized hotel with garden, bar and restaurant. Rooms L108,000–L151,000. Breakfast L18,500. Water-bus: Ferrovia.

Giorgione, SS. Apostoli, Cannaregio 4587. Tel. 5225 810. Tx. 420598. Fax 5239 092. Slightly shabby but very comfortable hotel in quiet and unspoiled part of the city Attractive courtyard restaurant. Rooms L100,000–L151,000. Breakfast L14,000. Water-bus: Ca' d'Oro.

Malibran, Cannaregio 5864. Tel. 5224 626. Tx. 420337. Fax 5239 243. Virtually next door to the theatre of the same name in a pretty secluded square. Rooms L76,000–L151,000. No breakfast. Water-bus: Rialto.

Spagna, Lista di Spagna 184. Tel. 715011. Tx. 420360. High season only. Recently renovated and reopened as 3-star hotel (was 2-star). Rooms L81,000. Breakfast L15,000. Water-bus: Ferrovia.

Union, Lista di Spagna 127. Tel. 715055. Largish hotel but very few rooms with private facilities. Cheap for area and for its rating. Rooms L75,000–L110.000. Breakfast L9,000. Water-bus: Ferrovia.

Universo e Nord, Lista di Spagna 121. Tel. 715076. Tx. 420818. Fax 717070. A comfortable hotel slightly cheaper than others of a comparable standard. Rooms L75,000–L142,000. Breakfast L14,000. Water-bus: Ferrovia.

2-star

Abbazia, Calle Priuli 66. Tel. 717333. Tx. 420680. In street running north from the Lista di Spagna. Bar and private garden. Rooms L65,000–L81,000. Water-bus: Ferrovia.

Atlantide, Cannaregio 375A. Tel. and Fax 716901. Quiet street running north from the Lista di Spagna. Rooms L50,000–L75,000. Breakfast L9,000. Water-bus: Ferrovia.

Caprera, Cannaregio 219. Tel. and Fax 715271. In another little street running north from the Lista di Spagna to open garden area. Only couple of rooms with private facilities. Rooms L65,000–L81,000. Breakfast L8,000.

Dolomiti, Calle Priuli 73/74. Tel. 715113. In street running north from the Lista di Spagna close to the railway station. Rooms L70,000–L81,000. Breakfast L7,000. Water-bus: Ferrovia.

Florida, Calle Priuli 106. Tel. 715253. Fax 718088. Rooms L50,000–L81,000. Breakfast L10,000. Water-bus:Ferrovia.

Guerrini, Cannaregio 265. Tel. 715333. In short street running north from the Campo S. Geremia at end of Lista di Spágna. Rooms L65,000–L81,000. Breakfast L12,500. Water-bus: Ferrovia.

Hesperia, Cannaregio 459. Tel. 715251. Fax 715112. In a street parallel to Lista di Spagna north of the gardens, overlooking the Cannaregio Canal. Restaurant and bar. Rooms L65,000–L81,000. Breakfast L12,000. Water-bus: Ferrovia.

La Forcolo, Cannaregio 2356. Tel. 720277. Between the Ghetto and the Maddalena Chuch in a little-explored part of the

Sestiere. Rooms L60,000–L81,000. Breakfast L10,000. Water-bus: S. Marcuola.

Leonardo, Cannaregio 1385. Tel. 718666. On one of the streets leading to the Ghetto. Rooms L70,000–L81,000. Breakfast L8,000. Water-bus: S. Marcuola.

Mignon, SS Apostoli 4535. Tel. 5237 388. Fax 5208 658. Close to the Grand Canal and the Ca' d'Oro. Small hotel with private garden. Rooms L70,000–L81,000.Breakfast L9,000. Water-bus: Ca' d'Oro.

Stella Alpina Edelweiss, Cannaregio 99D. Tel. 715179. Tx. 420166. Another hotel in a quieter location in the Calle Priuli. Private garden. Rooms L52,000–L81,000.Breakfast L12,000. Water-bus: Ferrovia.

1-star

Adua, Cannaregio 233a. Tel. 716184. On the Lista di Spagna. One visitor claims that the hotel raises tattiness of decoration to an art form. Rooms L60,000–L70,000. Breakfast L7,000. Water-bus: Ferrovia.

Bernardi Semenzato, Cannaregio 4366. Tel. 5227 257. Near Grand Canal and Ca' d'Oro. Couple of rooms with private facilities. Rooms L55,000–L65,000. Breakfast L5,000. Water-bus: Ca' d'Oro.

Casa Boccassini, Cannaregio 5295. Tel. 5229 892. Small hotel (10 rooms) in less-frequented centre of Cannaregio. Garden. High season only. Rooms L70,000. Breakfast L7,000. Water-bus:Fondamenta Nuova (route #5).

Casa Carettoni, Lista di Spagna 130. Tel. 716231. Homely atmosphere. No private facilities but most rooms have shower. Closed January-March and part of August. Rooms *L42,000*. No breakfast. Water-bus: Ferrovia.

Eden, Cannaregio 2357. Tel. 720228. Just north of the S. Marcuola Church. Only 8 rooms, half with private facilities. Rooms L46,500–L70,000. Breakfast L5,000. Water-bus: S. Marcuola.

Minerva e Nettuno, Cannaregio 230. Tel. 715968 Fax 5242 139. On the Lista di Spagna. Quite large and well-appointed for a 1-star hotel. Rooms L50,000–L70,000. Breakfast L8,000. Water-bus: Ferrovia.

Rossi, Cannaregio 262. Tel. 715164. In street running north from the Lista di Spagna, adjacent to open space. Recent renovation provided most rooms with private facilities. For first few nights liable to be charged with breakfast. Rooms L52,000–L70,000. Breakfast L5,000. Water-bus: Ferrovia.

Santa Lucia, Calle Misericordia 358. Tel. 715180. Quiet street running north from the Lista di Spagna. Private garden. High season only. Rooms L70,000. Breakfast L7,500. Water-bus: Ferrovia.

Tintoretto, S. Fosca 2316. Tel. 721522. Rooms L55,000–L70,000. Breakfast L5,000. Water-bus: Ca' d'Oro.

Vagon, Cannaregio 5619. Tel. 5285 626. In the SS Apostoli/Ca' d'Oro area. Only 10 rooms, all with private facilities. L65,000. Breakfast L6,000. Water-bus: Ca' d'Oro.

Villa Rosa, Calle della Misericordia 389. Tel. and Fax 716569. Quiet street off the Lista di Spagna. Quite large for a 1-star hotel (26 rooms) with restaurant and garden. Rooms L55,000–L70,000. Breakfast L8,000. Water-bus: Ferrovia.

Hostels

There is effectively only one Youth Hostel in Venice but a number of educational and religious institutions offer cheap but comfortable accommodation, some all year, others during school vacation periods. Some of the religious institutions accept females only, while others will only accept males as part of a family party. Again, some offer accommodation in dormitories while others have double or family rooms. Very few offer meals, although about half provide breakfast. Prices vary according to establishments, from season to season and from year to year. You should estimate for around L20,000 per person in double room, about L15,000 in a dormitory.

Ostello 'Venezia', Giudecca 86 (signposted from Zitelle landing-stage). Tel. 5238 211. The youth hostel, open all year — extra space in local school during summer months. 320 beds in 13 dormitories. Can telephone bookings Oct-May but personal bookings required June–Sept. (letter applications before April to secure space in July/Aug.). Must be member of YHA but can join at the hostel. Cost about L15,000 a night, including breakfast. Reasonable lunch and dinner served for about L10,000.

Casa Caburlotto, S. Croce 316. Tel. 5225 930. Open June 1–Oct. 31. For females or families only. 68 beds in 30 rooms. Breakfast available.

Domus Ciliota, Campo S. Stefano 2976. Tel. 5204 888. June 1–Sept. 30. 85 beds in 49 rooms. All meals available.

Domus Civica, Calle Campazzo, S. Polo 3082. Tel. 5227 139. June 1–July 31 and Sept. 1–Oct. 15. Females or families only. 95 beds in 67 rooms. No meals.

Domus 'Giustinian', Rio Tera dei Pensieri, S. Croce 326A. Tel. 5225 067. July 1–Sept. 30. Females only. 28 beds in 17 rooms. No meals.

Foresteria Chiesa Valdese, near S. Maria Formosa, Castello 5170. Tel. 5286 797. Open all year. 40 beds in 9 rooms. Breakfast available.

Foresteria Domus Cavanis, Rio Tera Foscarini, Dorsoduro 912. Tel. 5287 374. June 1–Sept. 30. 89 beds in 45 rooms (run by nuns so separate male and female rooms). Breakfast and evening meal available.

Foresteria Santa Fosca, near Campo S. Fosca, Cannaregio 2372. Tel. 715775. July 10–Sept. 10. 80 beds in 4 rooms. No meals.

Istituto Canossiano, Giudecca 428. Tel. 5222 157. Open all year. Females only. 35 beds in 2 rooms. No meals.

Istituto San Giuseppe, S.Lio, Castello 5402. Tel. 5225 352. Open all year. 42 beds in 15 rooms. No meals.

Istituto S. Maria del Soccorso, Ponte del Soccorso, Dorsoduro 2591. Tel. 5222 096. June 20–Sept. 15. 65 beds in 39 rooms. Breakfast available.

Istituto Solesin, Calle Larga Brusà, Dorsdoduro 624. Tel. 5224 356. July 1–Sept. 30. 17 beds in 10 rooms. No meals.

Patronato Salesiano Leone XIII, off the Via Garibaldi, Castello 1281. Tel. 5287 299. June 15–Oct.15. 60 beds in 32 rooms. All meals available.

Suore Mantellate, on island of S.Pietro di Castello, Castello 10. Tel. 5220 829. Sept.1–July 31. 30 beds in 5 rooms. Breakfast available.

Boarding Houses

There is a limited amount of accommodation in Venice which is somewhere between a hotel and a hostel and which can best be described by the English terms 'boarding house', 'b & b' or 'lodgings'. This class of accommodation is known as *Affittacamere* (meaning 'rooms to let') in Italian. This is very much an umbrella term as there is no clear definition as to what is included under this heading, and it can take many forms. Some establishments are no more than glorified hostels; some are restaurants or bars with a few rooms; others still are private houses which accept paying guests. There will usually be a sign outside advertising 'camere', often with the multi-lingual explanation — 'Rooms/Zimmer/Chambres'.

There is little point in listing them here since many of them tend to come and go with the seasons. Every year the APT Information Office in Venice produces a typewritten list of those families or establishments letting rooms to visitors. You could ask for the list at any of the information offices in the city, or obtain it by writing to the APT Office (see page 134 for address). The list you require is known as the 'elenco degli affittacamere di Venezia'.

Self-Catering

Venice does not offer much self-catering accommodation. There are indications that things are changing since **Citalia** does include two small apartments in its package tour brochure. They are small furnished flats to sleep 4/5, situated in Castello near the Riva degli Schiavoni and cost about the same per person as a 2-star hotel. But generally speaking the availability of self-catering accommodation is not listed or advertised. There are, however, a number of estate agents who deal with the short-term leasing of apartments and they could be approached to discover availability and cost.

ABC Immobiliare — San Marco 5467. Tel. 5237 759
Campanati — Castello 4710. Tel. 5226 635
Cera Immobiliare — San Marco 2956. Tel. 5220 601
Giaretta — Castello 5212. Tel. 5209 747
Immobiliare G & G — San Marco 1800. Tel. 5207 658
Narduzzi — Dorsoduro 930. Tel. 5208 111
Salerno — Castello 4987. Tel. 5223 594
S. Angelo — San Marco 3818. Tel. 5221 505
S. Marco — Castello 5620. Tel. 5235 935
Studio Immobiliare — Castello 5239A. Tel. 5230 200
Venezia — Cannaregio 1413A. Tel. 720401

Accommodation outside Venice

Outside the historic centre of Venice the islands around the Lagoon are the obvious place to stay, having an interest in themselves, as well as easy access to Venice proper. The Lido, of course, has a vast range of accommodation available but it tends to be as expensive, if not more so, as the historic centre: and just as crowded in the summer months. Accommodation on the Lido and other islands is listed on p. 254.

Turning to the mainland there is plenty of accommodation in Mestre and Marghera which is less expensive than in Venice. Lists of hotels in both places are available from the Venice Information Office. However, Mestre and Marghera represent the urban sprawl that Venice centre is spared because of the Lagoon and you might not find either place a very attractive setting for your stay.

Camping

Obviously there are no camp sites in Venice itself. The closest site to the historic centre is **San Nicolò** on the Lido. This is a small site, with just 150 places, which has a 1-star classification. The telephone number is 767415.

The most fruitful area is the Littorale del Cavallino where the road from the ferry at Punta Sabbioni is lined by camp-sites virtually as far as Lido di Jesolo. Some are luxurious indeed, five sites are classified as 4-star. There are something like 60,000 places available in the 10 kilometres between Punta Sabbioni and Jesolo. If you are interested in the possibility of camping write to the **Centro Nazionale Campeggiatori Stranieri**, Casella Postale 649, 50100 Firenze. They publish a guide to camp sites with full details.

For a camping holiday in a ready-erected, luxurious and well-appointed tent at Ca' Savio camp site, the cost for two people for a fortnight ranges from £200–£600 according to season, including Channel crossing with car. Contact **Canvas Holidays**, Bull Plain, Hertford, SG14 1DY. Tel. 0992 553535.

Barge selling fruit and vegetables at the side of the Campo S. Barnaba.

FIVE

Food and Drink
Restaurants, Cafés and Bars

The Italian Meal

Breakfast (*colazione*) is not really important in Italy, traditionally just a cup of coffee and perhaps a *brioche*. Most hotels
catering for foreign visitors will aim to do a little better, with at
least bread, croissants, jam and butter to go with the coffee.
The midday meal, taken between 12.30 and 14.00, is commonly
known as *Pranzo,* while the evening meal is served between
19.00 and 22.00, and is usually known as *Cena*, although both
terms are interchangeable and both meals can be known by a
variety of other names. Both are regarded as equally important,
although the midday meal is often the meal for serious eating
while the evening is more of a social occasion.

The standard pattern for a basic Italian meal is of two courses
and a sweet. The Italian for course is *piatto* (plate) and
therefore one speaks of the first and second courses as *primo
piatto* and *secondo piatto.* The visitor must understand that
although the *primo piatto* is often pasta, or rice, or a soup such
as *minestrone,* it is in no sense what the British call a 'starter'
but is a course in its own right and is often very substantial. The
secondo piatto is usually the meat or fish course that in Britain
would be regarded as the 'main course'. The dish is served as it
is without garnish or accompaniment; vegetables (*contorni*) or
salads (*insalate*) are usually ordered separately as side-dishes.
The *dolci* or sweet course is not regarded as particularly
important despite the Venetian reputation as pastry-cooks, and
in many restaurants these days it is disregarded, while in others
you will simply be offered a choice of *frutta, formaggio o gelato*
(fruit, cheese or ice cream).

Beyond the main courses the menu will often offer a 'starter' or *antipasto*. This, which literally means 'before the meal', is similar to the French *hors d'oeuvre* and can take many forms, although a perennial favourite is *prosciutto e melone* (wafer-thin slices of Parma ham with slices of melon). On a restaurant menu the first group of dishes are the *antipasti* on offer, the second group those that represent the *primo piatto,* sometimes called *minestre.* The third group represents the *secondo piatto* although they may be sub-divided into *carne* (meat) and *pesce* (fish). The group below this is made up of the *contorni* (vegetables, salads or side-dishes) on offer and the last group the *dolci.* Italian menus are flexible, there is nothing to prevent you choosing both courses from the same group of dishes so that you could have soup followed by pasta. Similarly, you may select a third, fourth or even fifth course if you wish.

In most restaurants VAT is included but there is usually a cover charge (*coperta*) for bread and the cruet which will add a couple of thousand lire to the bill. Service (*servizio*) charges of 12–16% are also added. The cover charge and service is, however, usually included in the fixed price menu, the *menù turistico* or *menù prezzo fisso*, which is on offer at most if not all Venetian restaurants. This fixed price meal offers a choice of three or four dishes for both *primo* and *secondo*, sometimes with a quarter bottle of wine included. A dessert course used to be normal as well but many trattorie have now dropped this to keep the cost down. Choice is restricted and portions are often smaller than those served *à la carte*, but the average cost is up to 25% less than the *à la carte* menu. If eating economically is important to you, remember to order the house wine with your meal and to go elsewhere for your after-dinner coffee.

Venetian specialities

Historically the Venetians can claim to be responsible for introducing *haute cuisine* to Western Europe through their medieval domination of the spice trade. And it has been claimed that the typically Italian dishes of pasta and risotto originated in China and were introduced to Venice and Italy at the time of Marco Polo. That being said, it must be admitted that Venice can no longer be regarded as a major gastronomic city and the number of Venetian specialities can be counted on the fingers of one hand. The one thing for which Venice is famed is the excellence of its fish dishes but nowadays, with pollution in the Lagoon and reduced fish stocks in the Adriatic, a large proportion of the fresh fish served in Venice has to be imported from Sicily and elsewhere. On most restaurant menus fish is much more expensive than meat. Do not eat fish on Monday when the fish market is closed and restaurants have recourse to the deep freeze.

Some of the fish to be found most regularly are sole, *branzino* — a sea-bass known as *loup de mer* in France, *San Pietro* or *Sampiero* — known in English as John Dory, and *dorate* — a kind of bream. Eels (*anguilla*) are very popular and can be served *alla Veneziana* with lemon and tunny or *in umido*, stewed with tomatoes. *Baccala* or salt cod is a regular Venetian staple, cooked in milk and then creamed, but it tends not to inspire the outsider. A favourite *antipasto* is *Sardine in saor*, which consists of sardines that have been fried and then marinated cold in a sweet and sour sauce of vinegar and onion. Another favourite start to a meal is a dish of *granseole* which are spider-crabs from Murano and *moleche* which are crabs that are changing their shells and which are dug from the sand where they hide their unprotected bodies. *Seppie* is ink-fish, or squid cooked in its own ink. It is either served as it is, accompanied by *polenta,* or used to make a *risotto nero* in which the rice is coloured black by the ink. Fish is also served frequently as a fish soup, known either simply as *Zuppa di pesce* or *Brodetto di pesce.* Venetian fish soup is not like the French thick and puréed *soupe de poissons* but is more like a fish stew, similar to *bouillabaisse. Fritto misto* is a common Italian dish and consists of a mixture of octopus, shrimp, prawns, squid etc. fried together. One Venetian fish dish that has become international is, of course, *Scampi.* Unfortunately, in Venice as elsewhere, the habit has grown of calling any kind of prawn 'scampi'.

The staple cereal food in Venice is neither rice nor pasta, yet both have delightful Venetian uses. There are a wide variety of risottos, many with shellfish, but *risotto alla sbiragglia* is served with chicken and *risotto in capro roman* is with lamb. The traditional Venetian rice dish is *Risi e Bisi*, which is rice cooked in a rich stock with peas and ham. It is rather more liquid than most risottos but it is a delicious and highly colourful dish. The full range of pastas are to be found in Venice but peculiar to the region is *Bigoli* which is a spaghetti-like pasta made with dark-coloured flour. It is normally served as *bigoli in salsa*, in a sauce made from onions and anchovies. Another Venetian dish employing pasta is *pasta e fagioli* which is another soup made from pasta and beans in a vegetable stock; very rich, tasty and filling. The staple cereal food in north-eastern Italy is *Polenta* which is a kind of porridge made from maize flour and boiled until it is so stiff it can be sliced like bread. There are two kinds of polenta — that made from *granturco* maize, which is yellow, and that made from the maize of Friuli which is white. Polenta is served as the natural accompaniment to traditional Venetian dishes such as ink-fish, salt-cod or veal's liver. It is a purely personal opinion but I categorise polenta as bland stodge and would say that it is definitely an acquired taste if it can be said to have a taste, although it can be made more interesting by frying it in slices and serving it with a piquant sauce.

Meat was always much scarcer than fish in Venice and there are therefore very few specifically Venetian meat dishes. There is *castradina alla griglia* which is grilled lamb and traditionally eaten on the Feast of the Salute in November. As a modern Venetian dish there is *Carpaccio*, invented by Giuseppe Cipriani, the founder of Harry's Bar. This is made up of transparently thin slices of raw beef in a mayonnaise sauce and therefore a variant of steak tartare. The other two meat dishes associated with Venice are both based on offal. The first is *Fegato alla Veneziana*, thin slices of calf's liver fried with onion rings and served with polenta. The second is borrowed from Treviso and is *Trippa alla trevisana*, well-seasoned tripe browned in the oven.

When it comes to the *dolci* it is hard to beat ice cream in Italy and, although the *gelati* of Venice do not have the reputation of the Neapolitan they are nevertheless superior to ices from most other parts of the world. Most restaurants will offer the standard Italian sweet of *tiramisù*. This, which literally means pick-me-up, comes in a variety of forms from a semi-liquid mousse to a solid cake-like slice. A tiramisù can contain sponge-cake or ice-cream but staple ingredients are cream, chocolate and a liberal dose of brandy. Most of the specifically Venetian sweets are legacies of the Austrian occupation and include *strudel* and *krapfen* — doughnuts filled with jam or whipped cream.

Wines

The wines of the Veneto that are commonly drunk in Venice are not great wines but are very palatable and have names that will be familiar to the reader. Probably the best known white wine of Italy is *Soave* from east of Verona, a semi-sweet (*abbocato*) white wine that is an ideal accompaniment to the fish dishes. If your preference is for a very dry (*asciutto* or *amaro*) wine then try the *Prosecco* or *Cartizze* sparkling wines from Conegliano. There is also a charming *Prosecco Rosé*. Of the reds the most common is *Valpolicella*, again from near Verona. Less ubiquitous but a good dry (*secco*) wine is *Bardolino* from the shores of Lake Garda. Both Soave and Valpolicella produce dessert versions known as *Recioto*. All these wines are produced by hundreds of different growers and vary in quality from superb to merely mediocre. To be safe buy Soave or Valpolicella that is sold under the vineyard's name, and also in dated bottles. Neither wine keeps and is best drunk young. Friuli produces a fair if unexciting range of wines, with a vaguely Balkan flavour — *Pinot nero, Merlot* and *Cabernet* among the reds; *Tocai, Pinot bianco* and *Sauvignon* among the whites. From between Venice and Friuli comes an interesting but little-known white, *Verduzzo di Piave*.

Most restaurants will have a house wine (*vino di casa*) which will be sold by the bottle or carafe (*carafa*) in quarter, half or full litre sizes. The house wine is worth ordering since it is often considerably cheaper than the bottled wine on offer, is frequently the same wine and, as the restaurateur is jealous of his reputation, is often selected with great care and taste.

Most restaurants will expect you to follow Italian custom and order a bottle of mineral water alongside the wine, even if it is only a half-litre bottle (*un mezzo*). Mineral water comes in two forms — *naturale* (still) or *gassata* (carbonated).

Before your meal the obvious aperitif (*aperitivo*) is the very Italian vermouth, of which *Cinzano* and *Martini* are the best-known names. Alternatively you can try the *bitter* or *amari* such as *Campari* or *Punt e Mes*. With your coffee after dinner a *digestivo* is recommended. There are a variety of liqueurs such as *Strega* to be had, or Italian brandy such as *Vecchia Romagna* or *Stock*. A typically Italian accompaniment to your after-dinner coffee, however, is *grappa*. This spirit, like the French *marc*, is a raw brandy made from the grape pressings, including pips and stalks, etc. It comes in a variety of types, coloured from straw to clear, and ranging in taste and effect from a fine brandy to something akin to paint-stripper.

Eating Out

The best rule of thumb when choosing the eating house that gives the best value for money is to get away from the immediate vicinity of St Mark's Square. That is not to say that the restaurants around the Piazza are all highly expensive; there are many offering quite reasonable menus in both quality and cost. But they tend to be heavily patronised and over-crowded so that the object of management is to get customers in and out as quickly as possible; portions are small and service is brusque. Other areas, such as the Rialto and the Lista di Spagna, seem to specialise in the cheap and cheerful tourist market — often very reasonable value but the food is not over-interesting and you might well be hurried. In the listings later in this chapter I attempt to outline the areas in each sestiere where the best value-for-money restaurants and trattorie are to be found.

By law all restaurants have to display their menu outside, together with details of the tourist menu they offer. You can therefore have some idea of what is available and what it is likely to cost without having to enter. A quick look at the interior decoration and the type of clientele they attract can also act as a guide. It is quite a pleasant activity for the hour between seven and eight to wander about, comparing menus to decide where you are to eat that evening. Even if you have made your preliminary choice from the restaurants listed in this chapter, there is nothing to stop you examining it from the outside and comparing it with some of the opposition before committing yourself.

An eating house might be known as a **ristorante, trattoria, locanda, osteria, tavola calda** or **pizzeria**, as well as a variety of other names. Sometimes the difference is obvious, sometimes it is more subtle. So here is an attempt at a rough definition of various terms you might encounter.

Ristoranti are at the top of the range. The setting is luxurious, the *à la carte* menu offers a wider range of dishes and there is a long wine list. Beware of paying over the odds for the ambience.

Trattorie are generally simpler and often family-run. Mostly they offer good regional cooking and wine at reasonable prices. The ambience varies from basic to luxurious, and of course the prices reflect this, but on the whole you are more likely to get your money's worth in a trattoria than in a restaurant.

Locande are often spoken of as 'inns'. They are usually trattorie but they have half-a-dozen, often simple, rooms to let. They are very like the French '*restaurant avec chambres*'. Again usually family-run they have often been in the same hands for two or more generations and have a proud reputation to maintain.

Tavola Calde: Literally meaning 'hot table' the tavola calda offers a range of hot and cold dishes, usually buffet-style self-service. Useful for snatching a quick and relatively inexpensive lunch while sightseeing.

Pizzerie: The term can cover a wide range of premises ranging from snack-bars to quite luxurious restaurants specialising in pizzas. Not that they only offer pizzas; many have a range of dishes, especially salads and pasta. They are useful at lunch-time when you want to be more comfortable than standing at a snack-bar counter but do not want either the quantity nor the expense of a full menu.

Gelaterie, osterie & enoteche: Or ice-cream parlours, pubs and wine-bars. All offer food that can be more than just a snack.

Restaurants by Sestiere

Who knows how many restaurants there are in Venice? The nearest thing we have to a list is a guide drawn up by the Venetian Association of Restaurant Owners, a copy of which you might be able to obtain from the Information Office, but it is not likely to be accurate. For one thing the list only contains association members and for another it was last compiled in 1989. Restaurants in Venice come and go very rapidly, often within the space of one season. The listing which follows is obviously not exhaustive and perhaps a few may have fallen by the wayside even as I write. I have selected restaurants which either offer good value within their price range, or where the menu is imaginative.

The list is divided into sestieri, with the restaurants divided into four broad price-bands — expensive, moderately expensive, reasonable and cheap. There is a subsidiary section for self-service restaurants, fast-food type snack bars and wine-bars that lay on a dish-of-the-day at meal-times. Suggested costs should be treated as relative rather than absolute and are intended to indicate roughly the price-range area into which a meal chosen from the *carte* is likely to fall.

For each restaurant I give its name, address and phone number. The price quoted is either the likely cost for the tourist menu or for a simple meal chosen with care from the *carte*. This is an approximation based on the likely impact of inflation since the restaurants last published their listings. Where the figure is followed by an asterisk the price also includes wine. Some restaurants do not offer a tourist menu, in which case the fact that they are *à la carte* only is noted. Not all of these are necessarily in the top price range but, in the majority of these cases, you can reckon that a meal chosen from the *carte* is likely to cost in excess of L40,000, however frugally you make your selection.

All restaurants close on at least one day a week; some close for two days, others close for an extra half-day either before or after their full closing day. The days on which restaurants are closed is noted in the list but it should also be considered that a number of restaurants close in the winter, and a few in August as well.

San Marco

This sestiere contains some of the finest and most expensive restaurants in Venice, particularly those centred on the luxury hotels along the Grand Canal, around the Fenice Theatre and in the area of the Calle Larga XXII Marzo. There are some restaurants of reasonable price and quality in the Frezzeria and the Calle Larga S. Marco but they suffer from the problems of proximity to the Piazza. Cheap and cheerful restaurants seem to proliferate around the Rialto. The most fruitful area for restaurants of reasonable quality but not unreasonable prices would seem to be the Calle dei Fabbri which runs south from the area of the Goldoni Theatre to the north side of St Mark's Square.

Expensive — over L40,000

Al Graspo de Ua — S. Salvador 5094. Tel. 5223 647. **à la carte.** Closed Mon. and Tues. a.m.

Al Theatro — S. Fantin 1916. Tel. 5237 214. **à la carte.** Stays open late to cater for theatre and orchestra artistes. Closed Mon.

Antico Calice — S. Salvador 5228. Tel. 5206 084. **à la carte.** Closed Wed.

Antico Martini — San Fantin 1983. Tel. 5224 121. **à la carte.** Closed Tues. and Dec.–March. One of Venice's most prestigious (and expensive) restaurants, with four crossed knives and forks and two rosettes in Michelin. For the special occasion.

Gorizia a la Valigia — Calle del Gambero 4696. Tel. 5223 737. **à la carte.** Closed Mon.

Il Cortile e La Caravella — Calle Larga XXII Marzo 2402. Tel. 5208 377. **à la carte.** These are the restaurants belonging to the Hotel Saturnia. *Il Cortile* is set out in the courtyard in summer. *La Caravella* has a Michelin rosette and specialises in fish dishes. Closed Wed.

Martini Scala — S. Fantin 1980. Tel 5224 121. **L45,000+.** Part of *Antico Martini* but classed as night-restaurant, open from 22.00 to 3.30. Closed Tues.

Osteria al Bacareto — S. Samuele 3447. Tel. 5289 336. **à la carte.** Closed Sat. p.m. and Sun.

Ristorante all'Angelo — Calle Larga S. Marco 403. Tel. 5209 299. **à la carte.** Closed Mon.

Ristorante Grand Canal — Calle Vallaresso 1325. Tel. 5200 211. **à la carte.** The restaurant of the Hotel Monaco & Grand Canal. Open-air terrace opposite the Salute. Closed Tues.

Taverna La Fenice — Campiello La Fenice 1937. Tel. 5223 856. **L50,000+*.** Closed Sun.

Moderately expensive — L30,000 to L40,000

Antica Carbonera — Calle Bembo 4648. Tel. 5225 479. **L33,000*.** Closed Tues.

Noemi — Calle Fabbri 912. Tel. 5225 238. **L35,000.** Locanda with Michelin rosette; good on Venetian specialities. Closed Sun.

Ristorante al Campiello — Calle dei Fuseri 4346. Tel. 5206 396. **L37,000.** Closed Mon.

Reasonable — L20,000 to L30,000
Al Conte Pescaor — S. Zulian 544. Tel. 5221 483. **L25,000**. Closed Sun. and Mon.
Alla Canonica — Calle di Canonica 339. Tel. 5225 365. **L23,000***. Closed Wed.
Alla Fava — Calle Stagneri 5242. Tel. 5285 147. **L23,000***. Closed Wed.
Alla Scala — Corte Lucatello 571. Tel. 5220 767. **L20,000**. Closed Tues p.m. and Wed.
Intermezzo alla Fenice S. Fantin 1847. Tel. 5204 878. **L25,000***. Closed Tues.
Ristorante Centrale — Calle Specchieri 425. Tel. 5205 730. **L23,000**. Closed Tues.
Ristorante Città di Milano — Campiello S. Zulian 599. Tel. 5285 437. **L22,000**. Closed Mon.
Ristorante da Raffaele — Calle delle Ostreghe 2347. Tel. 5232 317. **L25,000**. Pretty canal-side terrace. Closed Tues.
Ristorante Ridotto — Calle Vallaresso 1334. Tel. 5222 166. **L22,000**. Closed Thurs.
Ristorante S. Marco — Calle dei Fabbri 877. Tel. 5238 447. **L27,000**. Closed Tues.
Ristorante S. Stefano — Campo S. Stefano 2776. Tel. 5232 467. **L20,000**. Tables set outside on this very beautiful square. Closed Wed.
Rosa Rossa — Calle della Mandola 3709. Tel. 5234 605. **L25,000***. Closed Wed.
Sayonara — Calle dei Fabbri 4720. Tel. 5285 170. **L20,000**. Closed Tues.
Taverna al Pozzo — Calle dei Fabbri 1016. Tel. 5223 649. **L23,000**. Closed Sun.
Trattoria Città di Vittorio — Frezzeria 1591. Tel. 5230 537. **L23,000**. Closed Mon.
Inexpensive — Under L20,000 (or L20,000 inc. wine)
Al Gambero — Calle dei Fabbri 4685. Tel. 5224 384. **L20,000***. Closed Thurs.
Al Gazzettino — S. Salvador 4997. Tel. 5223 314. **L18,000–L20,000**. Closed Mon.
Al Teatro Goldoni — Calle dei Fabbri 4747. Tel. 5222 446. **L18,000 – L20,000***. Closed Tues.
Antico Marco Polo — Calle Stagneri 5185. Tel. 5285 669. **L18,000***. Closed Sun.

Birreria al Carbon — Riva del Carbon 4643. Tel. 5285 126. **L18,000**. Closed Wed.
Da Dino — Calle dei Fabbri 1053. Tel. 5223 075. **L18,000**. Closed Wed.
Rosticceria S. Bartolomeo — S. Bartolomeo, Calle della Bissa 5424A. Tel. 5223 569. **L18,000***. Has a cheaper self-service restaurant in basement. Closed Mon.
Taverna Pizzeria Bora Bora — Salizzada Fontego dei Tedeschi 5251. Tel. 5236 583. **L18,000**. Really a pizzeria but serves reasonably priced menu if you can stand the Polynesian decor. Closed Wed.
Self-service and Fast Food
Le Chat qui Rit — Calle Tron 1131. Tavola Calda. Closed Sat.
Italy & Italy — Campo S. Luca. Italy's answer to MacDonalds and Pizza Hut combined; burgers, pizza and pasta. Closed Tues.
Self Service Rialto — Riva del Carbon 4173. 2 courses with wine, **L15,000***. Closed Sun.
Vino Vino — S. Fantin 2007A. Really a wine bar but serves dish of the day, **L20,000***. Closed Tues.

Cannaregio
Some of the cheapest restaurants in Venice are in this sestiere: even the *à la carte* is not excessive. Along the Lista di Spagna and in the vicinity of the railway station they are essentially aimed at tourists in a hurry. North of here the eating houses cater for a largely working-class clientele; you can eat well and cheaply, if not in the most elegant of surroundings, and it helps if you speak Italian. Most productive in value for money eating is probably the small area between SS. Apostoli and San Canciano.
Expensive — over L40,000
Antica Mola — Fond. Misericordia 2800. Tel. 717492. **à la carte**. You might get away with paying less than L40,000 but this family-run restaurant has grown increasingly fashionable and expensive in recent years. Closed Wed.
Moderately expensive — L30,000 to L40,000
Ai Canottieri — S. Giobbe 690. Tel. 715408. **à la carte**. Closed Mon. and Tues. a.m. Sometimes music in the evening.
Trattoria alla Taverna — Calle Priuli 101.Tel. 716232. **à la carte**. Closed Sun.
Trattoria Antica Adelaide — Calle Larga Doge Priuli 3728. Tel.

5203 451. **à la carte**. Closed Mon.
Reasonable — L20,000 to L30,000
A la Vecia Cavana — SS. Apostoli 4624. Tel. 5238 644.
L23,000*. Closed Tues.
Alla Lanternine — S. Martino 2315. Tel. 721679. **L29,000***.
Closed Thurs.
Fiaschetteria Toscana — S. Giov. Crisostomo 5719. Tel. 5285
281. **L29,000***. Closed Tues.
Il Paradiso Perduto — Fond. Misericordia 2540. Tel. 720581.
L28,000*. Lively atmosphere, favoured by students and artists.
Music in evenings until 13.00. Closed Mon.
Rist. Pizzeria Malibran — S. Giov. Crisostomo 5864. Tel. 5228
028. **L25,000***. Closed Tues. p.m. and Wed.
Trattoria da Paolo — Sta. Fosca 2232. Tel. 721555. **L23,000***.
Not only wine and dessert included in tourist menu but
antipasto as well. Closed Wed.
Trattoria Tre Spiedi — Salizzada S. Cancian 5906.Tel. 5208
035. **L21,000***. Closed Sun. p.m. and Mon.
Inexpensive — Under L20,000 (or L20,000 inc. wine)
Bar Pizzeria Soldà — SS. Apostoli 4440. Tel. 5223 044.
L15,000* Closed Tues.
Casa Mia — SS. Apostoli, Calle Dragan 4430. Tel. 5285 590.
L18,000*. Very popular with the locals but the pizzas rather
than the menu are its strongpoint. Closed Tues.
Da Gianni — Strada Nova 4377. Tel. 5237 268. **L19,000**. Closed
Wed.
Dall'Aurelia — SS. Apostoli 4888. Tel. 5289 325. **L16,000***.
Closed Wed.
Da Rino — S. Canciano 5642. Tel. 5206 998. **L18,000**. Closed
Wed.
Gino's — Lista di Spagna 157. Tel. 716072. **L20,000***. Basically
a pizzeria with simple menu. Late-night opening, until 13.00.
Closed Thurs.
Pizzeria da Mimmo — S. Marcuola 1372. Tel. 5218 015.
L12,000. A pizzeria but with one of the cheapest menus in the
area. Closed Sun.
Pontini — S. Marcuola 1268. Tel. 715792. **L15,000**. Closed
Mon.
Trattoria alla Barca — S. Marcuola 5401. Tel. 5238 153.
L15,000*. Closed Sat.
Trattoria alla Cea — Fond. Nuova 5422A. Tel. 5237 450.
L15,000. Simple trattoria catering for local workers but with

attractive terrace in summer. Beware of hidden extras, not only are drink and dessert excluded from the tourist menu but also vegetables. Closed Sat. p.m. and Sun.

Trattoria alla Palazzina — Ponte delle Guglie 1509. Tel. 717725. **L18,000***. Closed Wed.

Castello

Some highly luxurious and expensive restaurants around the St Mark's end of the Riva degli Schiavoni, becoming less pretentious the further along the Riva you go. Some very reasonable and good-value eating-places at the Bragora end around the Arsenal and Via Garibaldi. Some interesting trattorie to be found in the S. Maria Formosa/SS. Giovanni e Paolo/S. Lio area.

Expensive — over L40,000 and à la carte only

Ai Barbacani — Calle del Paradiso 5746. Tel. 5210 234. **à la carte**. Closed Mon.

Les Deux Lions — Riva degli Schiavoni 4179. Tel. 5200 533. **à la carte**. More than expensive, this restaurant is classified as De Luxe by the municipality. A determinedly French ambience. Closed Tues.

Paganelli — Campo S. Zaccaria 4687. Tel. 5224 324. **à la carte**. Closed Wed.

Terrazza Principessa — Riva degli Schiavoni 4187. Tel. 5206 644. **à la carte**. Closed Tues.

Moderately expensive — à la carte only but under L40,000

Alla Rivetta — S. Provolo 4625. Tel. 5287 302. **à la carte**. Closed Mon.

Da Bruno — S. Martino 2338. Tel. 5210 660. **à la carte**. Closed Mon.

Osteria ai Schiavoni — Calle del Dose 3734. Tel.5226 763. **à la carte** Closed Wed.

Reasonable — L20,000 to L30,000

Al Giardinetto — Ruga Giuffa 4928. Tel. 5285 332. **L22,000**. Good selection of Venetian specialities on tourist menu. Closed Sat.

Bar Ristorante al Covo — Campiello Pescheria 3968. Tel. 5223 812. **L22,000**. Closed Thurs.

S. Provolo — Campo S. Provolo 4712. Tel. 5285 085. **L23,000**. Closed Fri.

Taverna dei Dogi — Calle Albanesi 4250. Tel. 5223 706. **L25,000**. Closed Mon.

Trattoria da Roberto — Campiello S. Provolo 4707. Tel. 5221 506. **L25,000**. Closed Mon.

Trattoria Giorgione — Via Garibaldi 1533. Tel. 5228 727. **L23,000***. Closed Mon.

Trattoria Nuova Speranza — Campo Ruga 145. Tel. 5289 524. **L21.000***. Closed Sat.

Inexpensive — Under L20,000 (or L20,000 inc. wine)

Aciugheta — SS. Filippo e Giacomo 4357. Tel. 5224 292. **L18,000**. Also a bar and pizzeria. The name means anchovy and the theme is developed in the décor. Closed Wed.

Al Giardinetto — SS. Giovanni e Paolo 6418. Tel. 5286 497. **L15,000**. Closed Sat.

Alla Conchiglia — Fond. S. Lorenzo 4990. Tel. 5289 095. **L20,000***. Closed Wed.

Al Mondo Novo — Salizzada S. Lio 5409. Tel. 5200 698. **L19,000**. Closed Fri.

Al Scalinetto — Calle del Dose, Bragora 3803. Tel. 5200 776. **L17,000**. Closed Fri.

Bar Bucintoro — Riva degli Schiavoni 4132. Tel. 5285 956. **L18,000**. Closed Tues.

Marco Polo — Salizzada S. Lio 5571. Tel. 5235 018. **L19,000**. Closed Tues.

Ristorante Belvedere — Via Garibaldi 1577. Tel. 5285 148. **L18,000**. Closed Mon.

Rist. Cantina Canaletto — Calle della Malvasia 5450. Tel. 5228 954. **L19,000***. Closed Wed.

Ristorante Laguna — S. Filippo Giacomo 4294. Tel. 5225 331. **L19,000***. Closed Fri.

Trattoria alla Rampa — Via Garibaldi 1138. Tel. 5285 365. **L17,000***. Closed Sun.

Trattoria al Marca — Via Garibaldi 1252A. Tel. 5231 179. **L20,000***. Closed Thurs.

Trattoria Chinellato — Calle Albanesi 4227. Tel. 5236 025. **L17,000**. Closed Sun p.m. & Mon.

Self-service and Fast Food

Da Elio Fritolin — S. Lio 5410. Tavola calda — **L16,000**. Closed Tues.

Sottoprova — Via Garibaldi 1698. Tavola calda — **L13,000**. Closed Tues.

Dorsoduro (and Giudecca):

In many ways, I believe, the most interesting sestiere for

finding places to eat. In the triangle formed by the Accademia, Salute and Zattere there are some very fine trattorie, while the student area between Ca' Foscari and the Campo S. Margherita is rich in cheap but satisfying eating places.

Expensive — over L40,000 or à la carte only

Ai Padovani — Campo S. Barnaba 2839. Tel. 5238 660. **à la carte**. Closed Sun.

Anzolo Raffaele — Campo dell'Angelo Raffaele 1722. Tel. 5237 456. **à la carte**. Closed Mon. and Tues. p.m.

Taverna S. Pantalon — S. Pantalon 3757. Tel. 5229 189. **à la carte**. Closed Tues.

All'Altanella — Calle delle Erbe, Giudecca 269. Tel. 5227 780. **à la carte**. Excellent fish dishes and attractive outdoor terrace. Closed Mon. and Tues. and winter.

Harry's Dolci — Fond. S. Biagio, Giudecca 773. Tel. 5224 844. **à la carte**. An outpost of Harry's Bar with just slightly less elevated prices. Closed Sun. p.m. and Mon.

Moderately expensive — L30,000 to L40,000

Antica Locanda Montin — Fond. di Borgo 1147. Tel. 5227 151. **L32,000+**. A Venetian institution since the 1920s. Hemingway ate here, Ezra Pound spent the best part of his life here, ditto Peggy Guggenheim, Visconti and the rest of the art/literary world. Best in summer when tables are set in the attractive garden, but dining rooms art-hung and cheerful. Closed Tues. p.m. and Wed.

Isola Misteriosa — Rio Terà della Scoazera 2894. Tel. 5238 366. **L30,000***. A little on the trendy side, with vegetarian specialities. Closed Mon.

Ristorante Pizzeria al Profeta — Calle lunga S. Barnaba 2671. Tel. 5237 466. **L32,000***. Closed Mon.

Reasonable — L20,000 to L30,000

Alle Zattere — Zattere 795. Tel. 5204 224. **L23,000***. In fact one of the best pizzerie in Venice. So proud of their pizzas that they occur as a possible secondo piatto on their trattoria menu. Closed Tues.

Gianni — Zattere 917. Tel. 5237 210. **L20,000**. Closed Wed.

Trattoria Ai Cugnai — S. Vio 857. Tel. 5289 238. **L25,000***. Run by pair of sisters in attractive if rather cramped premises. Favoured by the French which says something. Closed Mon.

Inexpensive — Under L20,000 (or L20,000 inc. wine)

Ai Sportivi — Campo S. Margherita 3052. Tel. 5234 690. **L17,000***. Closed Mon.

Antico Capon — Campo S. Margherita 3004. Tel. 5285 252. **L15,000**. Basically a superior pizzeria which offers a menu. Popular with students. Closed Wed.

Ca' Foscari — Calle Larga Foscari 854. Tel. 5229 216. **L15,000**. Closed Sun.

Cazzetta — Calle Larga Brusa 924. Tel. 5285 184. **L13,000**. Cheap but very restricted choice and no dessert. Closed Tues.

Friggitoria da Bruno — Calle Lunga S. Barnaba 2754A. Tel. 5206 978. **L14,000***. Plain, bourgeois Venetian cooking in basic surroundings. Closed Sat p.m. and Sun.

Taverna S. Trovaso — S. Trovaso 1016. Tel. 5203 703. **L18,000***. Same basic Venetian specialities as the *da Bruno* but a little more up-market. Closed Mon.

Al Redentore — Campo S. Giacomo, Giudecca 205. Tel. 5206 096. **L15,000***. Closed Sun.

El Cicheto Venexian — Fond. della Croce 68. Tel. 5235 268. **L14,000**. Closed Mon.

San Polo

A small but interesting sestiere as far as dining out is concerned. A smart area so tending to the pricey. Main concentrations of restaurants are in the market area just north of the Rialto, or strung out along the route from the Rialto to the Frari by way of Campo S. Polo.

Expensive — over L40,000 or à la carte only

Agli Amici — Calle dei Botteri. Tel. 5241 309. **à la carte**. Closed Wed.

Ai Mercanti — Pescheria 1588. Tel. 5240 282. **à la carte**. Closed Mon.

Al Gobbo di Rialto — Rialto 649. Tel. 5204 603. **à la carte**. Closed Tues.

Alla Madonna — Rialto 593. Tel. 5223 824. **à la carte**. Has

Opposite One of the more colourful points on the Grand Canal: the Accademia Bridge leads to the Campo S.Vidal, with the Campanile S.Vidal beyond.
Overleaf The rooftop statuary and domes of St. Mark's as seen from the Campanile.

received Michelin rosette. Always very busy — booking advised. Closed Wed.

Da Ignazio — Calle dei Saoneri 749. Tel. 5234 852, **à la carte**. Specialises in sea-food and menu changes according to the day's catch. Closed Sat.

Due Colonne — Campo S. Agostin 2343. Tel. 5240 685. **à la carte**. Closed Sun.

Moderately expensive — L30,000 to L40,000

Antica Trattoria Poste Vecie — Pescheria 1608. Tel. 721822. **L32,000***. 16th-century building; claims to be 'oldest trattoria in Venice'. Closed Mon. p.m. and Tues.

Reasonable — L20,000 to L30,000

All'Antico Pizzo — Calle S. Mattio 814. Tel. 5231 575. **L28,000***. Tourist menu with Venetian specialities such as *seppie, baccala & fegato.* Closed Mon.

Al Pordenone da Sandro — Calle della Madoneta 1457. Tel. 5289 482. **L25,000**. Run by family from Pordenone so mixes Venetian dishes with Friulian specialities.

Antica Trattoria Letizia — Rialto 692. Tel. 5229 526. **L20,000**. Closed Mon.

Ristorante al Giardinetto — S. Tomà 2910A. Tel. 5224 100. **L23,000***. Closed Mon.

Trattoria Rialto Novo — Calle Parangon 518. Tel. 5235 774. **L23,000***. Closed Mon.

Inexpensive — Under L20,000 (or L20,000 inc. wine)

Ai Tosi — Pescheria 1586. Tel. 5241 086. **L20,000***. Closed Sun.

Antica Trattoria Orsetta — Campo dei Frari 3004. Tel. 5327 229. **L17,000**.

S. Tomà — Campo S. Tomà 2864. Tel. 5238 819. **L17,000**. Closed Tues.

Trattoria Alla Rivetta — Campiello dei Meloni 1479. Tel. 5224 246. **L13,000***. Closed Mon.

Trattoria Antica Torre — Pescheria 833. Tel. 5238 315. **L19,000***. Closed Wed.

S. Croce

The sestiere with the fewest restaurants and not exactly a gourmet's paradise. Most eating places cluster around the Piazzale Roma and seem to cater largely for people with a bus to catch. In this sestiere those restaurants not offering a tourist menu are unlikely to be as expensive as elsewhere so, in this instance, the *à la carte* restaurants are grouped under that heading rather than classifying them as expensive.

A la carte only

Alle Burchielle — Piazzale Roma 393.Tel. 5231 342. Closed Mon.

Al Ponte del Megio — Calle Larga 1666. Tel. 719777. Closed Sun.

Pizzeria Snack Bar Vittoria — S. Simeon 745. Tel. 718500. Closed Mon.

Zanze — Fond.S. Croce 231. Tel. 5223 555. Closed Sun.

Moderately expensive — *L30,000 to L40,000*

Ristorante la Regina — Calle della Regina 2330A. Tel. 5241 402. **L36,000***. Closed Mon.

Reasonable — *L20,000 to L30,000*

Trattoria Nono Risorto — Campo S. Cassiano 2331. Tel. 5241 169. **L23,000***. Closed Tues.

Inexpensive — *Under L20,000 (or L20,000 inc. wine)*

Ai Bari — Lista Vecchia Bari 1175. Tel. 718900. **L15,000***. Closed Thurs.

Tende Rosse — Salizzada S. Pantalon 116. **L17,000**. Closed Sun.

Trattoria ai Tre Ponti — Tre Ponti 271. Tel. 5207 010. **L17,000***. Closed Sat.

Trattoria da Bepi — Fond. Minotto 159. Tel. 5226 735. **L17,000***. Closed Mon.

Trattoria Ferrata — Calle Larga dei Bari 1103. Tel. 718846. **L15,000**. Closed Sun.

Trattoria Mater Domini — S. Maria Mater Domini 2097. Tel. 5241 334. **L17,000***. Closed Mon.

Pizzerie

Pizzas are everywhere in Venice and the quality varies greatly. Many pizzerie have already been listed because either a trattoria will have a pizzeria attached, or pizzerie will serve meals. However, whether mentioned previously or not, about the best half-dozen pizzeria are reckoned to be —

Pizzeria Bora Bora — Calle dei Stagneri, S. Marco.

Casa Mia — Campo SS. Apostoli, Cannaregio.

Da Sandro — Campiello dei Meloni, S. Polo.

Alle Zattere — Zattere, Dorsoduro.

Antico Capon — Campo S. Margherita, Dorsoduro.
Al Profeta — Calle Lunga S. Barnaba, Dorsoduro.

Cafés and Bars

It is sometimes a little difficult to distinguish between cafés and
bars in Venice, since most bars will serve coffee and many a
caffè will serve alcoholic refreshment. However, among the
cafés we include *pasticcerie* (pastry-shops), *latterie* (milk-bars)
and *gelaterie* (ice-cream parlours). Also included are those cafés
in the grand style — what, in 18th-century London, would have
been called 'coffee houses'. Bars include *osterie* (hostelries —
like pubs) and *enoteche* (wine-bars). There is further confusion
arising from the fact that most bars serve food — not only
snacks and sandwiches but very often a 'dish-of-the-day' — and
some have previously appeared in the list of restaurants.
    Most bars and the *pasticceria* type of café are very small;
eating and drinking is done standing up at the bar or, at best,
seated on one of the couple of bar stools which might be set
against a counter on one wall. Some larger establishments do
have a few simple tables to which customers can retire having
bought what they want at the bar-counter. But mostly a bar or
café with tables will provide waiter-service and food and drink
will cost about twice what they do at the counter. In summer,
when bars and cafés with external space set out their tables in
the open air, this is even more true and what you order is likely
to cost even more at an outside table than at an interior table.
In the larger bars and cafés, when you intend to be served at
the counter, it is normal to order and pay at the cash-desk
(*cassa*) and then to hand the receipt you are given to the
barman, while repeating your order. If you sit down, and are
waited upon, you pay the waiter when you have finished.

Cafés
Coffee is an integral part of Italian life and no bar or café is
complete without its *espresso* machine. To the outsider it is
something of an acquired taste. A request for a coffee will
produce an *espresso*, a very small measure of very strong and
possibly bitter black coffee. If you want a larger and weaker
quantity you can have it diluted with hot water by asking for a
caffè lungo. White coffee is obtained by asking for a *cappuccino*

or a *caffè-latte* (with ordinary hot milk). In summer you can order iced coffee — *caffè freddo* for black or *caffè-latte freddo* for white. If you fear that the amount of milk added will make the coffee too weak and milky it must be remembered that the basic *espresso* is strong enough to resist any blandness introduced by the milk.

Tea (*tè*) is often a disappointment to British tastes since it frequently comes as a sort of do-it-yourself drink with a small tea-bag in a cup accompanied by a jug of hot water. Remember to ask for *tè-latte* if you want it with milk, or *tè con limone* if you want it with lemon. Otherwise it will come as just tea, without accompaniment. As a hot drink, chocolate is very popular. If you want it very rich you should ask for *cioccolata con panna* (with cream).

Of non-alcoholic drinks the pleasantest is probably a *spremuta* (fruit-juice). In the cheaper cafés this will probably take the form of bottled or tinned fruit-juice (which is more properly called a *succo di frutta*). But in a proper café it is the equivalent of the French *citron pressé*, and takes the form of the freshly-squeezed juice of the fruit, served with sugar and a jug of iced water for you to sweeten and dilute for yourself. Most fruits can be used and you normally ask for a *spremuta di* . . . and nominate your choice. In summer *fragolino* is delicious, being crushed strawberries served as a *spremuta*.

The three grand cafés of Venice are situated on St Mark's Square and rate as three of the foremost cafés in the world.

On the south side of the square, in the Procuratie Nuove, is the **Caffè Florian**. The first coffee-house to be opened in Venice (in 1720) it has long been the place to be seen. Inside it is a warren of small, mirrored rooms decorated in 18th-century style. In summer the tables are set out in the Piazza and the orchestra plays light classics and selections from operetta. Your drink here will cost you five times what it would cost in a simple café but the unique atmosphere and setting make it worthwhile. It is a relatively inexpensive way for anyone to mingle with high society and the jet set.

Opposite, in the Procuratie Vecchie, is the **Caffè Quadri**. Almost as old as Florian, and with the same outside tables, orchestra and elevated prices, yet it has always been the runner-up in the prestige stakes. Probably this is because Quadri was favoured by Austrian officers and their collaborators during the occupation period, while Florian was the meeting-place for those devoted to Italian nationalism.

Next door to Quadri, is the **Caffè Lavena**. It shares the location and atmosphere of the other two but, without the historical associations and orchestras, it does tend to be forgotten. Nevertheless, it was Wagner's favourite café.

Around the corner, in the Piazzetta, projecting from the Sansovino Library, is the **Caffè Chioggia**, less prestigious than the three cafés on the Piazza but still exacting a price for its location facing the facade of the Doge's Palace.

At a less elevated and less expensive level, other cafés, mostly *pasticcerie*, which are worth noting are —

Causin, Campo S. Margherita, Dorsoduro. Pastries and ices.

Il Golosone, Salizzada S. Lio, Castello. Delicious cakes. Try the *spremuta di mele* (apple-juice).

Latteria Zorzi, Calle dei Fuseri, S. Marco. As the name suggests, a milk-bar, but in the summer it also opens its dining-room and claims to be Venice's only vegetarian restaurant.

Marchini, Ponte San Maurizio, S. Marco. Claimed to be Venice's finest *pasticceria* its window displays can stop people dead in their tracks.

Rosa Salva, Campo S. Luca and Merceria S. Salvador, both in S. Marco. Branches of a catering group, noted for good coffee.

Vio, Rio Terà Toletta, Dorsoduro. Near the Accademia. Cakes and pastries.

Three *gelaterie* well worth visiting are —

Il Doge, Campo S. Margherita, Dorsoduro. Advertises *gelati artigianali* which means the ices are made on the premises in the traditional fashion. Try their *granita* — crushed ice flavoured by strong cordial or syrup.

Nico, Zattere, Dorsoduro. Speciality is *gianduiotto* - praline flavoured ice cream, a cup of which will do great damage to your bank balance and chloresterol level. If you want the effect to be lethal ask for it *con panna* — with whipped cream.

Paolin, Campo S. Stefano, S. Marco. Disputes with Nico the title of Venice's finest ice cream maker. In summer, delightful outside tables at the head of the square. Try the *coppa mista* in which *gianduiotto* and chocolate ice cream are swirled together around the kernel of an almond flavoured water-ice.

Bars

In the mornings the *pasticcerie* are largely filled with women having coffee and a pastry while the men are in bars eating savoury things and probably drinking a glass of wine. In Venice a glass of wine is known as an *ombra*, which means 'shade', remembering the days when the pleasure of a summer day would be to take a glass in the shade of a colonnaded square. Wine is red (*rosso*), white (*bianco*) or rosé (*rosato*) and it can be dry (*secco*), very dry (*asciutto*) or sweet (*dolce* or, more usually, *abbocato*). If you are ordering by the bottle or carafe they come in fractions of a litre — *un quarto* (quarter litre), *un mezzo* (half) or *un litro* (full litre).

Beer (*birra*) is treated as a summer drink by the Venetians. Bottled beer is more expensive and is often imported from Germany or Holland. Italian beer is quite acceptable, not unlike French. It will probably be Italian if you order draught (*alla spina*) and you must be careful to state the size you want; a small beer (*piccola*) is a quarter litre while a large (*grande*) is usually a half-litre. In some bars, however, a half litre is a *birra media* (middle-sized beer) and *una birra grande* is a full litre (nearly two pints!).

A drink once peculiar to Venice was the *spritz* but, as a 'spritzer' it has now made its appearance in the Anglo-Saxon world. It is basically a mixture of wine and fizzy (*gassata*) mineral water. The wine can be ordinary wine, or vermouth, or a *bitter* such as Campari. Also mixed with mineral water are a number of cordials like the French *sirops*, of which the most popular is the orange-coloured *aperol*.

All bars serve food of one kind or another. In a good, traditional bar there is usually a wide variety of interesting bite-sized snacks known as *cichetti*, not unlike the Spanish *tapas*. You can also usually obtain a slice cut from a large tray-based pizza, or a *pizzetta*, which is a miniature saucer-sized pizza. For sandwiches there are always the ubiquitous *pannini* (rolls), ask for either a *pannino prosciutto* (ham) or a *pannino formaggio* (cheese). Much more interesting are *tramezzini* (literally 'between two halves') which are sandwiches made from large *genovese* loaves, the crusts cut off and the round cut diagonally into two so that you get a triangular shaped sandwich, but a very thick sandwich because they positively bulge with interesting fillings — tuna and mayonnaise, eggs and anchovies etc. With a drink, one or two *tramezzini* make an excellent lunchtime break in your sightseeing. The best places to look for bars with interesting snacks are in Dorsoduro between the Accademia and the Campo S. Margherita; in the eastern part of Castello along the Via Garibaldi and in Cannareggio along the

Strada Nova between the Rialto and the Station. For that matter the station buffet itself is a very good bar with a very reasonable selection of *tramezzini*.

Beyond mentioning likely areas in which to look for bars I make no suggestions or recommendations. Bars are everywhere and it is easy enough to check from the street as to whether it appeals to your personal taste. But there is one bar which must be mentioned because it stands in relation to the other bars of Venice as the Caffè Florian stands in relation to the cafés. This is **Harry's Bar**, which has achieved such fame that there are imitative Harry's Bars all over the world. Situated at the bottom of the Calle Vallaresso, adjoining the San Marco landing-stage, the bar was founded over fifty years ago by an American, Harry Pickering, who set up the barman, Giuseppe Cipriani in his own establishment. The bar is now owned by Giuseppe's son, Harry, Italianised as 'Arrigo'. Arrigo's major innovation is the 'Bellini Cocktail', made by mixing champagne and peach juice but cocktails generally are the speciality of the house. The safest bet for visitors of average income is to drink the house wine. Harry's Bar also serves food and has acquired a Michelin rosette for its specialities. The food is not therefore an average bar-snack in either quality or cost. All the rich and famous drink in Harry's Bar; Hemingway was virtually a permanent fixture — but he had the money to pay the prices.

Enoteche

Enoteche are wine-bars, priding themselves on the range and quality of their wines even if they serve a full range of other drinks. Some recommended wine bars are —

Al Volto, near Campo S. Luca in the Calle Cavalli, S. Marco. Over a thousand different wines most, but not all, Italian.

Corner Pub, Calle della Chiesa, Dorsoduro. Obviously models itself on the English pub but, in drinks, service and opening hours is pure Venetian.

Da Codroma, Fondamenta Briati, Dorsoduro. Near the Accademia and has a quiet, academic atmosphere where you can savour your wine at leisure.

Osteria della Vedova, Calle del Pistor, Castello. Just over the boundary from Cannaregio near the Ca' d'Oro. Family-run hostelry with wide selection of wines and excellent snacks.

Vino Vino, S. Fantin, near the Fenice, S. Marco. Probably the most prestigious of the wine bars and this is reflected in the atmosphere and the prices. Still worth a visit.

The staircase that gives its name to the Martini Scala Restaurant, next to the Fenice Theatre.

SIX

Night Life, Cultural and Sporting Activities

Night Life

It has to be said that, in many ways, Venice has no night life. It is ironic to look back on the Venice of the 18th century when members of society would not even rise from their beds before eight in the evening. Today most cafés and bars close by about 21.30 while many restaurants stop serving by 22.00. Those hours may be extended during the high season when the tourists are unwilling to leave but, outside the peak months, it is possible to wander through deserted streets and squares after ten o'clock. The exception to this general rule is during the various festivals that punctuate the year. During Carnival, for instance, there are many night-time events. Consult *Un Ospite di Venezia* to check whether anything is happening during your stay.

Theatre, opera and concerts will be dealt with later in this chapter but, for less cultural entertainment, you must rely on Venice's solitary disco, a handful of piano bars and a number of bars that stay open late, sometimes with music.

The disco is **El Souk** on the Calle Corfù between the Accademia and the Campo S. Barnaba in Dorsoduro. An ordinary bar until 20.00 it re-opens at 22.00 as a disco and remains open until 3.00. There is an entrance charge of about L15,000 which includes the cost of your first drink. Customers are vetted at the door and those the management consider undesirable are refused entry. Closed Sun.

The piano bars are quietly luxurious and much more expensive. The principal ones are:
Ristorante Piano Bar 'Antico Martini' in S. Fantin near the Fenice. Open from around 22.00 until 3.00. Closed Tues. and Wed.

Piano Bar 'Do Leoni' attached to the 'Deux Lions' restaurant on the Riva degli Schiavoni. Open from 19.30 until 1.00 or 2.00. Closed Tues.

Enoteca Piano Bar 'Linea d'Ombra' on Zattere, not far from the Punta Dogana. Open until 2.00 during the season. A little more down-market than the previous two, although not by much. Closed Wed.

Bars and restaurants with live music have been mentioned before under other headings but the most noted are:

Music-Restaurant Paradiso Perduto, Fondamenta della Misericordia, Cannaregio. Already mentioned among the restaurants this is a lively establishment with a popular bar and art displays. Mostly jazz. Open until 1.00, or even later. Closed Wed.

Ai Canottieri, Ponte Tre Archi, Cannaregio. Music most evenings with some dancing. Open until around midnight. Closed Mon.

Other bars and cafés open until at least midnight are:

In S. Marco —

Ristorante Bar Al Theatro, S. Fantin near Fenice. Until midnight, closed Mon.

Caffè Bar Quadri, Piazza. Until half past midnight, closed Mon.

Bar Gelateria Gran Caffè Chioggia, Piazzetta. Until midnight, closed Sun.

Ristorante Taverna La Fenice, S. Fantin. Until 1.00, closed Sun.

In Cannaregio —

Bar S. Lucia, S. Geremia. Until 1.00, closed Sun.

Bar Sport Club dei Dardi, Misericordia. Until 1.00, closed Wed.

Birreria Beau Brummel, Lista di Spagna. Until 2.00, closed Wed.

Pizzeria Gino's, Lista di Spagna. Until 1.00, closed Tues.

In Dorsoduro and Giudecca —

Cantina Veneta, Fond. S. Croce, Giudecca. Until midnight, closed Tues.

Corner Pub, S. Vio. Until 1.00, closed Tues.

Snack bar Cicchetteria del Grigio, Campo S. Barnaba. Until midnight, closed Fri.

In Castello —

Birreria Forst, SS. Apostoli. Until midnight, closed Tues.

Ciro's Bar, Calle de la Malvasia. Until midnight, closed Sun.

The Casino

The Municipal Casino offers the usual gambling games — roulette, chemin de fer, trente et quarante, blackjack and craps. There is a minimum betting limit of L2,000. The Casino also hosts International Tournaments in bridge, backgammon and gin rummy. Outside the gaming rooms there is a theatre, piano bar, bars and restaurants. Fashion parades are also a regular feature laid on for customers.

During the winter months the Casino is housed in the **Palazzo Vendramin-Calergi**, next to the S. Marcuola landing stage. From April until November it transfers to the Lido, at **Lungomare G. Marconi 4**. Opening hours are from 15.00 until 3.00. During the summer months there is a direct *motoscafo* connection, the 'Casino Express' which leaves S. Marco every half hour. Entry to the Casino is L18,000 and clients are expected to be dressed for the occasion.

Cinema

There are a number of cinemas in Venice but the non-Italian speaker will be hard-pressed since, although all the latest Hollywood releases are shown here, the Italian fashion is to dub films rather than use sub-titles.

Two cinemas which offer art-film and critical showings as well as general releases are —

Accademia, near the Accademia in the Calle Corfù.

Olimpia, Campo San Gallo, just past the Cavaletto Hotel, north of the Piazza.

The two main general release houses are —

Ritz, Calle dei Segretaria, off the Campo S. Zulian.

Rossini, Salizzada del Teatro, between S. Luca and the Campo Manin.

In the Piscina di Frezzerie is the **Cinema Centrale** which functions as a normal cinema at night but, during the day, shows a continuous performance of a three-quarter hour film about Venice, *The Venice Experience.*

The Venice Film Festival

The International Film Festival, run by the Biennale Organisation, takes place every year in late August/early September. Activities are confined to the Lido, with the films shown at the **Palazzo del Cinema**, on the Lungomare G. Marconi, opposite the Casino and at the **Astra** in Via Corfù. The programme of films is announced about a month prior to the opening of the Festival and can be obtained from any information office or the two cinemas concerned. Tickets surplus to the needs of the invited audience are available to the general public but they cannot be pre-booked and have to be bought on the day of performance; be prepared for long queues!

Galleries, Museums and Monuments

In any city as full of history and art as Venice there are bound to be a great many museums and art galleries but, as I have stated previously, the last way to get the unique flavour of Venice is to spend your entire time in museums; the city itself is the best museum of them all. Faced with a menu so rich in cultural activities the visitor has to be selective, in case over-indulgence leads to a form of cultural indigestion.

The major museums, galleries and *palazzi* will, of course, be described in fuller detail at the relevant point in the chapters on sightseeing, but the principal ones are listed here so that you can plan your programme. Information is as complete and accurate as I can make it but opening hours can change four times a year, according to season, while entrance charges are currently increasing after a few years' stability. A few places are closed in the winter, many open for only half the day and most close on at least one day a week. Use the list for guidance but check with the Information Office in Venice, or in *Un Ospite di Venezia,* for the position at the time of your visit.

Galleria dell'Accademia: Probably the greatest collection of Venetian art under one roof, with all the major Venetian artists represented. Gems are works by Giorgione and Giovanni

Bellini. Open 9.00–14.00 daily (9.00–13.00 holidays). Entrance L.8,000.

Doge's Palace: The seat of the Republic's government for 900 years. The interior of the Palace is not as impressive as the exterior, although the entrance is magnificent enough. Open daily 8.30–14.00 winter, until 17.00 summer (no one admitted in the last hour before closing). Entrance L8,000. Guided tour of the private rooms (in Italian only) L5,000 — must be booked 24 hours in advance.

Ca' d'Oro: Reputedly the finest *palazzo* on the Grand Canal, restored by Baron Franchetti who left it, together with his art collection, to the nation. Opened as a museum in 1984 but just the building itself is well worth looking at, especially when the current work of restoring the facade is complete. Open 9.00–14.00 daily (9.00–13.00 Sun. and holidays). Entrance L2,000.

Museo Civico Correr: Housed on the south side of the Piazza the museum contains a picture gallery laid out to illustrate the history of Venetian art from early Gothic to the 17th century. Open daily 9.00–16.00 (9.00–12.30 holidays), evening openings Fri. (21.00–23.00), Sat. and Sun. (until 20.00). Closed Tues. Entrance L5,000.

Guggenheim Collection: Housed in the late Peggy Guggenheim's house, one of the finest collections of modern art in the world. All major artists represented — Picasso, Magritte, Moore, Dali etc. Open 11.00–18.00. Entrance L5,000; free entrance Sat. 18.00–21.00. Closed Tues.

Ca' Pesaro: *Palazzo* designed by Longhena which houses two museums. The **Museum of Oriental Art** is generally acknowledged to be mediocre at best. Open 9.00–13.30 daily (to 12.30 on Sun. and holidays). Entrance L2,000. The **Museum of Modern Art** consists largely of 19th- and 20th-century works purchased at the Biennale. Open 10.00–16.00 (9.30–12.30 Sun. and holidays). Closed Mon. Entrance L3,000. Both museums were closed in 1991 for extensive restoration work.

Ca' Rezzonico (Museum of 18th-Century Life): Longhena *palazzo* furnished and decorated to illustrate life in a patrician Venetian home of the 18th century. Open 10.00–16.00 (9.00–12.30 Sun. and holidays). Closed Fri. Entrance L5,000.

Museo Fortuny: Mariano Fortuny was an artist in textiles. The lower floors are devoted to the art of the man; the textiles fascinating, the paintings less so. Photographic exhibitions on the second floor. Open 9.00–19.00. Closed Mon. Entrance L5,000.

Museo di Storia Naturale: For those who like that sort of thing, the largest dinosaur skeleton in existence. Worth seeing for its setting in the Fondaco dei Turchi, trading base of the Turks in Venice. Open 9.00–13.30 (until 13.00 on Sundays and holidays). Closed Mon. Entrance L3,000.

Museo Storico Navale: Close to the Arsenal the museum contains some fascinating models of ships, galleys and gondolas from the heyday of the Republic, including a magnificent model of the *Bucintoro*. Open 9.00–13.00. Closed holidays. Entrance L2,000.

Scuole Grande dei Carmini: Home of the Carmelite co-fraternity. Designed by Longhena and decorated by Tiepolo, so successfully that he was admitted to the fraternity. Open 9.00–13.00 and 15.00–18.00. Closed Sun. Entrance L5,000.

Scuole di San Giorgio degli Schiavoni: Founded 1451 by the Dalmatians, its pride is a frieze by Carpaccio showing the lives of three Dalmatian saints, including St George. Open 10.00–12.30 and 15.30–18.00 Closed Mon. (and p.m. on Sun. and holidays). Entrance L4,000.

Scuole Grande di San Rocco: Given over to the works of Tintoretto with almost all his output between 1564 and 1588. Open 9.00–13.00 daily. 15.30–18.30 Sat. and Sun. only. Entrance L5,000.

Pala d'Oro, Treasury and Gallery of St Mark's: This way you get to see not only the Pala d'Oro but all the finest treasures of the Basilica including the original horses. As a bonus, the view from the *loggia*. Open 10.00–16.00 Mon.–Sat., 13.30–17.00 only on Sun. Entrance L2,000 for Treasury, L2,000 for Gallery, L2,000 for the Altar.

Campanile di San Marco: Open 10.00–16.00/19.30 (depending on season).Entrance L3000.

Campanile di San Giorgio: Equally good views but cheaper and less crowded. Open 9.00–12.00 and 14.30–18.00 daily. Entrance L2,000.

Museo Comunità Ebraica: At the heart of the Ghetto the museum of the Jewish community in Venice. Open 10.00–16.00. Closed Sat. and Jewish holidays. Guided tours of the Synagogues at hourly intervals between 10.30 and 14.30. Entrance L2,000.

There are many lesser museums, most of which will be

mentioned in the text. There are also a host of minor art galleries, many privately owned, which put on temporary exhibitions throughout the year; consult the guide *Un Ospite di Venezia* for the exhibitions in progress at the time of your visit. Supreme among exhibition sites is the **Palazzo Grassi** which was bought by Fiat in 1984 and made into a Cultural Centre which puts on some of the glitziest exhibitions ever seen. Another site where major art exhibitions are housed is the **Galleria di Palazzo Cini**, although the permanent collection here is of Tuscan art. Other major venues for seasonal exhibitions are the **Cini Foundation** on San Giorgio Maggiore, the **Doge's Palace** and the **Correr Museum**.

Most churches in Venice contain at least one work of art and the major churches are listed in the sightseeing chapters. Although entrance to churches is free, except for the Frari which charges L1,000, it may be necessary to tip a sacristan to open up some parts of the church for you. Alternatively the work of art may be placed in a dark corner where it cannot be seen under natural light; carry a supply of 100 and 200 lire coins to operate the meter-controlled lighting or hire the portable mirrors through which you can examine the roof.

The Performing Arts

Venice has long been famous for theatre, opera and music and all have their place today. An added bonus is the setting as much as the performance. The Fenice Theatre for example is a beautiful building, the interior of which can only be seen during performances. Many musical concerts are given in some of Venice's most beautiful churches. Consult *Un Ospite di Venezia* for information as to what is on during your visit.

Theatre
There are three principal prose theatres in Venice.
Teatro Goldoni, Calle Goldoni, San Marco. Built 1678. The classical theatre of Venice with a concentration on the works of Goldoni himself. For the foreigner the chief snag is that the plays are written in the Venetian dialect.
Teatro del Ridotto, Calle Vallareso, San Marco. On the site of the original 18th-century gambling den. Also paying more than lip-service to Goldoni but with a greater specialisation in 20th-century works.

The Commedia dell'Arte

The Commedia dell'Arte is the folk theatre of Italy, born of troops of strolling players and the ancestor of such diverse offspring as Comic Opera, Farce, Pantomime and the Punch and Judy Show. It reached its finest flowering in Venice where the playwright Carlo Goldoni is said to have discovered the Commedia, developed it into an art and then killed it off. The last statement is based on Goldoni having written 136 plays – once, it is said, writing a play a week for a year – all of them virtually indistinguishable but simply variations on the same theme.

The imagery of the Commedia dell'Arte pervades Venice, especially in Carnival costumes. The hero is *Arlechino* who is the cheeky and crafty servant who always gets the better of his master *Pantalone* who is the archetypal silly old man and cuckolded husband. The heroine is *Columbina*, although she can also be known as *Arlechina* if she wears a costume with a diamond pattern similar to Arlechino's. *Pulcinello*, quite unlike his English manifestation, Punch, is a sad-faced and white-dressed figure who speaks in a high-pitched voice and in the early morality plays represented the dead. While Arlechino is from Venice, Pulcinello is from the South. Also in the cast is the *Plague Doctor* from Bologna. He is dressed in black and wears a white mask with a very long nose. He is obviously very clever and speaks in impossibly long words that no one else can understand. The cast may also include the *Devil* who is dressed in red.

The **Teatro all'Avorgaria**, Campo S. Sebastian, Dorsoduro. Specialises in Venetian dialect plays.

There are open-air theatres next to the Palazzo Grassi and on S. Giorgio Maggiore which put on occasional productions during the summer.

Opera and Ballet

The **Fenice** means 'Phoenix' and commemorates the rebuilding of the theatre after a disastrous fire in 1836. The theatre had already seen the first performances of operas by Rossini, Bellini and Donnizetti but its reputation was made by Verdi who transferred here, through dissatisfaction with Milan's La Scala, in 1844. Many of his finest operas were premièred at the

Fenice, including *La Traviata*. Since then the Fenice has seen first performances of Wagner's *Rienzi*, Stravinsky's *The Rake's Progress* and Britten's *The Turn of the Screw*.

There are concerts, ballet and opera throughout the year although the opera season runs from November to July. The theatre is closed in August. Tickets start at about L15,000. Box office open 9.30–12.30 and 16.00–18.00. Tel. 5210 161.

The **Teatro Malibran** in Cannaregio is housed in a building of 1678 next door to the birth-place of Marco Polo. It is named after a Spanish singer of the early 19th century although it functioned as a theatre long before that and saw the first performance of Handel's *Agrippina* in 1710. Today it is principally a venue for ballet, although opera and orchestral concerts are also performed there. Seasonal. Box office Tel. 5225 339.

Music

For general information about musical presentations in Venice contact the music department of the Cultural Office, S. Marco 1221B. Tel. 5209 288. Regular choral and orchestral concerts are held at the Fenice and Malibran Theatres and jazz concerts at the Goldoni Theatre under the auspices of the Assessorato alla Cultura. Also, every year in November, the Goldoni Theatre hosts two musical contests — the **New Venetian Song Contest** and the **International Pop Festival** for the **Golden Lion** Award.

Church of Santa Maria della Pietà: This is Vivaldi's church and the tradition continues with chamber orchestra concerts of work by Vivaldi and others.

Frari Basilica: Full concerts, particularly of oratorios and church music.

For both the above, tickets are available through the agency Kele & Teo, Ponte de Bareteri, S. Marco 4930. Tel. 5208 722.

Other chamber concerts take place in the **Palazzo delle Prigioni Vecchie**. Information from the Secretary to the Circolo Artistico, tel. 5225 707.

Occasional concerts and recitals are held in other Venetian churches, principally in **S. Stefano** and the **Scuole Grande di S. Giovanni Evangelista**. It is sometimes possible to gain free entrance to concerts broadcast by RAI from its studios in the **Palazzo Labia**. Details of all musical entertainments are to be found in *Un Ospite di Venezia*.

The Biennale

The Biennale is one of the foremost international exhibitions of
modern art in the world. Founded in 1895, in celebration of the
Silver Wedding of King Umberto I and Queen Margherita, the
Exhibition is known as the Biennale because it is held every
two years — even-numbered years since 1914 — between June
and September.

There is a permanent exhibition site, the **Palazzo
dell'Esposizione**, in the **giardini pubblici** at the far eastern end
of the islands, between the Arsenal and S. Elena. Very early on
the number of potential exhibitors rapidly outpaced the
capacity of the exhibition centre and so the organisers sold
space in the public gardens on which various countries could
build their national pavilions. The Belgians were first in 1907
but many other countries followed suit until today there are 27
different pavilions on the exhibition site in imitation of the old
international expositions from the turn of the century.

The exhibition as a whole has long since outgrown the
exhibition grounds. Beyond the national displays of invited
artists, room had to be found for the new and less-established
artists. So, just as the Edinburgh Festival has its 'Fringe', so the
Biennale has its '**Aperto**' or 'Open' exhibition in the salt
warehouses on Zattere, or the rope works near the Arsenal.
Many people believe that the 'Aperto' is more vigorous and
exciting than the Biennale proper.

Tickets for the whole of the Biennale cost L10,000 but tickets
for separate sections can be bought. The Biennale has its
administrative headquarters in the Ca' Giustinian, Calle
Vallaresso, near the S. Marco landing stage. They can give
information about the exhibition. The **Archives** of the Biennale
are kept at the **Palazzo Corner della Regina** near the Ca'
Pesaro', entrance free. The **Museum of Modern Art** in the Ca'
Pesaro contains all the paintings which won the Biennale during
the early years, when it was a practice to buy the paintings
rather than give prizes.

Sports

It has to be said that Venice is not really the city to go to if you
wish to indulge in sporting activities. With very few exceptions
sport is banished to the Lido and, if you are interested in any

sporting activity you should make your enquiries to the **Centro Sportivo Turistico**, Piazzale S. Maria Elisabetta, Lido (just by the vaporetto landing stage).

Swimming: There is a 12km beach on the Lido but, with the exception of two public beaches at the northern and southern extremes of the island, at San Niccolò and Alberoni, most beaches are the private property of the hotels. The northern beach is 15 minutes walk from the landing stage while the southern beach must be reached by bus and is therefore less crowded. If you do not mind the expense you can hire a beach-hut for the day on one of the private beaches along the Lungomare Marconi.Contact the **Direzione Attività Balneari**, Gran Viale Santa Maria Elisabetta 2, Lido.

Golf: There is a full eighteen-hole golf course at Alberoni at the far south of the Lido.

Tennis: *Tennis Club Lido*, Via San Gallo 163, Lido Tel. 5260 954

       Tennis Club Venezia, Lungomare Marconi 41, Lido Tel. 5260 335

Non-residents are also able to play on some of the hotel tennis courts, especially since the Venezia Tennis Club is attached to the Hotel Excelsior.

Clay-Pigeon Shooting: *Tiro e Segno Nazionale*, S, Niccolò 23, Lido.

Wind-surfing: Enquire at the Hotel Excelsior, Lungomare Marconi 41, Lido.

Horse Riding: *Circolo Ippico Veneziano*, Ca' Bianca, Lido.

Some sports can be indulged in Venice proper.

Sailing: Enquiries should be made either to the offices of the *Compagna della Vela,* Giardinetti, San Marco. Tel. 5222 593 or at the Marina, Isola di San Giorgio Maggiore. Tel. 5289 287.

Boats can sometimes be hired by the hour from the boatyard at the corner of the Rio degli Ognissanti and the Rio di San Trovaso, Dorsoduro. The CIGA Yacht Club sometimes runs sailing courses in Spring and Summer as well as hiring out sailing boats.

Fencing: *Circolo Scherma*, Cannaregio 47.

For spectator sports there are of course the many regattas during the summer months.

Football: Venice play in the C1 Division of the National League. Matches are played on Sunday afternoons at the F. Baracca Sports Stadium, Mestre.

Basketball: The home team for Venice is Reyer-Hitachi and they play in the A2 division of the National Championship. Matches are played on Sunday evenings at the Arsenal Sports Pavilion, Castello.

The Ridotto

The Venetian authorities have always kept a firm control over gambling in the city. In the 18th century the most important gaming-house in Venice was the government-owned Ridotto, situated in the Calle Vallaresso where the Teatro del Ridotto stands today. Would-be gamesters had to wear masks when on the premises. Others were even more secretive; Casanova entered the Ridotto through a secret passage from what is now Room 287 of the Hotel Monaco. Government control spread through all manifestations of gambling. Having provided the Ridotto for the upper classes, it also organised a lottery for the common people, with tables set up at the foot of the Campanile.

Boating in the Lagoon — A Warning

In the Southern Lagoon in particular the sight of a sheet of water like an inland sea might lead the unwary into thinking that the Lagoon is a paradise for boating. However, the poles marking the channels are important. There are deep-water channels but much of the Lagoon is very shallow indeed. It is even possible to see a large oil tanker making its way towards Marghera, almost within touching distance of a fisherman standing on a sand-bank with the water not up to his knees. Navigation in the Lagoon requires a depth of knowledge and experience that the casual visitor cannot possess. The number of visitors who strand themselves on the shallows of the Lagoon is the reason so few boatyards in Venice will hire out boats to non-Venetians.

SEVEN

Shopping

Shopping areas

Venice is full of shops: far more than could possibly be needed by the dwindling local population and the vast majority are aimed exclusively at the tourist trade. Inevitably, there is an awful lot of rubbish on sale, and not always cheap rubbish at that! At the other extreme, because Venice is a smart city and an expensive city, there is a high proportion of high-quality, high-fashion goods on show that are beyond the reach of the average purse. It takes a certain degree of perseverance to steer the middle course between these two in order to find the attractive, yet reasonably priced, item: but it can be done.

The main shopping area lies between St Mark's Square and the Rialto Bridge in the series of streets known collectively as the **Mercerie**. The word '*merceria*', like the English 'mercer's', means 'draper's shop'. There are four main stems to the Mercerie. From the Clock Tower on the Piazza the **Merceria dell'Orologio** leads north although, by turning right along the Calle Larga S. Marco, you can reach the parallel **Spadaria**; the two coming together at the Campo S. Zulian to form the **Merceria S. Zulian**, which in turn runs as far as the Ponte di Bareteri, before becoming the **Merceria S. Salvador** leading to the Campo S. Bartolomeo and the Rialto Bridge. The Mercerie contain a wide variety of shops, with prestige names like *Gucci* and *Cartier* rubbing shoulders with middle-range chains such as *Benetton* and *Stefanel*; all mixed in alongside the cheap and shoddy. The shops on the Rialto Bridge are a continuation of the Mercerie.

The prestige names and quality shops largely cluster around the Piazza itself, and west of it along the **Salizzada S. Moisè** and the **Calle Larga XXII Marzo**, as well as their offshoots, the **Calle Vallaresso** and the **Frezzerie**. Continuing straight on from the Calle Larga XXII Marzo will bring you to the **Campo San Maurizio** which is not only the centre of the antiques trade but contains a number of attractive and interesting speciality shops.

Outside San Marco the most profitable area for shopping excursions is in San Polo along the route from the Rialto to the Campo S. Polo by way of the **Ruga Vecchia S. Giovanni,** the **Ruga Ravano** and the **Calle Madonnetta.** The area around the **Frari** is good for prints and papers. Between the **Accademia, Campo S. Barnaba** and the **Campo S. Margherita** you can find a good selection of arts and crafts goods. North and east of the Rialto there are busy shopping streets in the **Strada Nuova** and its continuations towards the Station, and in the **Salizzada S. Lio**, which loops back to join the Mercerie at S. Zulian.

Glass

You cannot be long in Venice without realising that the manufacture and sale of glassware plays an important role in the local economy. Every other shop seems to be devoted to the sale of glass, much of it, sadly, over-priced and pretentious *kitsch*. For those who like coloured and decorated glass tableware there is plenty here to choose from.

For those who favour the simple but adventurous use of glass the best bet is **L'Isola**, with two branches, in the Salizzada S. Moisè and the Mercerie dell'Orologio. They favour clean-cut lines and a subtle use of colour. Another area to look for good quality designer glass is along the calle between the Guggenheim Museum and the Salute in eastern Dorsoduro, where there are a number of showrooms, one of which has a furnace and glass-blowing room for demonstrations.

If your fancy is for the small ornamental item rather than tableware then the most creative and imaginative shop is that of **Pagnaco Glass** on the corner where the Merceria dell' Orologio becomes the Merceria S. Zulian. Their speciality is for minute figures and creatures made from glass. There are, for example, over sixty varieties of insect reproduced in blown glass and an entire orchestra of miniature instrumentalists in 18th-century costume. For glass jewellery or *millefiore* paperweights you could try **Bortoli Glass** on the corner of Salizzada S. Moisè and Calle Vallaresso.

If you wish to see glass being blown there are a couple of workshops beyond the north side of St Mark's Square, both of them well-advertised and well-signposted, as well as the workshop in Dorsoduro, mentioned above. But beware! In return for the ten minutes excellent and interesting demonstration you will have to face, for rather longer, the full rigours of a high-pressure sales-pitch.

If you are serious about glass, however, you will go to Murano where it is all made. It is not that glass is any cheaper in Murano than it is in Venice; often the reverse is true. But there is more of it in a more concentrated area. It is also more permissible to bargain in Murano than in Venice.

Lace

Like glass, lace has always been associated with Venice and with one island in the Lagoon in particular, in this case Burano. Unfortunately, the declining number of women with the skill to make lace, and the time taken to make any individual item, means that supply can no longer meet demand and much of the lace sold in Venice (and in some cases in Burano too) is machine-made in the Far East.

Unlike glass, it is far better and cheaper to buy lace at source, taking the boat to Burano and trying the various outlets there. Do not expect the lace to be cheap. There are seven different stitches in Venice or Burano point lace and an individual lace-maker will specialise in just one stitch. This means that for all but the simplest of items a piece of lace will be passed from one specialist to another. A lace place-setting or table-mat will take seven women over a month to produce. In terms of the time and effort that goes into its production lace is not expensive, costly though it may be in absolute terms. A small item will cost in the region of L10,000.

If you have no time for the trip to Burano the place to go in Venice is **Jesurum**, named after Michelangelo Jesurum who re-introduced the art of lace-making to Venice in 1870. The main salesroom, with a wide range of table-linen as well as lace, is at Ponte Canonica, across the Canonica Canal from the Calle Larga S. Marco. There is also a smaller shop on the Piazza itself.

Lace-making can be seen in the **Scuola dei Merletti** (see page 247) or at **Il Merletto** in the Sotoportego del Cavaletto on the south side of the Piazza.

Masks

Nowadays shops selling masks as souvenirs are almost as

common as shops selling glass. But this is quite a recent occurence. The wearing of masks, which was commonplace in the 18th century, was banned by Napoleon and discouraged by the Austrians. Early this century it was making a come-back when the practice was outlawed by the Fascist regime who, with the intolerance of a totalitarian state for secrecy on the part of its citizens, made it a capital offence. It is only since the revival of Carnival in the late 70s that the making and wearing of masks has come back into its own.

Types of mask range from the simple white half-mask, as worn with the *bautta,* to elaborate gilded sun-god creations or ceramic faces that can cost hundreds of thousands of lire. As with lace there are a lot of mass-produced, garish masks produced cheaply for the day-tripper market. There are still plenty of outlets for genuine, hand-produced and hand-painted masks and you should have no difficulty in recognising the genuine article in many shops. A few outstanding sources are:
Ca' Macara, on the corner of the Fondamenta Rezzonico and the Calle Botteghe, across the canal from the Campo S. Barnaba in Dorsoduro. Full range of *commedia dell'arte* character masks, many of which you can see being painted in the back of the shop. About L25,000 for the average mask.
Mondonovo, Rio Terà Canal, leading into the Campo S. Margherita. This is a theatrical costumiers as well as a mask-maker. Expect to pay a bit more but they are less standardised than elsewhere and, if you are there for Carnival, you can hire the costume to go with them.
Paolo Vasquez, Corte Lucatello, S. Zulian. Extremely beautiful masks painted in strict accordance with tradition.
Emile Massaro, Calle Vitturi. At the bottom end of the Campo S. Stefano take the calle in front of S. Vidal Church, as signposted for the Palazzo Grassi, and the Calle Vitturi crosses it a short distance along. This is a mask factory producing for half the shops in Venice but you can obtain them here at wholesale prices.

Leather
Like all Italian leather, that sold in Venice is beautifully made and crafted with style and skill. Quality for quality it is relatively cheap and very individual in style and design. Unfortunately, Venetian leather is rather more expensive than a similar item would be elsewhere in Italy.

For fairly reasonable leather goods try **Casella** in the Salizzada Pio X, on the approach to the Rialto Bridge from Campo S. Bartolomeo. Classier (and pricier) is **La Bauta** in the Merceria S. Zulian. Classiest of all is **Vogini** in the Calle Ascensione, just beyond the Piazza.

For shoes your best bet is certainly **Zecchi** on the corner of the Merceria dell'Orologio and the Calle Larga S. Marco. They specialise in discounted quality shoes so that for between 60,000 and 100,000 lire you can pick up beautifully crafted, all-leather shoes which would cost at least twice that elsewhere.

For a real bargain, look in the shoe shops for highly-coloured velour slippers. Expertly made and hard-wearing, they can be got for less than L20,000 a pair.

Clothes

For style and quality Italian fashion is hard to beat, both for men and women. Sadly, it is also hard to beat in terms of cost. Ironically, in some of the priciest shops such as the **Duca d'Aosta** in the Merceria S. Zulian (men's shop on the right, women's facing it on the left) half the labels in the window are from British clothiers (Burberrys, Aquascutum etc.). One Italian designer who is not exactly cheap but whose clothes are available in Venice for less than you would pay in London, and in a wider range, is **Armani**. The class outlet is **Giorgio Armani**

The Bautta

The traditional dress for Carnival is known as the *Bautta*. It consists of a long black cape with a hood. Over the face is worn a white half-mask that leaves the mouth free. The whole is topped by the black tricorne hat. Worn by both sexes and all classes it is the perfect guarantee of anonymity because the wearer could be man or woman, rich or poor, old or young. In Venice's heyday the Bautta was so popular that many Venetians would have worn it all the time. It was certainly the only disguise permitted outside the Carnival period. It could be worn in the afternoons between October 5th and December 16th; on St Mark's Day and the Feast of the Ascension; it could also be worn for any major event at St Mark's such as the Proclamation of the Doge. It still enjoys currency during the modern Carnival and the complete outfit can be hired from the more serious mask shops.

in the Frezzeria but prices are a little more reasonable in the **Emporio Armani** on Calle dei Fabbri.

Two clothing chains with many branches in Venice which sell clothes at moderate prices are **Benetton** and **Stefanel**, both well-represented in the Mercerie as well as elsewhere in the city. A department store specialising in clothing at very reasonable cost is **Coin**, the Venetian branch of which is just north of the Campo S. Bartolomeo.

For real bargains in silk scarves and ties as well as some very good knitwear (lambswool and angora), try the stalls on the north side of the Rialto Bridge; both on the bridge and in the Ruga dei Orefici.

Antiques

The antiques trade is concentrated in the S. Maurizio district, around the square of that name. Mostly the goods are bulky and pricey but you should keep your eyes open for the **antiques fairs** held on the **Campo S. Maurizio** about once a month. Check with the Information Office as to whether there is to be one during your stay. Small items at reasonable prices.

For less expensive items the best source, apart from the antiques fair, is to be found in the many little back-street bric-a-brac or junk shops which you are bound to stumble across if you wander freely about the city. Some of the alleyways between S. Zaccaria and SS. Giovanni e Paolo in Castello are rich in this kind of shop, although the best place to look is around the Campo S. Barnaba in Dorsoduro.

Jewellery

Gold, silver and precious stones are to be found in plenty around the Piazza. The traditional centre of the trade is north of the Rialto Bridge in the Ruga d'Orefici (*orefice* means 'goldsmith'). Naturally enough you will expect to pay accordingly for the genuine article but the area north of the Rialto and towards the Campo S. Polo is well known for jewellers selling very good imitation gold and silver jewellery. As long as you are knowledgeable enough not to be sold imitation for genuine there are useful bargains to be found. Here also, in the Ruga Vecchia and the Ruga Ravano you can find glass and ceramic jewellery, as well as ethnic items from Africa and the Far East.

For the unusual and relatively inexpensive, try the gallery that is to the left of the Accademia in the **Rio Terà Foscarini** which specialises in re-set Venetian glass rings, ear-rings and necklaces as well as other unusual items. It is possible to pick up a pair of ear-rings for little more than L10,000.

Papers, prints and posters

Marbled and decorative papers are to be found all over the city but the majority of such work is produced in Tuscany. For traditional wood-block Venetian printing you should try **Legatoria Piazzesi** in the Campiello della Feltrina between S. Maria del Giglio and Campo S. Maurizio. Some of their work is based on old wood-blocks, still in their possession, that date back to the 15th century. The beautiful marbling technique known as *ebrù* is shown at **Alberto Valese** with branches in the Salizzada S. Samuele and Calle del Teatro. Here the process is not only applied to paper but to textiles and wood as well.

Old prints and maps of the city, usually reprinted from engravings in old books, are to be found in many parts of Venice but are often expensive. By far the best value for reprints of old engravings is the Armenian Monastery's printing-house on the island of **San Lazzaro** (see page 251). Within Venice the most comprehensive source of maps, posters

Strada Nova: a thoroughfare driven through Cannaregio to provide a land route to the railway station.

and engravings at reasonable cost is **Artigiani Riuniti** on the Rio Terà dei Nomboli in San Polo between S. Polo and the Frari. Another inexpensive way of obtaining good engravings is a poster which reproduces no fewer than 25 18th-century engravings of Canaletto drawings but only costs about L12,000. These can be obtained from bookshops such as **Goldoni** and the **Libreria Sansovino** (see below).

Modern prints — aquatints, etchings etc. — are attractive and there are many small galleries selling them in the city. Recommended are **Luna** in the Calle dei Saoneri in San Polo, and **Bac**, with two branches, on the Campo S. Maurizio and on the Ruga Ravano. They produce limited editions of local engravings in all sizes from full-poster size down to stamp-sized vignettes on hand-produced writing paper. Most economical is a set of five postcard sized aquatints for around L10,000.

Books

Books in English about Venice, its art and architecture as well as straightforward guide-books and maps, can be obtained at **Libreria Sansovino**, Bacino Orseolo (just through the arch from the Piazza), **Libreria Serenissima** in the Merceria S. Zulian and **Libreria Internazionale S. Giorgio** on the Calle Larga XXII Marzo. The first of these has a very strong section on guide-books and histories in English, including Lorenzetti's *Venice and its Lagoon* (see page 37). They also have a useful selection of posters and remaindered art books. If you simply want something to read the best selection of English books is in the **Libraio a San Barnaba** just west of the Campo S. Barnaba.

For general books, but especially the glossy art books which are so well produced in Italy, the best bookshops are **Goldoni** in the Calle dei Fabbri, with a useful selection of posters and maps, and **Libreria della Toletta** in the Sacca della Toletta between the Accademia and Campo S. Barnaba, which often has a good selection of books at reduced prices. The glossiest and most expensive books are to be found at **Fantoni Libri** in the Salizzada S. Luca. For facsimile editions of old books about Venice in Italian see **Filippi Editore Venezia** in the Calle della Bissa off the Campo S. Bartolomeo.

Do not rely on the city's museums and art galleries as a source of art books and posters. They are mostly very disappointing. At the Accademia for example you are likely to do far better at the news-stand in front of the gallery than at the gallery's own sales-counter. One exception to this, however, is the **Correr Museum** which has an excellent choice of cards and books, together with some extremely fine poster-sized reproductions for only about L5000.

Miscellaneous

If you cannot make your mind up about what you want to remind you of Venice you could try **Veneziartigiani**, set in an 18th-century apothecary's shop on the Calle Larga San Marco, which houses more than fifty traditional craft workers.

If you are looking for the unusual without regard to cost take a look at **V. Trois** in the Campo S. Maurizio, a modern textile workshop whose aim is to reproduce all the original designs of Fortuny.

For music or records, if not for musical instruments, take a look at **Ricordi** in a courtyard set back from the calle leading from S. Maurizio into S. Stefano. Apart from having a superb selection of records they have undertaken the task of producing the entire *corpus* of Vivaldi's forgotten works.

Food

There is not much point in buying food in Venice unless you are one of the very few in self-catering accommodation. However, the food markets to the north of the Rialto Bridge are one of the most fascinating sights of Venice. Get there early in the morning to see the produce in all its glory, and all the locals stocking up for the day. The finest sight of all is the **pescheria** or fish market (any day bar Sunday and Monday) with mounds of gleaming fish, of species not seen in northern waters. Lesser, but still interesting, street markets are to be seen on the squares of S. Maria Formosa and S. Margherita and on the Rio Terà S. Leonardo and Via Garibaldi. See also the barge moored alongside the Campo S. Barnaba which sells a full range of fruit and vegetables. One kind of food that can be bought as a souvenir of Venice is the produce of the pasticcerie; cakes and pastries, chocolate and other confectionery.

To buy wine or *grappa* there are many wine-shops throughout the city but the best bargains are to be obtained in the food shops (*alimentari*) which are scattered through all the residential areas. Most have comprehensive stocks of Italian, and specifically Veneto, wines at very reasonable prices.

Gondolas parked alongside the Rio dell'Orseolo.

EIGHT

A–Z of Useful Information

Addresses

Venice has probably the most complex house-numbering system in the world. Numbering is continuous throughout each sestiere according to some logic long lost in the past. The normal address is therefore given as the sestiere followed by a number; as for example the Hotel Gritti Palace, the address of which is San Marco 2467. Even when, on rare occasions, the street name is given in the address the number is still the number within the sestiere rather than the street, as with the Hotel Bauer Grunwald whose address is San Marco, Campo S. Moisè 1459.

On the whole it does not matter, but if the reader wants to try to understand the system they should obtain a copy of *Il Nuovo Indicatore Anagrafico di Venezia* by Piero Pazzi, privately published at L9,500. This lists, by parishes within sestieri, the allocation of numbers to each street in Venice and the islands.

If writing to any of the addresses given in this book the correct address is the name of the sestiere followed by the number (the street name can be included if known) and on the next line the post code number is followed by the place-name. The correct postal address of the Bauer Grunwald is therefore: Hotel Bauer Grunwald, S. Marco, Campo S. Moisè 1459, 30124 VENEZIA

The post codes for the sestieri are:
Cannaregio — **30121**, Castello — **30122**, Dorsoduro and Giudecca — **30123**, S. Marco — **30124**, S. Polo and Santa Croce — **30125**

Alberghi Diurnali

Literally 'Day Hotels' the Alberghi Diurnali are useful institutions in most Italian cities. Their main purpose is to provide washing and bathing facilities for day-trippers or people who are unable to return to their hotel during the day, as well as such services as hair-dressers, laundry and dry-cleaning, shoe-cleaning, rest-rooms, telephones and writing-rooms. The charge is around L500 for the use of a wash-basin and WC; with an additional bath or shower the cost is around L4,000. There are three in Venice, details are given under the heading of 'Toilets' later in this section.

Annual Holidays

Italy has a fair number of holidays each year and Venice adds a few local holidays to the list. On the days listed below all shops and businesses operate as on Sunday; only bars and restaurants are open, together with some bakers, which open in the morning only.

January 1 (**New Year's Day**): January 6 (**Epiphany**): **Good Friday** and **Easter Monday**: April 25 (**St Mark's Day**): May 1 (**Labour Day**): August 15 (**Feast of the Assumption**): November 1 (**All Saints'**): November 21 (**Feast of the Salute**): December 8 (**Immaculate Conception**): December 25 and 26 (**Christmas Day** and **Feast of St Stephen**).

Banks

All the major Italian banks are represented in Venice together with several local banks. Most of the banks have their main offices close to St Mark's Square in the Via XXII Marzo or surrounding streets. These include:

Banca Commerciale Italiana, via XXII Marzo 2188
Banca d'America e d'Italia, via XXII Marzo 2216
Nuovo Banco Ambrosiano, via XXII Marzo 2378
Banco di Roma, Mercerie dell'Orologio 191

The other concentration of banks is further north, still in S.

Getting the postcards home

Sorting offices of the Italian Postal Service, particularly in northern cities, are chronically short-staffed. In summer, when holiday absences make the problem critical, the answer is to put non-urgent mail on one side to be dealt with later. The most common form of mail to be so treated in this way is, of course, the holiday postcard. I have known a postcard posted in Italy during August be delivered in Britain as late as October. Sometimes they are never seen again. The answer, if you want your cards to get home before you do, is to take a supply of envelopes with you, pop the card inside the envelope and send it as a letter. It will only cost you an extra L100 and it will ensure delivery in days rather than weeks.

Marco but between the Rialto and the Campo Manin, and includes:

Banca d'Italia, S. Marco 4799

Cassa di Risparmio di Venezia, Campo Manin 4216

Credito Italiano, Campo S. Salvador

In common with most European banks Italian banks operate the system whereby the transaction is conducted at one counter but you go to another counter (the *Cassa*) to obtain your money.

Bank opening hours are normally 8.30 to 13.30 and 15.00 to 16.00, Mondays to Fridays. When the banks are closed a useful place to change money is the **American Express** in Salizzada S. Moisè, west of the Piazza, which is normally open 8.00 to 20.00 Mondays to Saturdays. Another possibility is **Wagons-Lits** in the Calle Larga S. Marco, just past the clock tower off the Piazza or at **Thomas Cook** on St Mark's Square. There are many exchange bureaux (*Cambio*) throughout the city but, since they give a very unfavourable rate of exchange and charge high commission, they are best avoided except in an emergency.

Most banks have cash dispensing machines which accept **Eurocheque** cards. If you have one of these cards, together with the necessary PIN number, see p. 32, you will find the dispensers throughout the city.

Bargaining

Some tourists seem to believe that all Mediterranean countries thrive on haggling over prices. This is certainly not true in Venice where the price marked in the shops is the price they expect you to pay. You can, however, ask about discounts for cash on large purchases. You can also bargain when you are buying directly from the artisan or workshop, as in some Murano glass workshops. Although there is a fixed tariff for water-taxis, gondolas and porters always agree your payment before you hire. This is not so much to get a bargain low rate as to ensure that you are not over-charged. Finally, you can attempt to get a better bargain from the hotel-keeper in the depths of the low season. In any other situation an attempt to question prices would just be regarded as bad manners and will get you nowhere.

Cats

Venice swarms with cats which roam the open spaces and are known as *gatti di laguna*, the Venetian equivalent of our alley-cats. It has been estimated that there are two cats in Venice for every human inhabitant. Yet they lead a fairly pampered life and, despite living in near-wild conditions, most look remarkably sleek and well fed. This is because there is an army of old ladies whose mission it is in life to feed the cats, and most restaurateurs will put out their scraps for the cats.

In 1987 a group of students organised a Festival of the Cats. Among the activities was the gift of a cat to any tourist who wanted one, each cat complete with carrying basket and vaccination certificate. And the tourists queued up in their hundreds for such an unusual souvenir of their visit to Venice. Out of this success grew the 'Badoer' International Cat Adoption Agency. If there are no regulations to prevent you bringing home a Venetian cat, you should apply to the Centro Internazionale Adozione Gatti 'Badoer', Campo San Giovanni Evangelista, S. Polo. Tel. 5233 997.

Churches

All the famous churches in Venice are functioning places of worship and it can be a moving experience, even for a non-Catholic, to attend mass in these historic surroundings. Some of the more special services are —

St Mark's: Solemn High Mass in Latin at 10.00 each Sunday.

S. Moisè: Latin Mass with readings in English, French and German at 18.15.

S. Giorgio Maggiore: Sung Gregorian Mass at 11.00 each Sunday.

Many churches also sing Vespers on Saturday evenings or on the eve of Church Festivals. Confessions in English are heard on Sunday evenings between 19.00 and 22.00 in the churches of San Marco, the Gesuiti, the Scalzi, SS. Giovanni e Paolo, the Redentore and San Giorgio Maggiore.

Other denominations

Church of England — St. George's, Campo S. Vio, Dorsoduro — Matins 10.30; Communion 8.30, 11.30.

Methodist — Waldesian Church, S. Maria Formosa, Castello — 11.00.

Lutheran — Campo SS. Apostoli, Cannaregio.

Greek Orthodox — Ponte dei Greci, Castello — 11.00 and noon each Sunday.

Jewish — Sinagoga Ebraica, Ghetto Vecchio — 9.30 each Saturday.

Most churches close at lunch time, between 12.00 and 13.00 until 14.30 at least and until as late as 16.00 or 17.00 in some cases.

Climate

	Average daily max. temp.	Rainy days per month
January	6°C	6
February	8°C	6
March	12°C	7
April	17°C	9
May	21°C	8
June	25°C	8
July	27°C	7
August	27°C	7
September	24°C	5
October	19°C	7
November	12°C	9
December	8°C	8

Consulates

Austria: Piazzale Roma 416:Tel. 5200 459
Belgium: S. Marco 2632: Tel. 5224 124
Denmark: Campiello S. Agostino 2347: Tel. 5206 822
France (Consul-General): Dorsoduro 1387: Tel. 5222 392
Germany: S, Marco 2888:Tel. 5225 100
Great Britain: Palazzo Querini, Dorsoduro 1051:Tel 5227 207
Greece:Rialto 720:Tel. 5237 260
Luxembourg: Castello 5312:Tel. 5222 047
Netherlands: S. Marco 423: Tel. 5225 544
Norway: Rotonda Garibaldi 12, Mestre:Tel. 5340 447
Portugal: S. Marco 1253:Tel. 5223 446
Spain (Vice-Consul): Fond. Ostreghe 2442: Tel. 5204 510
Switzerland:Dorsoduro 810:Tel. 791611.
The United States does not have a consul in Venice, the consulate in Milan should be contacted on the Milan number (02) 652841. The consulates of Canada and Australia are also in Milan.

Conversion Tables

Italian weights and measures are fully metric, using kilos, litres, metres and degrees Celsius. It is worth bearing in mind, however, that whereas in Britain metres and litres are divided into millimetres and millilitres, the norm in Italy is to divide into centimetres and centilitres. A quarter bottle of wine or a small measure of beer is therefore 25cl and not 250ml. Food is mostly sold by the kilo (2.2 lb), 500 g. (1.1 lb) or 250g. (0.55 lb), but small quantities of things such as sweets, chocolate or cake are sold by the 100 grammes (3.5 oz). This measure is known as an *etto*, so, for anything which you would normally buy in quarter pound quantities you should ask for '*un etto di* . . .'

Clothing and shoe sizes equate as follows:

Dress sizes

British	10	12	14	16	18	20	22	24
Italian	44	46	48	50	52	54	56	58

Women's knitwear

British	10	12	14	16
Italian	46	48	50	52

Shoe sizes (Women's)

British	2	3	4	5	6	7	8	9
Italian	34	35	36	37	38	39	40	41

Shoe sizes (Men's)

British	4	5	6	7	8	9	10	11
Italian	39	40	41	42	43	44	45	46

Men's shirts (collar sizes)

British	14	14½	15	15½	16	16½	17	17½
Italian	36	37	38	39	40	42	43	44

Men's suits

British	36	38	40	42	44	46
Italian	46	48	50	52	54	56

Crime

Any major city has its fair share of petty crime, but Venice is freer of crime than most Italian cities. Indeed it is said, only half-jokingly, that a posting to Venice is death to a policeman's career. The commonest crimes in Italy are thefts from motor-vehicles and Vespa-thieving (where boys or girls on motor-scooters snatch bags or cameras from pedestrians), both impossible in traffic-free Venice. Take the same precautions you would take anywhere. If you have parked your car during your stay in Venice do not leave any valuables in it and remove, if possible, any radio/cassette-player. Do not leave money or valuables in your hotel room and keep a wary eye open for pickpockets in the packed streets between the Piazza and Rialto during the more crowded months.

Disabled

Unfortunately, Venice is not a good place for the disabled traveller. Hotels tend to be old buildings with steep staircases, not always with lifts; there is an awful lot of walking to be done; it is difficult getting in and out of water-buses and many of the bridges are steep and stepped.

However, the problem is being tackled by **Progetto Veneziaper-tutti** (the Venice for All Project) which is promoted by the University Architectural Department. Their work is based on the fact that disabled people can use the *vaporetti* but cannot cross bridges. The city is therefore divided into those areas that can be reached by *vaporetto* without crossing a bridge and they have produced a map showing these areas in yellow, and the inaccessible areas in white. This map is prominently displayed at the *vaporetto* stops: Ferrovia, Piazzale Roma, Rialto, Accademia and S. Marco. Copies can also be obtained from Information Offices. The same team also produces a larger, more detailed map which not only reproduces this information but lists the hotels available in the accessible areas, states which boat routes can handle passengers in wheelchairs, toilets with disabled facilities and also the monuments, museums and churches accessible to the disabled. This map can be obtained free by application to the Porter's Lodge, U.L.S.S. (Health Dept.), Piazzale Roma, Dorsoduro 3493, close to the Route 1 Water-bus stop.

In Britain, advice for the disabled wanting to travel is always available from **RADAR** (Royal Association for the Disabled and Rehabilitation), 25 Mortimer St, London W1N 8AB. Tel: 071 637 5400.

Duty Free Allowances

All countries place a limit on the amount of goods that can be purchased in a duty-free shop and imported without further taxation. For citizens of the EC, however, allowances free of customs duty are considerably greater when the goods have been bought in Italy and have paid Italian tax.

	Duty paid	Duty free
Cigarettes	300	200
Cigarillos	150	100
Cigars	75	50
Tobacco	400 gr	250 gr
Spirits (over 22% alcohol)	1.5 litres	1 litre
Fortified or sparkling wine	3 litres	2 litres
Still table wine	5 litres	2 litres
Perfume	90 ml	60 ml
Toilet water	375 ml	250 ml
Other goods	£265 worth	£32 worth

Electricity

The electricity supply in Venice is 220v, although all appliances 220–240v will work. All sockets are standard Continental two-pin and light bulbs are of the screw type. If you are taking any electrical appliances with you, also take a travel adaptor.

Emergency Telephone Numbers

Carabinieri	5235 333
Police	113
A.C.I. Road Service	116
Ambulance	5230 000
Fire Brigade	5222 222
Passport Office (Questura)	5203 222
Lost Property (Airport)	661262
(Railway)	716122
(Vaporetti)	780310
Tourist Information	5226 356
Travel Information (Actv)	780111
(Air)	661262
(Rail)	715555

Etiquette in Churches

Mention is made elsewhere of the etiquette relating to clothing in churches — no shorts or bare shoulders. Churches are not closed to visitors during services but the visitor is expected not to talk or move about too much. In many churches you will find a sign reminding you that this is a place of worship, not a museum. At other times, if a sacristan or church servant does you a favour, such as unlocking a chapel normally closed to the public or illuminating some work of art, it is considered right to give a generous tip.

Information Offices

Outside Italy information on Venice and the Veneto can be obtained from the Italian National Tourist Office (**E.N.I.T.**) at 1 Princes Street, London W1R 8AY (071 408 1254) or 630 Fifth Ave, New York, NY 10111 (212–245 4822).

In Venice the *Azienda Promozione Turistica*, or **APT** for short, has its head office at Castello 4421 (5226 110) with offices serving the public at Calle dell'Ascensione 71c, (under the arch at the far end of the Piazza), at the railway station, Piazzale

Roma, the Marghera Motorway exit and at the airport. Apart from the San Marco office these information offices tend to be seasonal, either closed or working short hours in the low season. As well as normal tourist information these offices can also arrange hotel bookings as discussed elsewhere (but beware that in the high season the San Marco office is usually too busy to offer this service). For information or advice by telephone dial 111.

Available from the information offices but also from most hotel receptions is the monthly (fortnightly in the high season) bilingual publication *Un Ospite di Venezia* (A Guest in Venice) which includes much valuable information as to what is on in Venice together with current timetables and tariffs for the water-bus, taxi and gondola services, etc.

Medical Emergencies

The hospital for casualties and emergencies is the **Ospedali Civili Riuniti di Venezia** on the Campo SS Giovanni e Paolo. The water ambulance can be called on 5230 000.

At least one chemist for each sestiere is open at night on a rota. A list of that week's chemists can be found in *Un Ospite di Venezia* but all chemists will have a notice in the window notifying the nearest night chemist available.

Mosquitos

Mosquitos are not quite the problem that might be expected but it would be unusual if the smaller internal canals with little water movement were entirely free. Visitors are advised to take an insect-repellant spray or cream with them as a precaution, particularly if they are likely to be eating out of doors on summer evenings.

Opening Hours

Official shop opening hours in Venice are 9.00 to 12.30 and 15.00 to 19.30 p.m. and are closed all day Sundays and on Monday mornings. Those shops with a large tourist clientele will often be open outside these times; certainly in the high season.

Package Tours

The following tour operators offer package deals for Venice. The list is by no means exhaustive and readers are recommended to check with their local travel agent:
British Airways, Leisure Traveller Short Breaks: Atlantic

House, Hazelwick Ave, Three Bridges, Crawley, West Sussex RH10 1NP. Tel. 0533 461000.

Citalia, CIT (England) Ltd, Marco Polo House, 3–5 Lansdowne Rd, Croydon CR9 1II. Tel. 081 686 5533.

Thomas Cook (Travelscene) Ltd, 11–15 St.Anne's Rd, Harrow, Middlesex HA1 1AS. Tel: 081 427 4445.

Cresta Holidays: Cresta House, Victoria St, Altrincham. Ches. WA14 1ET. Tel. 0345 056511 (London), 061 927 7000 (Manchester).

Italiatour (Alitalia), 241 Euston Rd, London NW1 2BT. Tel. 071 383 3886.

Thomson Citybreaks, Greater London House, Hampstead Rd, London NW1 7SD. Tel. 071 387 6534 (London), 021 432 6282 (Birmingham) 061 236 3828 (Manchester).

Photography

There are not many restrictions on where you can take photographs in Venice although you are requested not to use flash in churches or other interiors where the bright light might affect delicate frescoes or oil paintings. Individual churches sometimes impose limitations on photography and you should look out for any signs to that effect.

Be warned that film is very expensive in Italy. Since Venice is highly photogenic, remember to take plentiful supplies with you.

Post Offices

Post Offices are notoriously scarce in Italian cities.

Main Office — **Fondaco dei Tedeschi**, on Grand Canal, near the Rialto. Open for most services until 19.00 Monday to Saturday. Address for Poste Restante letters: Fermo Posta, Fondaco dei Tedeschi, 30100 VENEZIA.

There is at least one branch post office in each sestiere which is open until 13.30 Mondays to Fridays and until noon on Saturday. Offices that might be of use to the visitor are —

Calle dell'Ascensione, just behind St Mark's Square.

Via Garibaldi, at the eastern end of the Riva, just short of the Public Gardens.

Zattere, in Dorsoduro, just past the Zattere landing-stage.

A small post office is available at the railway station which is open in the afternoons, until 19.00 Mon.–Fri., until 18.00 Saturdays.

In Italy stamps are mostly sold by *rivenditori* — literally re-sellers — who act as agents for the post office. Virtually all hotels act as *rivenditori* and so do most shops selling picture postcards. Most commonly stamps are to be found at cafés and bars which have the 'T' for *Tabacchi* sign outside. These are cafés licensed to sell state monopoly goods such as tobacco, matches, salt and postage stamps.

Postal Rates

In recent years the postal tariff has risen at least once every year, so there is little point in giving outdated information. Check current rates before buying stamps. There are two points to bear in mind, however. Letters and postcards sent to countries in the European Community pay the same rate as internal letters or cards. As far as postcards are concerned there is a cheap rate for cards with a message of 5 words or less. Note that the five words should be what the Italians call *convenevole* — conventional greetings — such as 'Wish you were here' etc. The Post Office has been known to surcharge cards where the 5 words are used for an epistolary message.

Letters should be posted in the post-boxes normally painted red and marked either POSTE or LETTERE. If the post-box has two openings the one marked CITTA' is for local mail within Metropolitan Venice only.

Ricevuta fiscale

Italian tax law insists that restaurants issue an authorised receipt for all meals purchased, and also insists that the customer does not leave the restaurant without such a receipt. Try not to forget it and do not be alarmed if the waiter comes racing after you in the street to press the receipt into your hand; you could both be in trouble with the police if you do not have it.

At least that is the theoretical and legal position. Like many Italian laws it is more often disregarded than obeyed.

Study

A number of courses in art, architecture and the Italian language are organised in Venice for the benefit of foreign visitors. These are usually advertised in your home country and information can be obtained from E.N.I.T. You can however obtain a brochure from the Venice branch of the European Students' Union — *Ufficio Assistenza dell' ESU,* Ca' Foscari, Calle Giustiniàn 3246 Dorsoduro.

Specific departments arranging courses from time to time include:

Fine Arts and History of Art: *Accademia di Belle Arti*, Campo della Carità 1050 Dorsoduro

Language: *Università Ca' Foscari*, Calle Giustiniàn 3246 Dorsoduro

Architecture and Urban Studies: *Istituto di Architectura*, Campazzi di Tolentini 191, Santa Croce.

The *Società Italiana Dante Alighieri*, Italy's foremost cultural society, sometimes organises courses in Italian Language and Literature. Their base is adjacent to the Arsenal on the Fondamenta dell'Arsenale.

Telephoning

The code for Venice is 041 if telephoning from outside the province. If telephoning from abroad the code is whatever the international prefix is in that country (in the U.K. it is 010) followed by the code for Italy, which is 39, followed in turn by the provincial code minus the first 0 — i.e. 41. For example the telephone number of the Venice Tourist Office from Britain would be 010 39 41 5226 110.

The Italian telephone system has recently been totally re-organised in a sort of semi-privatisation, with responsibility devolved from the Ministry of P & T to an autonomous body known as SIP. A vastly increased number of public call boxes has sprung up all over the city, usually of the free-standing type under a clear plastic hood. They are identified by the letters SIP and four wavy lines in a bright brick-red colour. There is usually a disc above with the symbol of a hand-set in the same red on a white ground. Many bars and cafes also have pay-phones and are identified by the same red hand-set on a white disc over the bar door. Pay phones take 100, 200 or 500 lire coins but increasingly telephone boxes accept telephone cards (*schede telefoniche*) which can be bought at SIP offices, *tabachi* and some newspaper shops for L2,000, L5,000 or L10,000.

To telephone somewhere in the province of Venezia just dial the number; for elsewhere in Italy you must find the provincial code prefix. To dial somewhere outside Italy first dial the international prefix '00'. The dialling tone will then change and you should dial the country code (44 for the U.K., 1 for the U.S.A., 61 for Australia etc.) and then the area code minus the first 0, followed by the number. For long distance or international calls it is necessary to use telephone boxes marked **Interurbano**, although most are so marked these days. You will find the telephone boxes have very clear operating instructions in several languages including English.

To save you having to feed the coin slot at all-too-frequent intervals, the easiest way to make an international call is to use the services of the **SIP** offices. There are two main offices in Venice, on the Piazzale Roma and at the head post office in the Fondaco dei Tedeschi. At either of these two offices you book your call at the counter and are sent to a booth and your call is put through. The call is metered while you are speaking and when you have finished you pay at the counter for the time used. The booths at the main post office are air-conditioned; very important in the summer months. Many hotels offer the same service but at a hefty surcharge on SIP prices. The Italian for a reversed charge call is '*carico a destinario*'.

Time
Venice, like most of the Continent, observes Central European Time which is one hour ahead of Greenwich Mean Time. Between March and October clocks are put forward in Daylight Saving Time. In relation to the U.K. Venice is one hour ahead, except for about two weeks in the autumn when Italy puts its clocks back ahead of Britain.

Tipping
Service (*servizio*) is included in most hotel, restaurant or bar bills but, where it is not, an addition of 12–15% is customary. After a meal, or several drinks at a bar or café, even when service is included it is considered polite to leave the *piccole monete* when the waiter brings your change. In other words, you should pick up the notes but leave the coins. The usher who shows you to your seat in theatre, cinema or opera will also expect a small tip, as will a hairdresser, porter or water-taxi driver.

Toilets
Any traveller to European cities knows the problem of finding public toilets. Venice is not over-supplied with facilities but it is better endowed than many other cities.

By sestiere, the toilets available are:
S. Croce
Tronchetto; Stazione Marittima: Piazzale Roma (Municipal Garage); Calle Cassetti (on the far side of the Piazzale Roma, alongside the Rio Nuovo); Giardini Papadopoli; Lista dei Bari (men's urinal only).
Cannaregio
Railway Station (on platform 1) Free for men and disabled —

albergo diurno for ladies; Campo S. Leonardo; Campo SS. Apostoli (men's urinal only).

Dorsoduro
Set into the base of the Accademia Bridge.

S. Polo
Campo Rialto Novo (follow signs at end of Bridge); Campo S. Polo (men's urinal only).

Castello
Biennale Exhibition Site; Calle S. Domenico (men's urinal near entry to Public Gardens on Via Garibaldi); Castello 4052 (*albergo diurno* — difficult to find — up narrow alley alongside the Hotel Gabrielli Sandwirth)

S. Marco
Calle della Bissa (just off the Campo S. Bartolomeo); Giardini Reali (at far end, near S. Marco landing-stage); Calle Ascensione (the main *albergo diurno*, well signposted from St Mark's Square).

And within the following buildings:
Ca' Farsetti, Fenice Theatre, Ca' Giustinian, Doge's Palace.

These toilets are often hard to find because the signs leading to them are small green arrows that need some looking for, but practice makes perfect. Charges in public toilets are around L200 except for the S. Marco *albergo diurno* where the charge is L500. Many bars also have toilets which, by law, have to be accessible to the public. It is held to be a courtesy, even if not obligatory, to make a small purchase in a bar where you use the toilet.

Travel Agents

There are many travel agencies in Venice, most of which organise visits and excursions around the Lagoon and the Veneto, but the larger ones to deal with your travel problems are:

Acitour Veneto, Piazzale Roma 540b. Tel. 5208 828
Adriatic Shipping Co., S. Marco 2098. Tel. 5205 533
Alitalia, S. Marco 1463. Tel. 5216 222
American Express, S, Marco 1471. Tel. 5200 844
Bucintoro, S. Marco 2568. Tel. 5210 632
C.I.T.,Piazza S. Marco 48/50. Tel. 5210 241
ITALTravel, S. Marco — Ascensione 72b. Tel. 5229 111
Kele e Teo, Ponte di Bareteri (Mercerie), S. Marco 4930. Tel. 5208 722
Marco Polo, S. Zaccaria 4682b. Tel. 5203 200
Wagons Lits. S. Marco 289. Tel. 5223 405

Youth Pass

If you are between 16 and 27 it is possible to obtain a *carta giovani* which entitles you to discounts in certain hotels, restaurants, shops, cinemas and museums. You can be issued with one immediately at the S. Marco Information Office on production of a passport-sized photograph and proof of your age. The card comes complete with a list of the participating establishments.

A Linguistic Point

Remember that the Italian for postage stamp is *francobollo*. My father, who did not speak Italian, once attempted to buy postage stamps at the post office without knowing the word. Like many English people he thought he could make himself understood by tacking an 'o' or 'i' onto the end of an English word. 'Stampi, stampi' he kept saying to the postal clerk. It so happens that the Italian word '*stampe*' means 'printed papers' and is used for newspapers and magazines. 'No here,' repeated the postal official. Finally, the clerk left his counter and indicated a shop across the street which sold newspapers. As it happened, the shop was a *tabacchi* with an English-speaking assistant and my father got what he wanted. Ever afterwards he would inform people, with all the wisdom of a seasoned traveller, 'In Italy you don't buy stamps at the post office, you have to get them at the newspaper shop'.

The familiar Bridge of Sighs links the Doge's Palace to the Prisons.

NINE

Introduction

This section is designed to help you plan your sightseeing according to the time you have available. If you only have one or two days to spend in the city, the whole of your time can be given over to the obligatory sights around St Mark's Square as described in this chapter. If you have three or four days you should take at least one of the water-bus journeys described in Chapter Ten, since Venice is best seen from the water.

One hint that may help those for whom time is limited is that you need spend relatively little time on the interiors of buildings. Venice was built by an ostentatious people with an eye for outward show. The architecture is superb, the decoration exquisite and many vistas such as the Grand Canal and St Mark's Basin are incredibly beautiful. But they are meant to impress from the outside. With a few notable exceptions most Venetian interiors are disappointing. Many churches have one or two treasures within them but none that need detain the visitor for more than a few minutes. The greatest satisfaction lies not in seeing how many churches, galleries and museums you can pack into one day but in just walking around and looking at this marvellous city, which was designed to display the wealth and importance of the Venetian Republic. It is worth setting one day aside for simply wandering as the fancy takes you, seeking out Venice's hidden corners, the unexpected view or the charming wall-decoration. Areas that repay the casual stroller are the environs of San Polo and the Frari, west of the Grand Canal; the area between the Accademia and the Campo Santa Margherita and along the Zattere in Dorsoduro; or between S. Zaccaria and SS Giovanni e Paolo in Castello, as described in Chapter Eleven.

Sestiere of San Marco

The Centre

The best place to start is at the **Molo**, the water frontage on the Basin of St Mark's where distinguished visitors to Venice were received in the days of the Venetian Republic. The creaion of the Molo as landing stage, with the laying out of the Piazzetta and Piazza, was conceived as long ago as 1177 for the momentous visit of Pope and Emperor, and remained the ceremonial entry to the city for the next six centuries.

You can judge the impact it must have had on the visitor by standing on the Molo with your back to the Lagoon. Looking down the length of the **Piazzetta** you can see all the most important and impressive public buildings of the Venetian Republic at one glance. The **Palazzo Ducale** is on your right and the **Libreria Sansoviniana**, housing the **Biblioteca Marciana** (the Library of St Mark's) on the left. At the other end of the Piazzetta your view of the **Piazza San Marco** is restricted by the projections of the **Loggetta** and **Campanile** on the left and the

Some of the pigeons from St. Mark's Square take a rest at the base of the Morea flagpole.

Basilica di San Marco on the right. Closing your view from this standpoint, seen across the width of the Piazza, is the famous clock tower, the **Torre dell'Orologio**.

On the Molo, acting like ornate gateposts to the city, stand two massive pillars brought back from the East at the end of the 12th century. There should be three but the third fell off the barge carrying it and has lain in the mud of St Mark's Basin ever since. On the eastern column stands the Lion of St Mark, while the western bears a representation of Venice's original patron, St Theodore, accompanied by a dragon which looks suspiciously like a crocodile. Both statues are hybrid creations. Originally from Persia, or perhaps China, the lion is possibly a chimera to which wings, a halo and the open book have been added at various times; the whole thing being reassembled in the 19th century after damage caused by Napoleon's soldiers, who took it back to Paris as a trophy. St Theodore has a torso taken from a 1st-century Roman statue, while the head is that of a Mithridates from the 1st century BC. Until the 18th century the bodies of executed criminals were exhibited in the space between the two columns: even today superstitious Venetians avoid walking between them.

Before leaving the Molo it is worth looking left and right at two of Venice's more famous views. To the east the quay in front of the Doge's Palace ends at the Rio di Palazzo canal, crossed by the pretty **Ponte della Paglia**, on the summit of which all visitors pause in order to look down the Rio di Palazzo to the **Bridge of Sighs** which links the Doge's Palace with the Prisons. In the opposite direction the quay extends westwards in front of the building at the end of the Sansovino Library. This is the **Zecca** (Mint), which used to produce the famous Venetian gold coins, the *zecchini*. Unlike most Venetian buildings, which are timber or brick, faced with stone, the Zecca is solidly built of stone on an iron frame, for protection against fire from the smelting furnaces it once contained. Beyond the Zecca lie the **Giardinetti Reali** (Royal Gardens), laid out on the site of the Republic's state granaries, another product of Napoleon's restructuring of the San Marco area. The gardens are a pleasant haven but can become unpleasantly crowded in summer.

Advancing into the Piazzetta, turn and look back towards the Molo for one of the most famous views in Venice: the island church of **San Giorgio Maggiore** framed between the columns.

It is a view best seen in the early morning when the sun rising behind San Giorgio and the slight mist over the lagoon lend an insubstantial air to the facade and campanile of the church, which appears to float lightly on the waters. The waters of St Mark's Basin sparkle in the sunlight and throw into sharp relief the gondola stands that line the quayside of the Molo.

The Piazza and other Squares

Although the Italian for 'square' is Piazza, there is only one square bearing this name in Venice and that is the Piazza di San Marco, referred to by Venetians simply as the Piazza, without need of qualification. Apart from the Piazza there is the Piazzetta, or 'little square' which runs between the Doge's Palace and the Sansovino Library to the water's edge. The open space between the north end of St.Mark's and the Clock Tower was known as the Piazzetta Leoncini but now as the Piazzetta Giovanni XXIII. To the Piazza and two piazzettas we can add the Piazzale Roma. Other than these all squares in Venice go by the name of Campo, or Campiello in the case of a small square. The word *campo* which means 'field' is a memory of the time when this is what the squares were: fields where the Venetians grew their crops and grazed their animals.

The Piazzetta

The Piazzetta is flanked by the greatest secular Gothic building in the world on one side, and one of the greatest of Renaissance structures on the other, and is paved in grey, volcanic stone with a patterned inlay of white Istrian stone. In the days of the Republic the Piazzetta was used as an ante-room to government, where patrician members of the Grand Council met each morning to negotiate and fix deals. An alternative name for the Piazzetta was **il Broglio**, from the Italian word for 'intrigue'. Between ten and noon each day ordinary citizens were barred from the Piazzetta, giving patricians the freedom to pursue their own concerns in secret. The Piazzetta is dominated by the facade of the Doge's Palace which has a double frontage, on the Piazzetta and on the Lagoon. In fact the wing facing the Lagoon is the older section, begun in 1340 to provide a room large enough to accommodate all 1212 members of the Great Council. The work was finished in 1419 but was felt to be so satisfactory that in 1422 the old buildings facing onto the Piazzetta were demolished and the facade extended almost as far as the Basilica. If you look carefully at the columns of the ground floor colonnade facing the Piazzetta you will notice that the seventh column from the corner is thicker than the rest. This is where the wing facing the water-front originally ended and is the only remaining indication that the building was carried out in two stages.

The Piazzetta facade was completed in 1424 and attained its present appearance in 1438 with the addition of the **Porta della Carta**. Around the building at ground level runs a colonnaded portico, each arcade of which supports two arches of the loggia above. The facade is a little less graceful than was originally intended because the pavement has been raised by two steps over the years, hiding the base of the columns and making the arches of the portico noticeably less tall than the arches of the loggia. The three corners of the facade have shorter, thicker columns, surmounted by Old Testament statuary groups at portico level and carvings of archangels at loggia level. These groups are, starting by the Ponte della Paglia, *The Drunkenness of Noah/Archangel Raphael*; at the Piazzetta corner, *Adam and Eve/Archangel Michael* and, at the corner nearest the Basilica, *Judgment of Solomon/Archangel Gabriel*. The last group is attributed to the Sienese sculptor, Della Quercia. Above the loggia the building is faced in an intricate pattern of white Istrian stone and pink Verona marble and around the roof are ornamental crenellations of white marble, lending the building an Arabic or Moorish appearance. In the centre of the facade facing the water-front is a large balconied window built in florid Gothic style by Pier Paolo Dalle Masegne in 1404; the corresponding window facing the Piazzetta is an imitation constructed in 1536. Most of the columns were restored or renewed in the 1880s.

Such is the dominance of the Doge's Palace that the building opposite is often overlooked, which is a pity since the **Libreria Sansoviniana** is held to be the finest example of High Renaissance architecture in Venice and was said by Palladio to be, 'the richest and most ornate building to be created since the days of Ancient Greece and Rome'. The intention to build a National Venetian Library dates from the 14th century when the Republic either failed to obtain, or obtained and mislaid, the library of the poet Petrarch. The real starting-point, however, was the bequest to St Mark's of the Cardinal

Bessarion Collection of Greek and Latin manuscripts in 1468. For a time the collection of documents was housed in St Mark's, and then later in the Doge's Palace, but the importance of the collection was realised in the early 16th century and it was decided that a special library would have to be built. The task was given to Sansovino, who did more than any other single individual to change the face of the Piazza and Piazzetta.

The Library, construction of which began in 1537, was built of Istrian stone along classical Roman lines, with a Doric ground floor and an Ionic upper storey or *piano nobile*. A balustrade runs around the roof and is crowned by a series of statues. Initially Sansovino failed to realise that vaults were not a good idea in a city with unstable foundations. In 1545, while it was being built, the main hall's vaulted ceiling collapsed and the architect was imprisoned for incompetence. Released thanks to the intervention of Titian, Sansovino substituted a flat ceiling with a false wooden vault attached. After the death of Sansovino, in 1570, responsibility for the Library's construction passed to Scamozzi and the building was finished in 1591.

The library buildings house three collections. The **Biblioteca Nazionale Marciana** is situated at the lagoon end of the Piazzetta. It is entered through the door to number 7, formerly the entrance to the Zecca. One of the major libraries of Italy, the Biblioteca contains a million books, 13,000 manuscripts and 3,000 *incunabula* (books printed before 1500). Of special interest to Venice is a nearly complete collection of 1,000 works produced by the Aldine Press in the last decade of the 15th century. (*The library is open to genuine students wishing to consult the books or manuscripts and opens for this purpose between 9.00 and 19.00 Mondays to Fridays and from 9.00 to 13.00 on Saturdays. Permission should be sought from the Library Director on 5208 788.*) The historical **Original Library** is reached through the main entrance at number 13A and, again, access is by permission of the Library Director. The interior includes a monumental staircase, decorated by Vittoria, and a Grand Hall with paintings by Titian, Tintoretto and Veronese among others. Books in the library's possession include the Flemish *Grimani Breviary* of 1500, the 'Map of the World' by Fra Mauro of 1450 and a late 14th-century illuminated copy of Dante's *Inferno*. The oldest book in the library's possession is half an 8th-century Byzantine bible (the other half is in the Vatican Library). Other treasures include

Marco Polo's Will and a Petrarch manuscript. Finally there is the **Archaeological Museum**, entered either through number 17 on the Piazzetta or number 52 on the Piazza. Based on a collection bequeathed to the state by Cardinal Domenico Grimani in 1523, the museum contains a very fine selection of Greek and Roman sculptures, the most famous of which are a *Persephone* from the 5th century BC and a Roman head of *Vitellius* from the 2nd century AD. The museum has been closed for complete restoration but was expected to re-open on December 1, 1991. An entry fee will be charged. In any other city the museum would rank high on any list of things to see but, in Venice, there is so much else to visit that a museum like this, which is not specifically Venetian, must come low in the order of priorities. Unless you are here for more than a week, save it for a rainy day.

The Junction of Piazza and Piazzetta
Since the Library buildings are shorter than the Doge's Palace facade there is a sense in which the far northern end of the Piazzetta is also the south-eastern corner of the Piazza. Into this small area are concentrated — the main entrance to the Doge's Palace, the **Porta della Carta**; the southern facade of the Basilica, including the **Baptistery Doors**; and several interesting features such as the **Pietra del Bando**, the **Three Tetrarchs** and the **Acritan Pillars**. On the other side of the Piazzetta is the **Loggetta di Sansovino** at the base of the **Campanile**.

The **Porta della Carta** (Paper Gate) is set back between the facade of the Doge's Palace and the wall of the Basilica Treasury. It was erected between 1438 and 1443 to a design by Giovanni and Bartolomeo Bon in the same florid Gothic style as the facade. The origin of its name is uncertain since according to some it commemorates the State Archives being kept nearby, some think it recalls the clerks' working benches set up in its shelter, while others believe it is because copies of State decrees would be posted on the sides of the gateway. Above the door is a relief of Doge Francesco Foscari, who commissioned the gateway, kneeling in front of the Lion of St Mark. This is not the original work since, shortly after the Napoleonic conquest, a collaborating stone-mason, wishing to ingratiate himself with the French took a sledge-hammer to Foscari and his Lion. The present sculpture is an excellent reproduction installed in 1885. The head of the Doge from the original statue was preserved and is displayed inside the Doge's Palace. Above the carving is a Gothic window and above that a pinnacle crowned by the figure of *Venice as Justice*, attributed to Bartolomeo Bon, as are the flanking statues of *Temperance, Fortitude, Prudence* and *Charity*. The whole gateway was restored between 1976 and 1979 by the British Venice in Peril Fund.

The solid, marble-faced wall to the left of the entry to the Porta della Carta is the exterior of St Mark's Treasury, believed by some to be part of the original Doge's Palace. On the front corner a sculptured porphyry group is set into the angle of the wall near its base. It is known as **The Three Tetrarchs**, although there are four figures. This 4th-century work, probably Egyptian, supposedly represents the Emperor Diocletian and three of his co-governors. Popular legend, however, turns them into four Moors who raided the Treasury and then killed each other in a quarrel over dividing the spoils.

The southern facade of the Basilica is worth more attention than is usually given to it. The large arch to the left, blocked off now, was once the principal entrance to the Basilica for those arriving from the Molo. Next to it, and adjacent to the Treasury, is the **Baptistery** with fine 14th-century bronze doors. Above on the facade is a 13th-century Byzantine mosaic of the Madonna at prayer. Flanking the Baptistery doorway are two free-standing pillars known as the **Acritan Pillars**, alleged to have been brought from Acre in 1256 to celebrate a victory over the Genoese. The carving on the pillars is 5th- or 6th-century Syrian work. In front of the far corner of the Basilica, where it turns into the Piazzetta, stands another looted item from Acre. This is a truncated porphyry column known as the **Pietra del Bando** which served as a tribunal from which new decrees of the Republic were proclaimed to the people. In 1902 it acted as a buffer when the Campanile collapsed, preventing the Basilica itself from suffering any damage from the rubble.

Opposite this south-western corner of the Basilica rises the **Campanile** with the **Loggetta di Sansovino** at its base. The Campanile rises nearly 100 metres and was originally constructed at the start of the 10th century. In the beginning it was part of the city's defences and shared the duties of watch-tower and lighthouse, as well as housing the bells of St Mark's. An impression of the Campanile under construction can be gained from a 13th-century mosaic in the narthex of the Basilica where

The porphyry sculpture known as 'The Tetrarchs', a 4th century work from Egypt, thought to represent Diocletian and three other emperors at the corner of the Treasury of the Basilica of St Mark's.

it is shown representing the building of the Tower of Babel. The tower as we see it today was completed as far as the bell-chamber by 1173. The finishing touch of the upper storey, with the Lion of St Mark on two sides and an angel on the other two, was constructed in the early 16th century under the supervision of Bartolomeo Bon the Younger, who also added the pyramid-shaped spire on top. The work was completed in 1515 when a golden angel was hoisted to the tip of the spire 'to the sound of trumpets and pipes'.

The Collapse of the Campanile

The Campanile was the pride and symbol of Venice, something that was always there, visible from all parts of the city. The strongest way in which a Venetian could swear that something was unthinkable was to say, '*Gnanca se cascasse el campaniel*' (Not even if the Campanile falls down).

Yet, at 9.45 in the morning of Monday July 14, 1902, the unthinkable happened. 'Gently, almost noiselessly, as if in a curtsey . . .', the great tower crumbled and fell. It was as though the Campanile had never been, except for the rubble which spread out virtually to fill the Piazza. By a miracle no one was hurt except for one unfortunate cat. By an even greater miracle the Basilica over which the Campanile loomed was untouched. But the tower was gone, the Loggetta of Sansovino was destroyed and all but one of the Campanile's five bells were damaged beyond repair. The greatest damage of all was to Venetian pride. Near riots followed as angry crowds sought out those they held responsible for the disaster.

That same evening of July 14 the Council of the Municipality of Venice voted that the Campanile would be rebuilt in exactly the same place and exactly as it had been, giving the motto to those charged with the task, ' . . . *come era, dove era* . . .' The foundation stone of the new Campanile was laid on St Mark's Day, April 25 1903. The brick shaft of the new tower began to rise over the Piazza, Sansovino's Loggetta was reconstructed from the rubble and, by St Mark's Day 1912, the boast had been made good and the Campanile once more stood where it had always stood, looking as it had always looked.

In 1902, when the Campanile collapsed, happily without injury to humans, there was surprisingly little damage to other buildings, except for the end wall of the Library. Totally crushed, however, was the **Loggetta** at the base of the tower, eventually reconstructed from the rubble like a giant jig-saw puzzle. This interesting little building was originally built by Sansovino between 1537 and 1549. It had been intended to build a full loggia around all sides of the Campanile to act as a gentlemen's club or meeting-place for patricians during their morning discussions. That plan was abandoned after only one quarter had been built and we are left with the side facing the Porta della Carta. Its main function in the Republican period was to act as a guard-room for the *Arsenalotti* — trained bands of workers from the Arsenal who guarded the Great Council when it was sitting. The Loggetta is built of red Verona marble, with Carrara marble and Istrian stone for the decorative details. The design is meant to look like a Roman Triumphal Arch with three arches separated by twin columns, and bronze statues by Sansovino between the columns representing *Pallas, Apollo, Mercury* and *Peace*. The reliefs on the attic storey are allegories of Venice and her Empire — *Justice (Venice), Jupiter (Crete)* and *Venus (Cyprus)*. The Loggetta today acts as the entrance for those wishing to ascend the Campanile. (*The Campanile is open to the public every day, including Sundays and holidays, from 10.00 until a time which varies, according to the season, from 15.30 to 19.30. Entrance L3000.*) Having obtained your tickets in the Loggetta, you move on into the base of the bell-tower and take the high-speed lift to the open-sided bell chamber.

The view from the top is breath-taking. The whole of the city can be seen, with its maze of red-tiled roofs, broken by the white or brick-coloured fingers of *campanili* and the massive brick walls of the mendicant churches of SS. Giovanni e Paolo and the Frari. Amazingly enough, not a single canal can be seen, even though there are more than a hundred down there, buried between the buildings. Beyond the city the whole Lagoon is visible, bounded by the Lido on one side and the mainland on the other, with all the islands dotting the spaces between. In the days of the Republic no foreigner would have been allowed up here because, at low tide, all the secret deep-water channels through the Lagoon are revealed. On a clear day it is possible to see as far as the mountains and on a crisp, frosty winter's day the snow-covered Dolomites can seem remarkably close. There is only limited space in the bell-chamber and on a summer's day you will probably have to queue to gain admission and have your time at the top limited. At such times it is worth considering the Campanile of San Giorgio Maggiore as an alternative.

The Bells of the Campanile

The bell-tower of the Campanile contained five bells, each of which had a name and a purpose. The largest, the **Marangona**, was the bell which concerned everyone in the city since it signalled the beginning and end of the working day. The **Nona** or 'noon-time' bell, as the name suggests, rang the hour of midday. The **Mezza Terza** proclaimed a meeting of the Senate while the **Trottiere** was rung continuously to hurry up members of the Grand Council who might be late for a session. The fifth, the **Renghiera** or **Maleficio**, was the most sinister as it was rung to announce an execution. Of the five bells, only the Marangona survived the Campanile's fall of 1902. The other four were re-cast and presented to the rebuilt Campanile by Pope Pius X.

The Palazzo Ducale — Doge's Palace

Pass through the Porta della Carta to the ticket office in the **Cortile** (courtyard). (*The Palace is open from 8.30 to 14.00 in winter, until 17.00 in summer [the ticket office closes an hour beforehand]. Entrance L8000. The* itinerari segreti *(see page 000) costs L5000 and must be booked 24 hours in advance. Tickets from the administration office on the first floor.*) In the summer months you are recommended to get here as early as possible, since the rooms are already crowded by ten o'clock with tourist groups and their guides. The Doge's Palace is subject to a continuous programme of restoration and some of the rooms mentioned are bound to be closed to visitors. In 1991 the whole of the eastern front of the Cortile was shrouded behind timber screens.

You enter the Cortile through the **Arco Foscari**, so-called because it was commissioned by the same Doge Foscari as built the Porta della Carta, but only completed after his death. Most of the work was done by Antonio Rizzo who also designed the ceremonial staircase opposite, at the head of which the Doge was crowned. The staircase is known as the **Scala dei Giganti** (Giants' Staircase) because of the monumental statues of Neptune and Mars at the top of the stairway; the statues were sculpted by Sansovino in the 1560s. Rizzo also originally designed the arcaded east side of the Cortile. The arcades were extended to the south and west sides in the 17th century by Bartolomeo Monopola who also designed the baroque facade on the side backing on to the Basilica.

The entrance at the moment is in the north-eastern corner behind the Scala dei Giganti but it can be moved without warning. Notices will guide you to the main staircase, the **Scala d'Oro**, so-called because of the gold on white stucco decorations by Vittoria that coat the columns and vaulted roof of the stairway. This takes you to the second floor, or **Primo Piano Nobile** where the Doge's private apartments are located. The rooms in this eastern wing of the second floor have been stripped of their furnishings and decorations and are now mainly used for art exhibitions. At other times the rooms are closed to the public. Continue up one more flight of the Scala d'Oro to the **Secondo Piano Nobile** where the main government offices were located.

These official rooms were totally rebuilt and redecorated after a disastrous fire in 1574. After the small ante-chamber, the **Atrio Quadrato**, at the head of the stairs, you pass into the **Sala delle Quattro Porte** which was where ambassadors and others waited to be received by the Doge and his ministers. The ceiling frescoes are by Tintoretto but were damaged in restoration. The next room is the **Anticollegio**, or inner waiting room, one of the most richly decorated rooms in the Palace with four Tintorettos and Veronese's *The Rape of Europa*. After a second period of waiting the ambassador would be shown into the **Sala del Collegio** where the actual government of Venice met. The room is therefore decorated with all the splendour its importance warranted. The last in this series of rooms (there are private chapels beyond but they are closed to the public) is the **Sala del Senato**, another heavily gilded chamber where the sixty Senators met. It is decorated by a number of late 16th-century artists of whom Tintoretto is the most prominent. After the Senate Room the visitor recrosses the Sala delle Quattro Porte to gain the other half of this third floor.

The first room you come to here is the **Sala del Consiglio dei Dieci**. The Council of Ten was the much-dreaded state security body that achieved such a terrible reputation in the 18th century and this room, with paintings by the ubiquitous

Veronese, was where the Council questioned the accused. The accused waited for their inquisition in the next room, the **Sala della Bussola**, where it is possible to see a *Bocca di Leone,* the post-box shaped like a lion's head with an open mouth into which Venetians could slip a denunciation addressed to the Council of Ten. A door in the corner of the room is the first step in the route that leads to the torture chamber and prison. These rooms are now available to the public on the *itinerari segreti* (see below).

The remaining four rooms on this floor are given over to the **Armoury**. Take the **Scala dei Censori** down to the second floor and reach the **Sala del Maggior Consiglio**, the Great Council Chamber which occupies the entire frontage of the Palace. First built in 1340 to house the entire Grand Council, it was rebuilt to the same plan after a fire of 1577 and continued to contain a Grand Council that ultimately came to number 2,500. It is an immense room, 53 metres long, 25 metres wide and nearly 12 metres high.Unfortunately the paintings which decorated the original room, by Titian, Bellini and Carpaccio, were destroyed in the fire. Most of the paintings done to replace them are Mannerist works that serve little purpose except to cover some of the vast amount of wall space. Notable exceptions are some ceiling panels, especially those by Veronese and Palma the Younger. On one wall is the immense *Paradiso* by Tintoretto and his son Domenico. At 22×7 metres this is the largest oil painting in the world. Paintings on the wall, by a variety of painters, refer to incidents in the history of Venice — the Reconciliation of Pope and Emperor, the Fourth Crusade and the defeat of the Genoese at Chioggia. Around the walls runs a frieze of the first 76 Doges, commissioned from Tintoretto but carried out after his death by Domenico Tintoretto. Look for the space on the Piazzetta wall where a doge's face has been blacked out. This was Marin Falier who was executed in 1355 on suspicion of trying to make the dogeship hereditary in his family.

From the far end of the Council Chamber a door opens into a small room meant for the *Quarantia Civil Nuova* which was the civil court for Venetians living outside the city, in Crete or the other colonies for example. It is notable only for being decorated by the gilt leatherwork that was once a Venetian speciality. Beyond this small room you pass into the **Sala dello Scrutinio** which occupies the rest of the floor space on this

Piazzetta side of the Palace. This was the room in which all votes of the Council were counted and checked, as the name suggests. The Venetian Constitution was immensely complicated and the election of a doge could require more than a hundred separate ballots, took at least five days and was known to go on for weeks. Perhaps so as to bore rather than detain the voters, the paintings and decorations are singularly uninspired in this room. Most interesting is the line of portrait medallions of doges, continued from where the younger Tintoretto left off in the Council Chamber, each doge was painted by a contemporary down to the last, Doge Lodovico Manin.

From a door in the Council Chamber you can regain the Scala dei Censori and descend to see the **Ponte dei Sospiri** (the Bridge of Sighs). The bridge, linking the rooms of the Council of Ten with the Prisons, is supposed to have got its name from the sighs of prisoners being taken to a terrible fate. In fact the prisons only held minor criminals so it is unlikely that any felt the need to sigh. The important and condemned prisoners were kept in cells under the roof of the Doge's Palace.

The way out is by way of the **Avogaria** which was a sort of legal chancery where documents were prepared for the law courts. Before leaving it is worth going up to the first floor loggia with excellent views from the Porta della Carta right round to the Molo. The stairs up to the loggia are on the Piazzetta side of the Cortile.

The Itinerari Segreti

About 6 or 7 years ago it was decided to open the hidden rooms of the Doge's Palace to the public. These were rooms used by bureaucrats in the service of the State, discreetly hidden, like servants in a stately home. There are two visits each morning which have to be accompanied and must be booked at least 24 hours in advance. As yet the commentary by the guide is in Italian only. During the tour the area of most interest is that belonging to the Council of Ten. You can see the famous **Torture Chamber** and be duly disappointed that the worst torture ever applied was merely suspending a prisoner by their tied wrists. The tour ends under the roof, or leads **(Piombi)** where the real cells were located. According to Casanova who was imprisoned here (and claims to have escaped) the cells immediately beneath the lead-covered roof were unbearably hot in summer. Two benefits from this trip to the roof space are the view through those small circular windows that can be seen in the facade, and an insight as to how the huge ceiling of the Council Chamber is suspended.

Where the Piazzetta meets the Piazza.

The Piazza

The first impression one has of the **Piazza San Marco** — St Mark's Square — is of how large it is. Even at the height of a summer's day, when the square is full of visitors and the café tables from Florian's, Quadri's and Lavena encroach on the central space, the square seems vast. See it on a winter's day, or late in the evening, when it is all but deserted, and it appears immense. Yet it is no more than 175 × 80 metres. There are squares elsewhere that are as large, or larger, but there are two factors that combine to emphasise this sense of space. Apart from the three flag-poles in front of the basilica there are no monuments on the Piazza: no columns, obelisks, statues or fountains. And, of course, there is no traffic.

In the 9th century the first Doge's Palace (or Castle as it was then) was erected and it was decided to build a chapel to house the relics of St Mark alongside it. The area now occupied by the Piazza was a meadow and orchard, with a canal running across it and with a huddle of buildings around the growing Basilica. The Piazza as we now see it dates from the dogeship of Sebastiano Ziani between 1173 and 1178. He demolished the church of S. Geminiano that lay just in front of the Basilica, filled in the canal and bought the orchard from the nuns of S. Zaccaria. The space he had created was then paved in herring-bone brick and all the buildings round the square joined together by arches and collonades. The watch-tower near the Basilica was incorporated into the square as the bell-tower to St Mark's. What the Piazza must have looked like after this can probably be seen in Gentile Bellini's *Procession of the Cross on the Piazza S. Marco* in the Accademia. The picture was painted in 1496, just at the start of the hectic building programme that, within a century, gave the Piazza the look we know today.

The Piazza is closed on three sides by continuous ranges of buildings. From the corner by the Campanile the southern side of the square is bounded by the **Procuratie Nuove**, the western end is closed by the despised **Ala Napoleonica** and the northern side is made up of the **Procuratie Vecchie**, set at a tangent from the central axis so that the square is much wider at its eastern end than at the west, forming a trapezoid in shape. At the end of the Procuratie Vecchie, facing down the Piazzetta, is the clock-tower, the **Torre dell'Orologio**. The range of buildings continues beyond the northern facade of the Basilica to form the **Piazzetta dei Leoncini** (or **Piazzetta Giovanni XXIII**). The fourth and eastern side of the Piazza is wholly occupied by the western and main facade of the **Basilica di San Marco**.

The herring-bone brick surface was replaced in the early 18th century by paving stones of grey, volcanic rock, inlaid with a pattern of white Istrian stone that represents the route taken by ceremonial processions through the Piazza. If you look again at the Bellini picture you can see the ordered pattern by which the participants processed through the Piazza, marked by the white bands running the length of the square. The behaviour is mirrored today by the citizens of Venice during their evening *passeggiata*. Watch the groups move slowly down one side of the Piazza and back up the other. The dialect term for this pattern on the floor of the Piazza, whether drawn in stone or moving people, is the *Liston*, which roughly means 'patterned edging' or 'border'.

Nothing stands on the surface of the Piazza, not even the beautiful street-lamps which are such a feature of the Piazzetta. The only exceptions are the three massive flag-masts arranged across the face of the Basilica. These were placed here in 1505 and have elaborate carved bases, cast in bronze by Alessandro de' Leopardi. The three bases represent the major Venetian colonies of Cyprus, Candia (Crete) and Morea (Southern Greece). Each mast is surmounted by a gilded Lion of St Mark and on special days the central mast flies a huge Italian tricolour while the two flanking masts bear the equally huge, fork-tailed, crimson and gold banners of the Venetian Republic.

Contemporary with the raising of the flag-masts on the Piazza was the construction of the **Torre dell'Orologio**, built to face down the Piazzetta and to surmount the entrance to the Mercerie. The Tower itself was designed by Mauro Coducci and was built between 1496 and 1499; the clock mechanism was by Paolo and Carlo Rainieri and the two side wings were added by Pietro Lombardo in 1506. Above the archway (*sottoportego*) that leads to the Mercerie is the huge clock face, brightly decorated with gilt and enamel, impossibly complex and showing phases of the sun, moon and zodiac. If you want to know the time you have to look up to the third level and the gilt doors on either side of a statue of the Virgin and Child. The doors contain blue panels with white Roman numerals to the left representing the hour and Arabic numerals to the right to show the minutes. The minute display changes every five minutes, so do not look for precision in time-keeping, but this must represent the first digital clock in existence! The Madonna has a semi-circular balcony in front of her and, at Epiphany and during Ascension Week, the doors on either side open every time the clock strikes and the Three Magi preceded by a Herald come out of one door, circle round the balcony, bowing to the Virgin and Child as they do so, and return though the other door. At the fourth level, above the Madonna, is a bas-relief of

the Lion of St Mark set against a blue enamel ground studded with gold stars. On the flat roof of the Tower are two bronze figures with hammers who strike the bell on the hour. Properly speaking the figures are of skin-clad 'wild men' but the dark patina of the bronze has led the Venetians to refer to them as Moors and '*I Mori*' they remain. They were cast at the Arsenal in 1497, to the design of Ambrogio dalle Anchore.

It was possible to ascend to the roof of the Clock Tower where there is a viewing terrace with a coin-operated telescope alongside the Moors. Entrance is under the Sottoportego at the start of the Merceria dell'Orologio, number 147, but there is no lift. However, the Tower was closed for restoration in 1989 and had still not re-opened in 1991.

The Old Woman who put down a Rebellion

As you leave St Mark's Square beneath the Clock Tower look up to the first floor level of the house on your left as you leave the archway and enter the Merceria dell'Orologio. On the wall you will see a relief plaque showing an old woman holding a heavy object in her arms. This commemorates a remarkable event of 1310 when the Querini family, in alliance with an adventurer called Bajamonte Tiepolo, was in revolt against the Doge. On the night of June 15th the rebels set out from their base in S. Polo to attack the Doge's Palace. Marco and Benedetto Querini, father and son, arrived on the Piazza first but immediately fell victim to an ambush mounted by the Doge's party and were killed. Tiepolo, following along the Mercerie had paused by S. Zulian but became worried when he did not hear the shouts of victory he was expecting. Cautiously he advanced to the very edge of the Piazza and there he halted. An old lady, Giustina Rossi, opened her upstairs window and threw out the stone mortar she used to grind her corn. She missed Tiepolo himself but hit his standard-bearer and killed him outright. Seeing the man dead and their flag lying in the mud, the rebels lost heart and ran for their lives. In honour of her part in putting down the rebellion Signora Rossi won the right to fly the banner of the Republic, had her rent pegged at its then level by the Procurators of St Mark's and, of course, had the above-mentioned plaque raised to her memory in 1841.

Overleaf The Colleoni Statue in front of the Scuola San Marco, instead of on the Piazza San Marco as the condottiere wished.
Opposite The Piazzetta.

On the wall of the Sottoportego dell'Orologio a plaque commemorates the events of June 25, 1310, when an old lady, Giustina Rossi, quelled a rebellion by dropping a stone mortar onto the head of the rebel standard bearer.

Even while his Clock Tower was being built Coducci began the task of building the **Procuratie Vecchie**. These were the offices and living quarters of the Procurators of St Mark, in effect the state's Ministry of Works. Elected for life, the six to nine procurators were the most senior officers after the Doge and had an army of bureaucrats to do the actual work for them. They had been based in a variety of buildings along the north side of the Piazza ever since Doge Ziani had laid out the square in the 12th century but Coducci now had the task of building a set of premises that unified all the old offices under one roof. The building he designed is one of the finest examples of early Renaissance work in Venice and consists of three open galleries one above the other, with 50 arches in the ground level arcade and 100 arches on the two upper floors. Work on the building was halted by a fire in 1512 and, Coducci having died in 1504, supervision of the work passed first to Bartolomeo Bon the Younger and later to Sansovino. The building was completed in 1532, three years after Sansovino had become chief architect.

Apart from the Sottoportego dell'Orologio there are three exits from the square on this northern side. The first, midway along, crosses the Rio di Procuratie to become the Calle dei Fabbri. The second crosses the end of the Bacino Orseolo to pass in front of the Hotel Cavaletto to reach the *campo* and church of S. Gallo. The third and furthest arch leads out onto the Fondamento Orseolo and is worth a brief detour if only to see the tightly-packed ranks of gondolas bobbing gently on the waters. The Bacino Orseolo is used as a gondola park during off-duty hours.

Within a few years of moving into the Procuratie Vecchie the Procurators found the accommodation inadequate and San-sovino began planning a new range of buildings, the **Procuratie Nuove**. To accommodate this several old buildings near the campanile were demolished (including a hospice built by Pietro Orseolo, the only Doge to be canonised and the man who presented the *Pala d'Oro* to St Mark's in 976). Sansovino's idea was to continue the plan and elevation of his library round the corner from the Piazzetta into the Piazza. In fact work did not begin until after Sansovino's death, and the plans were therefore those of Scamozzi. His design, however, only extends as far as the 10th arch from the corner by the campanile. The building was completed by Longhena in 1640.

The Procuratie Nuove are not unlike the Procuratie Vecchie with three galleries above each other but the style is that of the High Renaissance with loftier galleries and a more spacious appearance. This range of buildings contains the **Caffè Florian**, the oldest coffee-house in Venice, founded by Floriano Francesconi in 1720 and decorated in 18th-century style in 1858. The café tables fan out into the Piazza as does the orchestra which, during the summer months, conducts musical duels with the rival Caffè Quadri across the square. The upper floors of the Procuratie Nuove were used as a Royal Palace from the fall of the Republic to 1920 when they were presented to the municipality by King Victor Emmanuel III. Since 1923 they have housed the civic museum.

The western end of the Piazza is closed by the **Procuratie**

Nuovissime, otherwise known as the **Ala Napoleonica** (or Napoleonic Wing). Originally the two procuratie buildings turned the corner with angles along the western side, with the gap between the two filled by the new Church of San Geminiano, built in Renaissance style by Sansovino to replace finally the church demolished by Doge Ziani. However, when Napoleon took the city in 1797 and turned the Procuratie Nuove into a royal palace he found that the new palace lacked a ballroom. So S. Geminiano was demolished once again and a wing built linking the Procuratie Nuove with the Procuratie Vecchie; a wing which contained the desired ballroom, although Napoleon never visited Venice in order to use it. On its two lower floors the Ala Napoleonica is a precise copy of the Procuratie Nuove, with fifteen divisions. But it succeeds in looking far less graceful because, instead of the third galleried storey, it has a heavy attic storey on which are the statues of 14 Roman Emperors, seven on either side. Note the wide gap in the middle where a statue of Napoleon himself should have gone.

There are two exits from the Piazza at this western end. One, at the bottom left-hand corner connects directly with the Salizzada S. Moisè and the route to the Accademia. A larger archway in the centre of the buildings leads into the Calle Ascensione opposite the post office and en route for the *albergo diurno*. Within this archway, on the right as you come from the Piazza, is the entrance to the **Museo Correr**, the city museum of Venice.

The Museo Civico Correr

(*The museum is open every day except Tuesday, from 9.00 until 16.00, hours extended to 20.00 on Saturdays and Sundays. It is also open in the evening on Fridays between 21.00 and 23.00. Entrance L5000.*) Tickets are sold on the first floor which is reached by way of a magnificent staircase in First Empire style with some excellent *trompe l'oeil* paintings on the wall.

From the ticket office you move along the Loggia Napoleonica with its views of the Piazza and alongside Napoleon's ballroom. The first room you come to is the Throne Room followed by the Dining Room. These rooms retain their First Empire neo-classical decorations and are notable for the works of Canova displayed here. From the dining room you turn into what was the first floor of the Procuratie Nuove. The sequence of 21 rooms that follow make up the civic museum and are devoted to items related to the history of Venice. The exhibits are of varied interest. Unless you have a good grasp of Venetian history the succession of portraits of doges, pictures of sea battles such as Lepanto etc. will tend to leave you cold. But there are some nice antique costumes, old book bindings, a superb collection of Venetian gold coins and a pretty model of the *Bucintoro*.

About three-quarters of the way down the gallery, off Room 16, is the staircase up to the second floor. At the top the way divides. To the left is the **Museo del Risorgimento** with displays relating to the unification of Italy, about a third of the space given over to Manin's Venetian Republic of 1848. But this museum has been closed for some time due to lack of staff. To the right lies the **Quadreria** or art gallery. The works in the art gallery are selected and displayed chronologically to illustrate the development of Venetian art. Beginning with pure Byzantine art the successive rooms show how this developed into Venetian-Gothic with influences from Ferrara, Tuscany and Flanders. You then pass into the early Renaissance with paintings by Giovanni Bellini, Gentile Bellini and Carpaccio among others. One unusual room is given over to Greek artists working in Venice, including an absolutely terrible early El Greco. A final section displays early maps and engravings of Venice. This last is a fascinating collection but it is housed in rooms regularly used for special exhibitions and is often displaced by them. The art gallery is, however, beautifully arranged, descriptions of the exhibits and explanations of their significance are lucidly explained in bilingual Italian/English captions. The museum shop is also superb value for cards and posters.

St Mark's Cathedral — Basilica di San Marco

From outside the Correr Museum you can look at the panorama of the Piazza virtually as it would have looked at the end of the 16th century. The purist and cynic would say that this is the only possible place from which to view the Piazza because this is the only place from which the Ala Napoleonica cannot be seen. What can be seen in its entirety is the main western facade of the Basilica. Ruskin, who loved the Basilica passionately, described it as, '. . . a multitude of pillars and white domes, clustered into a long low pyramid of coloured light.' And so on, for pages of ever more purple prose. Others have been more guarded in their praise:Mark Twain spoke of its, 'entrancing, tranquillising, soul-satisfying ugliness . . . like a vast and warty bug taking a meditative walk.' Whatever one's opinion the building has to be seen as an exotic rarity, a cathedral whose roots are fixed firmly in Byzantium and which is set totally apart from the Romanesque or Gothic cathedrals of Western Europe.

The Exterior

The fabric as we see it today is that of the third church to be built on this site, which was completed in 1094. The main facade begins with a porch extending across the entire width of the building, pierced by five arches, of which the central is the largest and main entrance. Each arch contains a semi-circular mosaic in the curve of the arch, with below it a carved lunette arch over the door. This porch, which is the Narthex of the Basilica, is roofed by a terrace from which the Doge used to watch ceremonies in the Piazza. The terrace is known as the **Loggia dei Cavalli** because in the centre, over the main archway, stand the **Four Bronze Horses** or **Quadriga**, looted from the Hippodrome at Constantinople during the Fourth Crusade. Today the horses are copies, the originals are inside, to protect them from pollution.

Very few of the original exterior mosaics remain. The process of replacing them began with Sansovino when he was chief architect in 1529. Generally they are insipid with the exception of the **Door of Sant'Alipio** to the extreme left, which contains a mosaic of 1260 showing *The Translation of the Body of St Mark to the Basilica*, the earliest known representation of the Basilica, its plan recognisable as that of today and with the bronze horses already in place. The mosaics on the four flanking arches all relate the story of St Mark being brought to Venice. The rather banal mosaic of the Last Judgment on the central arch was executed in 1836. The finest carvings are on the three arches of the **Central Portal**, carried out between 1235 and 1265, and representing, among a wealth of allegorical figures, the signs of the Zodiac and the trades of Venice. Most of the carvings and reliefs on the lower facade are 13th-century but, of the marble panels above the arches, one, *Hercules and the Erymanthean Boar*, is Roman. The bronze doors date from around 1300 but the doors of the **San Clemente Door** were cast in the Levant and are said to have been a gift of the 11th-century Byzantine Emperor, Alexius Comnenus. The many columns and capitals decorating the lower facade are an amazing mixture of styles and materials: marble, granite, alabaster and porphyry, from Dalmatia, Byzantium, Greece and Syria. They are the fruit of generations of merchant venturers, each of whom brought something back from his voyages to embellish the Basilica.

The upper facade has a large blank semi-circular window above the Central Portal. Above this is a gilded Lion of St Mark on a blue and gold ground which rises to a point on which there is a pinnacle surmounted by the statue of St Mark by Niccolò Lamberti. The four flanking arches have mosaics depicting the Death and Resurrection of Christ executed by Luigi Gaetano between 1617 and 1618, to cartoons by Matteo da Verona. All around the arches and along the roof line rises a forest of pinnacles, statues, tabernacles and tracery in Gothic style, begun in 1385 by the Dalle Masegne family and continued by Lombard and Tuscan artists, including the Sienese Della Quercia. Crowning all this from a distance are the Basilica's five domes or cupolas. The domes and details of the statues and carvings on the top of the Basilica are best seen from above in the view from the Campanile.

The Interior

The interior of the Basilica is so complex and so crowded with treasures that it is impossible to take it all in during the course of one visit. Also, the whole appearance of the interior alters constantly through the day according to the changing light. To see the interior to best effect it is advisable not to spend hours on one prolonged visit but to make a number of short visits at different times of the day. In the same way it is impossible to give a full description of the interior in a book of this length when there have been volumes devoted to nothing else. If you want to know everything about the mosaics and other decorations of the Basilica you would be well-advised to obtain a specific guide. Recommended is *The Basilica of San Marco* by Eugenio Bacchion, published by Ardo Editore and on sale at the bookshop in the Narthex. Alternatively, if you want a detailed account of the mosaics, there is *The Mosaics of St Mark's* published in the Electa Guides series and on sale in the city's bookshops. For hire in the Basilica are portable recorders with multi-language commentary but the sound quality is poor and the commentary itself rather unsatisfactory.

As a working church the Basilica is of course open all day and every day but visitors are requested to follow certain ground rules of courtesy and to confine their visits to the period from 9.30 to 17.30. On Sundays and holy days when there are morning services visitors are requested to keep out until 14.00. If a service is in progress during your visit you should not talk, move about too much or take flash photographs.

As with the exterior there are always parts of the interior closed to the public for restoration. Currently the areas affected are the Zen Chapel and Baptistery. There are three areas of the Basilica which require payment for entrance. These are the **Treasury**, the Altar and **Pala d'Oro** and the **Marciano Museum** (including the original four horses). Combined entrance charges for all three total L6000.

The Narthex

The Narthex forms the vestibule or porch to the Basilica proper and as a result is often crossed quickly, missing the many interesting things to be seen there. At one time the Narthex ran round all three sides of the west end of the church but, first the Baptistery in the mid-14th century, and then the Capella Zen, in the early 16th, were located in the southern arm of the Narthex so that it now runs continuously only along the west facade and along the north facade as far as the northern Transept. The bookshop for the Basilica is located in the Narthex close to the main doorway.

Often walked over without its significance being realised is a small white stone lozenge set into a slab of red Verona marble in the pavement within the main door. This is the spot where the Emperor Frederick Barabarossa knelt before Pope Alexander III in 1177 in the ceremony of reconciliation that did so much for Venice's reputation for diplomacy. The floor is largely stone-work of the 11th and 12th centuries and continues the floor mosaics of the interior. The lower part of the walls is marble but the upper portions and the ceiling are mosaic. The roofing of the Narthex is formed of six small domes with intervening vaults. The mosaics are largely based on the Old Testament and tell a more or less continuous narrative from the first dome in the southernmost part of the Narthex — which contains the story of the Creation in the upper two bands and

Adam and Eve in the lowest — to the story of Moses in the sixth dome near the North Transept. Some of the intervening scenes are famous in their way and all are charming. See the story of Noah on the first arch for example, or the building of the Tower of Babel in the second arch which, as has been said earlier, was modelled on the building of the Campanile. The mosaics in the northern arm of the Narthex, dealing with the stories of Joseph and Moses, were largely restored in the 19th century. In niches facing the main entrance are the oldest mosaics in the Basilica showing the Madonna with Apostles and Evangelists and which date from around 1065, only two years after the present structure was begun.

Near the first arch is the oldest funerary monument in Venice, the **Tomb of Vitale Falier:** the Doge who consecrated the new Basilica in 1094. He died in 1096 and the tomb was erected shortly thereafter from Byzantine materials. Two other doges, Bartolomeo Gradenigo and Marin Morosini, and a dogaressa, Felicita Michiel, are also buried in the Narthex.

Facing the main entrance seven steps lead up to the doors into the Basilica itself but a doorway and flight of steep steps to the right of those doors lead up to:

The Museo Marciano, Galleria and Loggia dei Cavalli

(*Open daily from 10.00 (13.30 on Sundays) until 16.00 or later (dependent on season). Entrance L2000.*) Climbing the stairs to the Gallery gives you the opportunity to go out onto the Loggia overlooking the Piazza, to see the world as the Doge once saw it. Within the Museum are the four bronze horses in their new home.

The horses were a *Quadriga*, the 4-horse team that pulled a chariot and this is the only quadriga to survive intact from the classical period. There is much controversy about the provenance of the horses. For many years it was believed that they were Greek from the 5th century BC but modern opinion has them as Roman from the 2nd century AD. Their colour is due to the bronze having a particularly high copper content. Close to, it can be seen that the surface is scratched and the gilding is only partial. It was once thought that this was due to wear and damage but it transpired during restoration that these partial markings were deliberate in their manufacture and were intended to make the horses sparkle in the sun's rays. The horses were brought inside and replaced by copies on the loggia after their restoration in 1979; the move was sponsored by

The four horses looted from Constantinople and now saved from pollution in the Gallery of St Mark's.

Olivetti. They were first removed from the loggia in 1797 when they were stolen by Napoleon's representatives and taken to Paris, but were returned in 1815. During both World Wars they were moved to Rome for safe-keeping.

The Main Basilica

Built when Venice was still theoretically part of the Byzantine Empire the church follows eastern principles and is laid out as a Greek cross with the four arms of the church — Nave, North Transept, South Transept and Presbytery — of equal length. St Mark's has five domes arranged so as to have lesser domes over each of the four arms and the largest dome over the central crossing. The church is laid out strictly according to the compass points; the Nave-Presbytery axis running due east-west and the Transepts due north-south. The model for the church was the Church of the Twelve Apostles in Constantinople. Although it is always known as the Basilica in Italian, it is not in fact a basilica in the architectural sense, since it has a transept, absent in a conventional basilica.

The first impression on entering the Basilica is of how dark it is. Here there are no great windows as in northern cathedrals; most light filters in from high under the domes, lending a mystical air to the interior that is part of its attraction. The gold and glass in the mosaics reacts with the light, shining brightly in the direct rays but retreating to a dull sheen when the light is removed. As the sun rises, sinks and moves from east to west so do the areas and proportions of the interior change their appearance, which is why I suggest that you should visit the interior on several occasions, at different times of the day.

The five domes are separated by barrel vaults and the aisles of all four arms are vaulted, supporting a gallery. So that everywhere there are curving, soaring surfaces, all covered with gold mosaics, making up more than 4,000 square metres of mosaic within the Basilica. Most of the mosaics were in place by the 13th century but a steady programme of additions and renewals has continued virtually to the present day. There are two rather unusual mosaics which deserve special mention. On the wall of the right-hand aisle in the Nave is an *Agony in the Garden* which, because Matthew, Mark and Luke do not agree on how Jesus prostrated himself, shows Christ in all the positions described by the three evangelists. On the west wall of the South Transept is a picture of the *Re-discovery of the Body of St Mark*. The story behind this is that they lost the relics of St Mark when the Basilica was being rebuilt but, during the Consecration in 1094 a portion of wall collapsed and the evangelist's arm fell out. The body was then transferred, amid rejoicing, to its present site beneath the High Altar.

The mosaics above might well distract you from a study of the floor, which would be a great shame because the inlaid marble and mosaic pavement is as much a wonder as the gold mosaics above. Most of the patterns are abstract or geometrical with hints of Islamic work but other designs feature religious symbols as well as beasts and mythical creatures. The books on mosaics mentioned earlier will help you to understand them but it is also possible to obtain poster sized floor-plans showing the lay-out of all the floor mosaics.

In the Central Crossing is the **Rood Screen** dividing the Sanctuary from the body of the church. This is the work of Jacobello and Pierpaolo Dalle Massegne and dates from 1394.

It consists of marble figures of the Virgin with St Mark and the Apostles, surmounted by a bronze and silver cross. The screen is flanked by two 14th-century pulpits, from the right-hand one of which a new Doge was presented to the people after his election. From the dome a huge Byzantine chandelier is suspended over the entrance to the Nave.

Sanctuary and Pala d'Oro

The Sanctuary was the preserve of the Venetian hierarchy and it was here that state religious ceremonies like the Coronation of the Doge took place. It is raised above the level of the church over the crypt. Entrance to the Sanctuary is normally from the South Transept through the **Capella di San Clemente** but on occasions this can be moved to the North Transept. (*Entrance L2000. Visiting is possible between 10.00 and 16.00, after 14.00 on Sundays*).

Beneath the **High Altar** lies the **Sarcophagus of St Mark**, as can be seen through a bronze grating. Here are interred the bones found in the 'Re-Discovery' of 1094 mentioned earlier but there are those who believe that the original relics were totally consumed in the fire of 976. Over the altar is a baldacchino supported by four alabaster columns interestingly carved with scenes from the New Testament. Experts disagree as to whether these columns are Byzantine or Coptic work of the 5th century, or Venetian work of the 14th.

Behind the altar is the **Pala d'Oro**, the Basilica's most priceless possession, acknowledged to be one of the finest examples of the goldsmith's craft. It was made in Byzantium in 976; re-worked in 1105, again in Constantinople; expanded, in Venice, to take loot from the Fourth Crusade in 1209 and finally re-modelled, again in Venice, by Giampaolo Boninsegna, in 1345. It is a large rectangle of gold set with gems, icons, enamels and carvings. An inventory of the gem-stones set into its surface comes up with 300 sapphires, 300 emeralds, 400 garnets and 1300 pearls as well as rubies, amethysts, topaz and hundreds of other stones. The enamels are noted for their antiquity as well as their artistic merit. The details of the work are impossible to see, given the distance at which sightseers are kept and the crowds that usually surround it, but the main panels show the Archangel Michael in the upper area and Christ Pantocrator in the lower. It is probably no bad thing to be kept at a distance because it is the total impact of the work that is most important in what it tells us about the wealth, prestige and artistic taste of medieval Venice.

The Treasury
(*The Treasury is open to the public at the same times as the Pala d'Oro and also costs L2000. The entrance is in the corner of the South Transept.*) The thick stone walls are almost certainly relics of a much older structure although there is disagreement as to whether this was the original 9th-century Basilica or the first castle-like Doge's Palace of the same period. Inside the Treasury is an amazing collection of gold and silver work, almost all Byzantine looted during the Fourth Crusade. There was once much more but quantities were taken by the French after 1797: which might be no more than fair dealing with what was stolen property anyway but at least the Venetians preserved the artistic objects for their beauty, the French melted theirs down for the value of the gold and silver.

The Baptistery
Next to the Treasury the entrance to the **Baptistery** is by way of the west aisle of the South Transept (when restoration work permits). The font is by Sansovino whose tomb is also here. The large granite slab by the altar was brought back from the Holy Land in 1126. It was recently found to conceal an ancient bath for baptism by total immersion. Two doges are buried here, Giovanni Soranzo, who died in 1328, and Andrea Dandolo, Doge from 1343 to 1354. Dandolo was a cultured man who commissioned the particularly fine mosaics showing the *Life of John the Baptist* and *Early Life of Christ*. One of my own favourite pieces of Venetian art is the representation of Salome, looking remarkably happy despite holding aloft John's head on a platter. Anyone who believes medieval art is wooden, stylised and religiously chaste should look closely at this figure. Note the coy tilt to Salome's head and the half-smile on her lips, her right leg thrust provocatively forward and a gown that clings revealingly to her body; the picture oozes sensuality.

The **Capella Zen** (currently undergoing restoration), entered from the Baptistery, was once that part of the Narthex forming the portico to the Piazzetta but was blocked off in 1504. The cause of this was Cardinal Giambattista Zen who died in 1501, leaving his entire estate to the Republic on condition that he was buried in St Mark's. His tomb was begun by Leopardi and Antonio Lombardi and finished by Paolo Savin. Most of the work in the chapel was executed by Tullio Lombardi. The mosaics, 12th- to 14th-century, were originally placed there to decorate the Narthex.

Capella della Madonna di Nicopeia

In a side chapel on the eastern side of the North Transept is housed what is, after the four bronze horses, the most famous property looted from Constantinople. The **Icon of the Madonna of Nicopeia**, a 10th-century work, was the most sacred relic of Byzantium and was carried in front of the Emperor's army. After its transfer it was adopted as the Patroness of the Venetian Republic. The gold frame was damaged in 1979 when the jewels were stolen but they were recovered and the frame restored.

Piazzetta dei Leoncini

Leave the Basilica by the door in the North Transept leading into the Narthex and exit onto the piazzetta north of St Mark's. The piazzetta has changed its name several times over the years having begun as the Piazzetta di S. Basso from the church of that name, built by Longhena in 1675. The church is now unused but is sometimes open as an exhibition centre. In 1722 Doge Alvise Mocenigo presented the Republic with two lions in red marble, after which the space became known as the Piazzetta dei Leoncini. For 200 years the lions have been the favourites of Venetian children who enjoy climbing on them. More recently, after the papacy of John XXIII, the piazzetta was renamed as the **Piazzetta Giovanni XXIII** but, as is often the case with re-named spaces in Venice, the locals continue to refer to the piazzetta as being of the *Leoncini*. At the end of the piazzetta is the **Patriarchal Palace** built in the 1830s after the Patriarch moved from S. Pietro di Castello with the designation of St Mark's as the Cathedral of Venice.

North from the Piazza — to the Rialto Bridge

Ninety percent of visitors to Venice do not move outside the immediate vicinity of the Piazza except for one excursion: to see the Rialto Bridge. Let us therefore round off this chapter on the historic centre by considering some of the sights between the Piazza and Rialto. Begin at the Torre dell'Orologio beneath which the Sottoportego leads into the Merceria dell'Orologio. Emerging from the Sottoportego look up to your left to see the bas-relief plaque on the wall commemorating the window from where a woman called Giustina Rossi ended a rebellion against the Doge by dropping a stone mortar on the head of the rebel's standard-bearer. The plaque bears the date of the event, June 15, 1310.

The **Mercerie** are described at length in the chapter on shopping so I shall say no more than that they become almost intolerably crowded in the summer months and visitors may find themselves diverted onto parallel streets as the urban police attempt to impose a sort of one-way system. To the left of the Merceria dell'Orologio, between it and the Calle dei Fabbri, is the old Armenian quarter, almost always deserted and containing the city's best-hidden church, **Santa Croce degli Armeni**. It is a very tiny church, built in the last years of the 17th century, and contains little of interest. But it remains one of those hidden corners of Venice that give constant pleasure to a wandering visitor. The **Church of S. Giuliano (San Zulian** in dialect) stands on the *campo* of that name at the end of the first stretch of the Mercerie. Not very distinguished, the church's main attraction is a ceiling painted by Palma Giovane. There is also a late Veronese and a stuccoed vault by Vittoria. The church's patron was Tommaso Rangone whose portrait statue by Sansovino is on the facade.

Follow the Rialto signs to where the Merceria bends around the **Church of San Salvatore (Salvador** in dialect). The baroque facade, by Sardi, is a late addition and not of great importance. The church itself was begun in 1508 by Spavento and completed by Tullio Lombardi. Its plan is a unique compromise between the Greek cross model of the Byzantine period and the long nave design demanded in the 16th century. The answer was to set three domed Greek crosses end to end. There is much of Sansovino's sculpture inside but his most famous work here is the **Tomb of Doge Francesco Venier**. Over the altar to the left hangs Titian's *Annunciation,* while his *Transfiguration* (much in need of cleaning) is over the High Altar. This latter painting hides a beautiful silver reredos which can be revealed on application to the sacristan who will lower the Titian mechanically. The other major tomb in the church is that of the tragic Queen of Cyprus, **Caterina Cornaro** (see page 178). The tomb post-dates her death because she was originally buried in SS.

Apostoli. Most guides tend to ignore the floor of the church and yet it is one of its splendours with crosses on circles in black, cream and red marble, mirroring the design of the roof. In the centre of the third circle is a small window set into the pavement through which a recently discovered merchant's tomb can be seen.

From S. Salvador a very short stretch of the Merceria brings you into the **Campo San Bartolomeo**. At the hour of the *passeggiata* when the fashionable and sociable flock to the Piazza the businessmen and merchants gather in the Campo S. Bartolomeo to gossip and do deals in a tradition that dates back to the days when Shakespeare had Solanio say, 'Now, what news on the Rialto?' See the square after six in the evening and it is full of groups and huddles of men in suits, often clasping briefcases. Sometimes they walk about, sometimes they pop into a bar for a coffee or glass of wine. But mostly they just talk and the buzz of their conversation can be heard two blocks away. In the centre rises the statue of Carlo Goldoni the playwright, very fittingly since he so loved gossip and conversation. At the north end of the square is the **Fondaco dei Tedeschi**, the old German warehouse, now the Head Post Office. The whole area was once the centre for German merchants and the **Church of S. Bartolomeo** in the Salizzada Pio X was the German church. The church is now disused and its altarpiece by Albrecht Dürer has been transferred to Prague. The Salizzada Pio X leads to the foot of the **Rialto Bridge**.

Over the centuries there were a number of bridges across the Grand Canal at this point, on pontoons at first and then on wooden piles. The last wooden bridge, with shops on it and a central drawbridge to let galleys move up and down the Grand Canal, can be seen in a famous painting by Carpaccio in the Accademia. But it was decided to rebuild in stone in the middle of the 16th century and designs were submitted by such giants as Palladio, Michelangelo and Sansovino. Yet in the end, the architect chosen was one whose only claim to the job would seem to be his name of 'Bridge': Antonio da Ponte. He shared the task with his nephew Antonio Contin who also built the Bridge of Sighs. The design is heavy, with three walkways, the central one between two arcades of shops, the two outer open on one side to the Canal. The arch of the bridge is particularly steep because one requirement of the design was that a fully-armed galley should be able to pass beneath it. If it were not as much a symbol of Venice as the Doge's Palace or St Mark's we might allow ourselves to recognise that the bridge is, in fact, downright ugly and wish we could have seen Michelangelo's construction or the five graceful arches devised by Palladio. As it is we greet the Rialto Bridge with the familiarity of an old friend who is not particularly good-looking but who is down-to-earth and good-hearted.

A view of the Rialto Bridge that shows how surprisingly wide it is.

If you cross the Rialto Bridge you come into the **Ruga degli Orefici**, lined with stalls and shops and a continuation of the shops on the Bridge. The *campo* on the Canal side of the *ruga* contains the tiny church of **S. Giacomo di Rialto**. Legend claims it as the oldest church in Venice and dates it to 421, the year the Consuls of Padua supposedly proclaimed the founding of the city. It is certainly very old but its known existence dates from around 1070, when St Mark's was being built. In plan it is a domed Greek cross and the pillars in the interior are 11th-century Greek. It seems as though the church has always been associated with the market which was established here in 1097 and a 12th-century inscription on the apse urges market traders

The Tragic Queen of Cyprus

One of the saddest stories in Venetian history is what befell a daughter of the Corner Family, although she is normally known by the Italian form of her name, Caterina Cornaro. Her hand was requested in marriage by James of Lusignan, an illegitimate son of King John II of Cyprus, who had seized the throne in 1460 from the House of Savoy. Aged 14 in 1468, the girl was hastily married off by the Republic which could see political advantages in the match; the Doge himself gave the bride away and she was given the honorary title of 'Daughter of St Mark'. For four years the union was a proxy marriage only, until Caterina sailed for Cyprus to become the true wife of King James. Unfortunately, the girl's husband died within a year of the marriage being consumated, leaving the 19-year old girl as ruler of Cyprus in the name of the son with whom she was pregnant at the time.

Afraid of Venetian influence, plot after plot was hatched against Caterina, largely with the object of giving the throne to Alfonso of Naples. The young queen was only maintained on the throne by Venetian support, Venetian representatives ruling the island in her name. This was even more the case after Caterina's young son died within a year of his birth. For fourteen years the young queen struggled on as a puppet ruler while many plots against her were put down by Venetian forces who were steadily growing in influence. In 1488 a plot was discovered to marry Caterina to Alfonso of Naples and there were hints that the lady was not unwilling. Fearing to lose their influence the Venetians made Caterina an offer she could not refuse: untold wealth and honour if only she would abdicate from the throne in favour of Venice.

In 1489 Caterina left the island of Cyprus, now a colony of the Venetian Empire, and returned to Venice in scenes of such pageantry and splendour that paintings of the event are to be seen everywhere in the Correr Museum, the Accademia and Doge's Palace. She was given the hill-town of Asolo where she could hold empty court like Napoleon on Elba and here she lived for twenty years. Her troubles were not quite at an end however. In 1509 she was forced to retreat in the face of the invading armies of the Emperor Maximilian and she fled back to her native city. And it was there she died in 1510, aged little more than fifty. Originally she was buried in the Church of the Apostoli but the tomb was transferred to S. Salvatore later that century. And there she lies under an inscription crediting her with being Queen of Cyprus, Jerusalem and Armenia.

to be fair and honest. The clock tower and portico were added in 1410 and it is a standing joke in Venice that the clock has never told the right time since the day it was installed. Across the *campo* from the church is the **Gobbo di Rialto**, a 16th-century figure of a hunchback that supports a rostrum from which proclamations of the Republic were made to the people, simultaneously with the same proclamation being read from the Pietra del Bando in the Piazza. Another function linked the Pietra and Gobbo since certain crimes were punished by the guilty party being stripped and made to run the gauntlet between the two rostra.

Return across the Rialto Bridge, descend to the canal-side and walk down past the water-bus landing stages. This *riva* and the corresponding *fondamenta* on the opposite bank are two of only half a dozen places where it is possible to walk alongside the Grand Canal, which is mostly shut off to the pedestrian. Make your way through the café and restaurant tables, and round the queues for the water-bus, and continue along the side of the Canal in front of the **Palazzo Dolfin-Manin** and **Palazzo Bembo**. Turn left into the Calle Bembo and then right into the Calle del Teatro. Straight ahead the Calle Bembo becomes the Calle dei Fabbri, full of shops, hotels and restaurants, which leads directly back to the Piazza. The Calle del Teatro passes in front of the **Teatro Goldoni**, the leading prose theatre in Venice, to reach the **Campo S. Luca**.

The Campo S. Luca is another social square like the Campo S. Bartolomeo. Approaching it in the evening there is the same hum of conversation audible long before you reach the square. But this is more high-pitched and less measured, because S. Luca is the square of the young: teenagers and students, young men and women in their early twenties, congregating in the same sort of groups and huddles as their elders. The **Campo Manin**, a little further on, was enlarged and re-named in 1871 in memory of **Daniele Manin**, leader of the revolt against Austria and head of Venice's short-lived Republic of 1848–9. This square was Manin's birthplace and his statue stands outside his former home. On the southern side of the square a narrow alleyway is signposted (the sign is very small and obscure) to **La Scala del Bovolo**. This landmark, found in every rack of postcards in the city but seldom visited by tourists, is in the courtyard of the **Palazzo Contarini del Bovolo** and is an external spiral staircase set against a corner of the palazzo. Built around 1500 it is the finest example of its type to be found in Venice. Unfortunately for the photographer it is set in such a small courtyard that it is impossible to capture the whole staircase without an extremely wide-angle lens. The garden at the foot of the stairs is dotted with several well-heads and is caged in to form a haven for some of Venice's many cats.

From the bottom end of the Campo Manin take either of the bridges over the canal, as if headed for the Accademia. Take the first right in front of the **Teatro Rossini** and continue into the **Campo S. Benedetto**. On the north side of the square is the small **Church of San Benedetto** with a few nice paintings but generally closed. The real reason for coming here, however, is the **Palazzo Pesaro degli Orfei** on the western side of the square, containing the **Museo di Palazzo Fortuny**. (*The museum is open from 9.00 to 19.00 every day except Monday. Entrance L5000.*) Mariano Fortuny y Madrazo was born in Granada in 1871 and studied to become a painter. He became increasingly interested in the theatre, especially through his friendship with D'Annunzio and Diaghelev and, displeased with the current attitude to costume design, began to design costumes himself, working for Eleonora Duse and Sarah Bernhardt among others. Later he turned to fashion designing, initially dressing those actresses he had worked with in the theatre but rapidly building up a devoted following of his own. He owned an establishment on Giudecca and began to produce textiles of extreme richness and high quality, it was said that one of his silk dresses was so fine that it could be pulled through a wedding ring. He died in 1950 and his widow gave his house, the 15th-century Palazzo Pesaro, to the Commune, on condition that at least half was devoted to the work of her late husband.

The lower floors contain a collection of clothes, textiles and theatrical costumes by Fortuny and also some of his paintings, sculptures and photographs (about which the best one can say is that it is a good thing that he turned from painting to theatrical design). The top floor was designated for cultural events by the widow and is in fact used for important international photographic exhibitions. Structurally the buildings are not sound and the number of visitors is limited.

From the Campo S. Benedetto retrace your steps to the *calle* between Campo Manin and the Campo S. Angelo and take the Calle di Verona southwards to the **Campo S. Fantin**. The principal building in the *campo* is the **Teatro La Fenice**, originally opened in 1792 but rebuilt phoenix-like (*Fenice* means Phoenix) in 1836, after a fire. The neo-classical exterior is not very exciting, the glory is the auditorium in gilt, red velvet and serried ranks of boxes. Normally the interior can only be seen if you attend a performance but try your powers of persuasion on the theatre staff if there is no production or rehearsal in progress. Look at the back of the theatre where a canal basin in front of the large doorway reminds you that, in Venice, the scenery and heavy equipment has to be brought to the theatre by water. The Campo S. Fantin and its environs contain some of the more expensive Venetian restaurants. The finest and most expensive, the **Antico Martini**, is on the southern side of the square. Behind and to the left of the theatre look for the pretty little 15th-century **Casa Molin** with its outside staircase that gives its name to the **Martini Scala Restarant**. The **Church of S. Fantin** is notable principally for a domed Sanctuary and Apse by Sansovino. The **Scuola di San Fantin** is closed to the public; it was the home of a co-fraternity devoted to comforting condemned prisoners before their execution. It is now the base of a cultural association, the *Ateneo Veneto*. Take the *calle* on the north side of the church, which ultimately becomes the Frezzeria and leads you back to the Piazza.

The Legend of St Mark

According to legend St Mark was travelling through the Lagoon on a visit to Italy and his ship happened to touch on the islands of the Rialto where the saint spent the night. As he slept, the saint was visited by an angel. '*Pax tibi Marce, evangelista mea,*' said the angel, 'Peace unto you Mark, my Evangelist. Here in this place is where your body will rest.' It is a story that proved very useful when justifying the seizure of St Mark's body from Alexandria and, the cynic would say, might well have been invented at that time. The words *Pax tibi Marce, evangelista mea* are those inscribed on the book held by the winged lion that is the symbol of St Mark. As such the inscription is seen everywhere in the city.

The bargain way to travel by gondola, the *traghetto* gondola-ferry nears the Ca' d'Oro with the arcade of the Fish Market behind it.

TEN

Seeing Venice from the Water

To see Venice from the water is to see the city as it ought to be seen. The canals were, and are, the city's main thoroughfares and everything is oriented towards them. The great *palazzi* were built with the architectural and decorative display of their facades on the canal frontage; to approach them from the land is to enter by the back door. Ideally, the way to see Venice from the water is by gondola but to do so extensively would be inordinately expensive. Luckily it is possible to see a great deal of the city by using two of **Actv**'s public *vaporetto* routes. The first covers the entire length of the Grand Canal, where the view from the water is especially important, because there are no more than half a dozen short stretches where it is possible to walk alongside the Canal. And the second is the circular route which circumnavigates the entire historic centre and which not only permits the traveller a view of places to which they are not admitted on foot, such as the Commercial Port and the interior of the Arsenal, but takes in the closest of the adjacent islands such as San Michele, Murano, Giudecca and San Giorgio Maggiore.

In describing the two routes I pause occasionally to describe some places in more detail, but that does not mean you have to break your journey at that point. For the moment it is intended that you treat your excursion on the canals as something to be enjoyed for itself. However, if you want to give a day over to these tours, stopping off periodically to view the sights described, you should obtain a 24-hour ticket, at a cost of L10,000.

Vaporetto Route Number 1 — The Grand Canal from Piazzale Roma to San Marco

This route is described from north to south, from Piazzale Roma to San Marco, but you do not need to do the journey in the same direction. This is the route followed by those who arrive in Venice at the Piazzale Roma or railway station and head for St Mark's. So sightseeing can become part of your arrival in Venice.

In all but the quietest of times you might have difficulty in obtaining a good vantage point on the water-bus. A *vaporetto* has a large covered cabin with plenty of seating accommodation but, once seated, it is a little difficult to see both sides of the Canal at once. Amidships, where you board, there is a large standing area open to both sides, but this gets very crowded and you are likely to find your view blocked by the people around you. There are a few seats in the open at the very front and back and these offer by far the best vantage-points, but places get taken very quickly. It is worth considering going back as far as Tronchetto in order to be first on board and have your pick of where to sit. Do not attempt to stand in the front of the boat as this will obstruct the view of the man at the wheel and you will be asked to move in no uncertain manner.

The Grand Canal is four kilometres long, between thirty and seventy metres wide and five metres deep. It follows the old river-bed of a Brenta outlet and describes a long double curve like a reversed 'S'. It is bridged in only three places. On its banks are over 100 *palazzi* built largely between the 14th and 18th centuries. Styles vary from Veneto-Byzantine to late Renaissance neo-Classicism but all follow the basic plan of the *casa fondaco*. The floor at Canal level was used for commercial activities, as warehouse and salesroom. The floor above, the *mezzanine*, contained offices and some living accommodation. The upper floor, the *piano nobile*, formed the main living quarters for the family while the servants lived in the attics. Most of the larger *palazzi* had two upper floors, the *primo piano nobile* and the *secondo piano nobile*. The plan for each floor was roughly the same: a hallway running the entire depth of the building with rooms opening off it. From the outside you can see the wide windows or loggia that illuminated the hallway, flanked by smaller windows in the front rooms. In the earlier buildings these rooms tended to be on one side of the hallway only, but later buildings have rooms on both sides and the loggia is central. On the roof, take note of two typically Venetian features: the strangely shaped chimney-pots which functioned as spark-traps in a city terrified of fire, and the roof-platform or *altane*, necessary in a city which has little room to spare for gardens, and the place where the family took the air or dried their laundry.

I only have space to name and describe the principal *palazzi* in this account. If you want to be certain in your identification of those I do mention, and some that I do not, it would help to have with you the city-plan published by L.A.C. of Florence, which not only locates all the *palazzi* along the Grand Canal but has pictorial representations of fifty of them to make identification easier.

To the First Bend — Piazzale Roma to Rialto

At the Piazzale Roma the Grand Canal is distinctly shabby, with nothing on the far side except the high brick walls of the State Railways offices, while the view back to the Lagoon is obstructed by bridges carrying the railway into the docks and the road into Piazzale Roma. Soon after leaving the landing stage, however, the boat makes a sharp turn left towards the railway station and the Canal proper begins. On the right-hand side, is the bridge over the **Rio Nuovo**, that rarity in Venice, a canal that was especially created rather than existing by nature and constructed in 1933 as a short cut from the railway station and Piazzale Roma to the last bend of the Grand Canal. The gardens are the **Giardini Papadopoli**, occupying the site of the Church of Santa Croce, which gave its name to the sestiere but was demolished as part of the 1930s reconstruction of this part of Venice. As the *vaporetto* pulls into the *Ferrovia* landing stage on the left bank the imposing building opposite, with the Greek portico and lofty grey-green dome, is the 18th-century **Church of San Simeone Piccolo**, now closed.

The **Santa Lucia Railway Station** was only completed in 1955. It is known as 'Santa Lucia' after the church of that name, demolished by the Austrians in 1860 to make way for an expanded rail terminus. As the boat pulls away from the landing stage the church at the end of the station forecourt is the **Scalzi Church**, built in the 17th century by Longhena, with a Baroque facade by Sardi, described by Henry James as having 'a costly, curly ugliness'. The word *scalzi* means 'shoeless' as the church was commissioned by the mendicant 'Barefoot' Carmelites. It was one of the first historic buildings to suffer from aerial warfare, being hit by an Austrian bomb in 1915, when a ceiling painted by Tiepolo was destroyed. The artist's original drawing for the painting, together with some surviving fragments can be seen in the Accademia.

Built by the Austrians in 1858–60, after the arrival of the railway, the original **Scalzi Bridge** was an iron construction too low for water-buses to pass beneath. It was replaced by the present structure, to a design by Miozzi, in 1934. Like the Rio Nuovo, Giardini Papadopoli and Piazzale Roma, the Scalzi Bridge forms part of the redevelopment programme carried out by the fascist-administered municipality after the opening of the road link in 1933.

Beyond the bridge are a number of not very exciting *palazzi*. Just past the Rio Manin on the right-hand side it is possible to see the Campo S. Simeone Grande beyond an attractive garden. The next stop for the water-bus is on the right bank at S. Biasio. On the opposite bank can be seen the **Church of S. Geremia**, built in the 1750s by Corbellini. The inscription on the facade facing the Grand Canal is dedicated to St Lucia, a much travelled saint, martyred in Syracuse in 304, her body stolen from Constantinople during the Fourth Crusade and her relics transferred here in 1863 when the Church of Santa Lucia was demolished.

To the right of S. Geremia is the opening of the Cannaregio Canal, the second largest canal in Venice proper. Looking down the canal a pleasanter facade of S. Geremia can be seen, together with the Campanile, relic of an earlier building and one of the oldest bell-towers in Venice. Almost wrapped around the Campanile and with its main facade on the Cannaregio Canal is the **Palazzo Labia**. This building belongs to the state broadcasting organisation, RAI, as can be seen by the array of aerials on its roof. The *palazzo* was originally built in 1750 for a wealthy Spanish family who had bought their way into the Venetian nobility in the 17th century. The building contains a ballroom, with paintings by Tiepolo, to which the public are admitted on request if the studio is not in use. The ballroom is also used for recording concerts to which the public are admitted (*at least weekly, tickets by request at the door or by telephone — 781111 or 716666*).

The water-bus now moves across the Canal to the landing stage of **S. Marcuola**. The church, with an unfinished facade by Massari, is not very noteworthy but the site has been that of a church since the 9th century. The impressive facade adjacent to the landing stage is the **Palazzo Vendramin-Calergi**, begun by

Coducci at the end of the 15th century and finished by Tullio Lombardo in 1509. The building is typical of the Renaissance buildings that were rising on the Piazza at the same time, like Coducci's own Procuratie Vecchie, and provides a model for Renaissance architecture in the city. It has a three-storey facade, topped by a classical cornice. Corinthian columns on each storey separate five arched windows, each containing two interior arches. Richard Wagner died here in 1883, a plaque recording the event is near the land entry at the rear of the building. During the winter it houses the **Casino** but is the venue for concerts during the summer.

Facing the Palazzo Vendramin across the Canal is the **Fondaco dei Turchi**, so-called because it was the base of Turkish merchants in the city between 1621 and 1838. The building was constructed as a private residence in 1225 by a rich merchant from Pesaro, Giacomo Palmieri. The long portico giving onto a central courtyard is typical of the Byzantine period in Venetian architecture. Between 1380 and 1621 it was the official guest-house of the Venetian Republic and housed visitors like the Byzantine Emperor. When the Turks left in 1838 the building was in ruins. After much agitation from conservationists such as Ruskin, a complete restoration was undertaken by Camillo Boito in 1858. The result was so bad that opinion is divided as to whether the restored building is any improvement on the ruins it replaced. From 1880 it housed the Correr Collection but, in 1923, the building became the **Natural History Museum**. As such the interior can be visited today (*open 9.00–13.30 every day except Monday. Entrance L3000*). The museum's prize exhibits include one of the largest dinosaur skeletons ever discovered (a *Duranosaurus nigeriensis*) and a 12-metre long crocodile found in the Sahara. Under the portico is the tomb of Doge Marin Falier, executed in 1355 for attempting to suborn the state.

The plain building to the right of the Fondaco dei Turchi is the **Casa Correr**, home of Teodoro Correr, who formed the collection bearing his name. The brick, crenellated building on the left of the Fondaco is the **Deposito del Megio**, the old State Granaries. A 15th-century construction, the Lion of St Mark on the facade is a replica, the original was smashed during the Napoleonic occupation. Next is the **Palazzo Belloni-Battagia**, designed by Longhena in the 17th century, with an elaborate facade, crowned by two obelisks and decorated by coats of arms. The cost of building the *palazzo* ruined the owner and he had to rent it out and live elsewhere himself. These last two buildings can best be seen as the water-bus crosses the Canal to reach **S. Stae**.

S. Stae is one of the strange contractions of Venetian dialect and is short for Sant' Eustachio. The present church was rebuilt in 1709 with a Baroque facade by Rossi. Recently restored it is now used for concerts and exhibitions. Also used for exhibitions is the adjoining building, the **Scuola dei Battiloro e Tiraoro**, belonging to the co-fraternity of goldsmiths. Across a small canal from the Campo S. Stae is the **Ca' Pesaro**, one of Longhena's finest works, occupying a site on which three houses formerly stood. It took 51 years to build, from 1652 to 1703, and was only completed 20 years after Longhena's death. Gaspari was responsible for the facade along the side-canal, an unusual feature in Venetian houses where stone was usually kept for the main facade, with the sides in brick. The upper floors of the facade are taller than had previously been the practice which gives a solid yet graceful appearance to the *palazzo,* and prevents the flamboyant baroque decorations Longhena had used from becoming over-powering. The building now houses two museums but the **Museum of Oriental Art**, based on the collection of Count Bardi who died in 1906, has been shut for some years through lack of staff. The **International Gallery of Modern Art**. which occupies the lower storeys, is based mainly on works purchased from the Biennale. After 1910 the museum began to make its own purchases, the most renowned being *Judita II* by Gustav Klimt. Sculptures and paintings include works by Rodin, Chagall and Matisse. Many of those purchased from the Biennale were fine in their day but seem unmemorable today. As a gallery of modern art it cannot compete with the Guggenheim Collection. In 1991 the Ca' Pesaro was temporarily closed for restoration.

As the water-bus leaves S. Stae and begins to move towards the opposite bank we come to a series of particularly fine *palazzi.* Opposite the Ca' Pesaro is the **Palazzo Gussoni Grimani della Vida** (or **Palazzo Gusson** in dialect), a building re-modelled in the 1550s by Sanmicheli and originally decorated by Tintoretto frescoes, unfortunately long-since lost. The most famous inhabitant of the *palazzo* was Sir Henry Wotton, English ambassador to Venice between 1604 and 1624. Sir Henry spent half his time in Venice as agent for James I and the Duke of Buckingham, buying pictures to be sent back to England. The other half of his time was spent securing freedom of worship for protestants in Venice and importing protestant texts with which he hoped to convert the Venetians to the Church of England! He was not in Venice for the full 20 years as he kept on being suspended for putting his foot in it, including his dismissal by King James for the famous remark that an ambassador was, 'an honest man sent to lie abroad for the good of his country'.

On the right bank, the next large building after the Ca' Pesaro is the **Palazzo Corner della Regina**, a *palazzo* dating from 1724 but so-called because the site was the birthplace of the tragic Caterina Cornaro (or Corner), Queen of Cyprus (see page 178). The building, once a state-run pawn-shop (*Monte di Pietà*), now houses the archives of the Biennale, which were transferred here in 1976 and contain material on film, theatre, dance and photography as well as painting and sculpture. (*Entry free on application.*) On the left bank, after the Palazzo Gusson, there is a succession of attractive frontages offering a cross-section of Venetian architecture. The *vaporetto* now comes to rest on the left bank, in front ot the most famous *palazzo* on the Grand Canal, the **Ca' d'Oro**.

The **Ca' d'Oro** is the culmination of Gothic domestic architecture before the onset of the Renaissance. Its elaborate facade was once gilded, hence the name 'Golden House' and was built between 1425 and 1440 by Matteo Raverti and the Bon brothers for a procurator of St Mark's, Marino Contarini. In 1922 the house, together with his own art collection, was bequeathed to the state by Baron Giorgio Franchetti who had done much to rectify some heavy-handed 19th-century restoration. Five years later the **Galleria Franchetti** was opened within the Ca' d'Oro and, many times restored and reorganised, especially after the floods of 1966, the gallery has become one of the finest and most beautifully presented art collections in the city. (*Open 9.00–14.00 every day except Sunday when it closes at 13.00. Entrance L2000.*) Works of note are a *St Sebastian* by Mantegna and two scenes, *Piazzetta* and *Molo*, by Guardi; two of the very few Guardis left in Venice. Other fine works are by Carpaccio, Titian and Van Dyck. Also displayed are frescoes by Giorgione and Titian, formerly on the exterior of the Fondaco dei Tedeschi. Apart from the art displayed the interior is beautiful in itself, with an attractive courtyard. When

Acclaimed as the finest building on the Grand Canal, the once-gilded facade of the Ca' d'Oro.

the current restoration of the facade is complete there should be wonderful views of the Grand Canal from the first floor loggia.

As the water-bus leaves Ca' d'Oro it seems to be heading into a dead-end. The high-walled building which appears to close off the Canal is the **Fondaco dei Tedeschi** (see page 176), the warehouse of the German merchants, built in 1508 by Spavento and Scarpagnino, with a portico of five arches running the width of the central block. The two truncated corner blocks were towers, and there are crenellations along the coping. The exterior was once covered in frescoes by Titian and Giorgione, some fragments of which are preserved in the Ca' d'Oro.

Between Ca' d'Oro and the Fondaco dei Tedeschi are several fine *palazzi*. One of interest to British visitors is the **Palazzo Mangili-Valmarana** on the left bank of the Rio SS. Apostoli, built at the request of Joseph Smith, an Englishman who lived in Venice from 1700 to 1770. A collector and patron of the arts he acted as agent for Canaletto, ensuring that almost all the artist's work is to be found in Britain. In 1762 Smith sold his collection to George III for £20,000, which is why there are more Canalettos in Windsor Castle than anywhere else. Smith is buried in the English Church at S. Vio after being uprooted from the Protestant cemetery on the Lido. On the opposite bank of the Rio SS. Apostoli is **Ca' da Mosto**, which has a ground floor portico and first floor arches from the 13th century. This is one of the oldest structures to be seen on the Grand Canal. Alvise da Mosto who discovered the Cape Verde Islands was born here in 1432. In the 16th century, as the '*Albergo del Lion Bianco*', it became one of Venice's first hotels, whose most famous guest was Turner.

On the right bank the approach to Rialto is dominated by the markets. The first building, passed soon after the boat leaves Ca' d'Oro, is the **Pescheria** fish market, built as a neo-Gothic open market hall in 1907. The two longer ranges of market buildings are older. The one following the curve of the canal, with a long arcade, is the **Fabbriche Nuove di Rialto** built by Sansovino in 1554. Behind is the older **Fabbriche Vecchie di Rialto** built by Scarpagnino in 1520. The last large building on this side before the bend is the **Palazzo dei Camerlenghi** built in 1525 as the Exchequer of the Republic. The building also doubled as the debtors' prison.

The height of the buildings and the narrowness of the Canal, added to the bend, lends a claustrophobic feeling of enclosure and a sense of entering a cul-de-sac. Then the *vaporetto* moves into mid-channel, turns sharply right and passes beneath the surprisingly deep **Rialto Bridge**. The Canal is always crowded here and the boat will often have to queue at the landing stages situated a little way down the Canal on the left bank.

To the Second Bend — Rialto to the Volta del Canal

Along this immediate stretch below the bridge, where the *vaporetti* landing stages are situated, runs one of the few canalside walks along the Grand Canal. These quaysides were the wharves at which goods were unloaded and their names reflect this, as witness the Riva del Ferro (iron), which runs from the foot of the bridge and which becomes the Fondamenta del Carbon (coal), extending along the Canal for 250 metres. This quayside is mirrored on the right bank by the even longer Fondamenta del Vin (wine).

Immediately below the water-bus landing stages there is a succession of imposing and important *palazzi*. The first of these, with blue *pali* in front, and a *sottoportego* under the facade, is the **Palazzo Dolfin-Manin**, built for the Dolfin family by Sansovino in the 1530s. It acquired its hyphenated name because it was the home of Lodovico Manin, the last Doge. It now houses offices belonging to the Banca d'Italia. Immediately after the Palazzo Dolfin-Manin comes the huge **Palazzo Bembo**, a 15th-century Gothic structure, birthplace of the writer, Pietro Bembo. A range of buildings follow, in the midst of which is the Gothic **Palazzo Dandolo**, one of the smallest *palazzi* on the Grand Canal. The Fondamenta del Carbon terminates with two twinned *palazzi* from the Veneto-Byzantine 13th century, the **Palazzi Loredan** and **Farsetti**, both heavily restored in the 19th century. The first of the two is noted for having been the birthplace of Elena Corner Piscopia, the first woman ever to gain a university degree; she graduated in philosophy from Padua University in 1678. Today, the two *palazzi* together form the *Municipio*, the Town Hall of Venice.

The water-bus now crosses the Canal to the landing stage of S. Silvestro. Immediately at the right bank end of the Rialto Bridge is the **Palazzo dei Dieci Savi**, built by Scarpagnino in the early 16th century to house the Republic's finance ministers. Other than that the buildings along the quayside are mostly nondescript.

Diagonally opposite the S. Silvestro stop, on the left bank, the imposing Renaissance *palazzo* in white Istrian stone is the **Palazzo Grimani di S. Luca**, built to the design of Sanmicheli, whose last great work it was. It took nearly twenty years to build, from 1559 to 1575, aiming to be as large and impressive as possible, in order to spite the owner of the **Palazzo Coccina-Tiepolo** opposite. The Palazzo Grimani now houses the Court of Appeal. The Palazzo Coccina-Tiepolo is also known as the **Palazzo Papadopoli**; changing family ownerships over the years has led to many of these *palazzi* having hyphenated or alternative names. This *palazzo* is much more conservative than its rival across the Canal, despite being built at about the same time and by the same builder, Giangiacomo dei Grigi, who completed the Palazzo Grimani after Sanmicheli's death.

On the other side of the Rio S. Luca from the Palazzo Grimani is the **Palazzo Corner Contarini dei Cavalli**, originally built in flamboyant Gothic style in 1445. Only the central section with the six-light window remains Gothic, the ground and upper floors were re-modelled in Renaissance style. The facade has two coats of arms bearing horses in the design, hence the name '*dei cavalli*'. A little further on, the pink *palazzo* is the **Palazzo Benzon** where, in the early 19th century, the Countess Marina Benzon held a literary salon which attracted the most fashionable members of Venetian society together with such literary or artistic giants as Byron and Canova. The Countess has a claim to fame in her own right as she was the model for a song still traditionally sung by gondoliers, '*La biondina in gondoleta*' (the blonde in the gondola).

Opposite the Palazzo Benzon on the right bank is a substantial Gothic *palazzo* with a brick facade and a second floor loggia, the columns and arches of which imitate those of the Doge's Palace. This is the **Palazzo Bernardo** built around 1420. Meanwhile the *vaporetto* has been approaching the S. Angelo landing stage on the left bank. Adjacent to the landing stage towards Rialto is the **Palazzo Corner-Spinelli**, an early

(**Overleaf**) **Top:** The island and church of S. Giorgio Maggiore.
Bottom: A gondola makes its way along the Rio Canonica towards the Bridge of Sighs.
Opposite The Torre dell'Orologio and the entrance to the Mercerie seen from above.

Renaissance building by Coducci, begun in 1490 and preceding the Palazzo Vendramin. In contrast to this elegant 15th-century building are the modern brick offices of the **Actv** organisation. This is where you must come to obtain a *Carta Veneziana*.

From S. Angelo it is only a short leg to the next landing stage, at S. Tomà on the right bank. Here you can see the buildings on the **Volta del Canal**, the name given to the apex of this second major bend in the Grand Canal, a bend sharper than that at Rialto but not apparently as acute because the Canal is twice as wide. A considerable stretch of the left bank between S. Angelo and the Volta is taken up with four *palazzi* all joined together as property of the Mocenigo family: the **Palazzo Mocenigo Nuovo** (or **Nero**), rebuilt in 1579 by Vittoria, the **Casa Mocenigo Vecchia**, re-modelled in the 18th century but with a Gothic base; and a double-fronted facade known jointly as the **Palazzo Mocenigo**. In the 1690s the Casa Vecchia saw the betrayal to the Inquisition of the philosopher Giordano Bruno, whose ghost is said to haunt the palace seeking revenge on the host who denounced him. The Palazzo Nuovo's most tempestuous guest was Byron who not only wrote part of *Don Juan* there but conducted a heated love affair with a Venetian lady who attacked the poet with a knife and was thrown into the Grand Canal for her pains. The less controversial side of Byron's visit is marked by a plaque on the facade of the *palazzo*.

The next leg of the water-bus route, from S. Tomà to Ca' Rezzonico, takes us round the Volta and past the magnificent sequence of *palazzi* situated on the right bank within the bend. These cluster around the wide outlet of the **Rio Ca' Foscari** which links up with the Rio Nuovo to provide a short cut through to the Piazzale Roma. On the right-hand side of the Rio is the **Palazzo Balbi**, built in the 1580s by Alessandro Vittoria who designed the Scala d'Oro in the Doge's Palace. Considering that it is a Renaissance building it is a precursor of baroque styles with a rusticated ground floor facade, elaborate window decorations, coats of arms on the facade and two obelisks on the roof. The building is now the administrative headquarters of the Veneto region. In the 1950s there was a plan to put up an adjoining building designed in aggressively modern style by Frank Lloyd Wright, but a concerted resistance campaign, already alarmed by modern extensions to the Danieli and Bauer Grunwald Hotels, succeeded in having planning permission refused.

Across the mouth of the Rio is a group of three buildings which seem to merge into a triple facade since all three are in late Gothic style with second floor loggias modelled on that of the Doge's Palace. The first of the three is the oldest, tallest and biggest. This is **Ca' Foscari**, built in 1434 for Doge Francesco Foscari, who was doge for 34 years, pushed the mainland possessions of Venice to their widest extent, guided Venice after the fall of Constantinople to the Turks and built the Porta della Carta. He was finally forced to abdicate in 1457, to die of a broken heart a few weeks later. When it was built, the Ca' Foscari was the largest private house in Venice and, after the Doge's Palace, one of the finest examples of secular Gothic architecture. It is now part of the University. Adjoining the Ca' Foscari and making an *ensemble* of buildings is the double **Palazzo Giustinian**. Also late Gothic, from the second half of the 15th century, this was built for two brothers who wanted adjacent but separate houses. The original architect was Bartolomeo Bon. One of the house's most distinguished residents was Wagner who wrote the second act of *Tristan und Isolde* here. It too is now a central part of the university.

After a couple of less prominent houses the water-bus comes in to the landing stage alongside the **Ca' Rezzonico**. This is a 17th-century house, begun by Longhena and very similar to his Ca' Pesaro. The ambitious project was commissioned by the Bon family but their money ran out before the building was complete and it remained unfinished until 1750 when the house was sold to the Rezzonico family, an up and coming group of immigrants from Genoa, who not only had the money to buy their way into the Venetian nobility but could afford Massari to finish off their *palazzo* and add a second *piano nobile*, a ballroom and a grand staircase not envisaged by Longhena. The Rezzonico family died out in 1810 and the house passed through various hands including the Browning family: the poet Robert Browning died here in 1889. When the building was acquired by the Commune in 1935 it was completely empty except for the ballroom chandeliers, two statues of the sculptor Vittoria and a bureau.

The Ca' Rezzonico now houses the **Museo del Settecento veneziano** (Museum of 18th Century Venetian Life). (*Entry L5000. Open 10.00–16.00 daily except Fridays. Sundays 9.00–12.00.*) Inside, the palace has been restored to give an idealised picture of a patrician household in the 18th century.

One of the great *palazzi* of the Grand Canal, the Ca' Rezzonico now houses the Museum of 18th-century Venetian life.

Most of the rooms have been beautifully set up with some magnificent furnishings. Notable among the paintings are the only two views of the Grand Canal by Canaletto that remain in Venice. On the top floor is a reconstructed apothecary's shop of the 17th century, *Ai do San Marchi*. In the room beyond this is a puppet theatre with costumes and paintings that illustrate the themes and characters of the *Commedia dell'Arte*.

The Final Curve — Ca' Rezzonico to San Marco

Across the Canal is the bulk of the **Palazzo Grassi**, built in 1748 by Massari who was simultaneously completing the Ca' Rezzonico opposite. It had been commissioned by a rich Bolognese family who admired the Ca' Rezzonico and wanted to live in a *palazzo* that mirrored the style of the older building in many ways. Like the Genoese Rezzonico family, the

Bolognese Grassi bought their way into the nobility by making a substantial contribution to the Turkish War of 1718. In 1984 the *palazzo* was bought by the Agnelli family, owners of the FIAT car company, and it has been turned into a cultural centre which stages some of the glossiest and most prestigious exhibitions seen in Venice. The open space immediately after the Palazzo Grassi is the Campo S. Samuele which has a water-bus landing stage used by the Number 2 service. Visible on the *campo* is the 12th-century **Campanile di San Samuele**. Just before the next canal there is a building, the lower portion of which represents an unfinished Gothic *palazzo*, commissioned by the Corner family from Bartolomeo Bon, but left incomplete in 1461 when it was sold to Francesco Sforza, Duke of Milan, after whom it is named **Ca' del Duca**. Across the *rio* is the 15th-century **Palazzetto Falier** which is chiefly distinguished for the two roofed loggias projecting from the facade. Such covered balconies, known by the dialect word *liagò*, were once a feature of Venetian architecture and were to be found everywhere in the city. Nowadays most of them have disappeared.

Opposite the Ca' del Duca on the right bank is the **Palazzo Loredan dell'Ambasciatore**, so called because it was the residence of the Austrian Ambassador between 1574 and 1797. It is a 15th-century building, chiefly notable for the statues of two pages that are believed to be the work of the Rizzo studio. It has a plain brick facade that anticipates the change from Gothic to Renaissance style. Across the Rio S. Trovaso is the double *palazzo* made up of the **Palazzo Contarini-Corfù** and the **Palazzo Contarini degli Scrigni**. The former was built first, in the 15th century, presumably for a branch of the Contarini that held lands or offices in Corfu, while the latter was built as an extension to the first in 1609 by Scamozzi, who did not quite manage a harmonious marriage of styles between his work and the earlier Gothic building.

The *vaporetto* now stops at the Accademia landing stage. The **Accademia Bridge** was the second bridge to be built across the Grand Canal, erected in 1854 by the Austrians. That bridge, like the original Scalzi Bridge, was an iron construction too low for the *vaporetti* to get beneath, as can be seen from the historic picture postcards that are still sold at Venetian news stands. In 1933 the iron bridge was replaced by a single-arch wooden construction intended as a temporary measure but the temporary seems to have become permanent because the wooden bridge remains, despite having been restored and virtually rebuilt on several occasions.

The right bank end of the bridge, near the *vaporetto* stop, is set in a square known as the **Campo della Carità**. The 18th-century brick facade facing the Canal, designed by Massari, belongs to the **Scuola della Carità**, while the adjacent church is **Santa Maria della Carità**. These two buildings, together with the former convent of the same name, now form part of the **Accademia** (see page 221). On the opposite bank of the Canal the end of the bridge is situated in the **Campo San Vitale**, one of the most attractive and colourful open spaces along the Grand Canal, with houses brightly colour-washed in red and yellow and with the **Campanile di San Vidal** rising over the trees that flourish here. The large *palazzo* at the foot of the bridge is the **Palazzo Franchetti**, originally a 15th-century construction, but heavily (and heavy-handedly) restored in the last century.

As the *vaporetto* pulls away from the landing stage, under the bridge, and moves across the canal towards S. Maria del Giglio you can see the Palazzo Franchetti more clearly with, beyond it, on the other side of a *rio*, the twin buildings of the **Palazzo Barbaro**. The houses were built in the early 15th and late 17th centuries but the two have been better blended than was the case with the similar Contarini *palazzi* on the other side of the Canal. Owned by the Curtis family, the older of the two houses had the most prestigious guest list of any 19th century Venetian home. Whistler, Sargent and Monet were among the painters, and Robert Browning and Henry James among the writers, who stayed here as the family's guests. James wrote *The Aspern Papers* while staying here and used the house as a setting for *The Wings of a Dove*.

On the other bank of the Canal, the first building after the Accademia is the **Palazzo Contarini-Polignac** (also known as **Dal Zaffo** from the family's estates in Jaffa). The facade, which was added to an earlier Gothic house in the 15th century, represents a transitional phase between the late-Gothic work of Lombardo and the early-Renaissance style of Coducci. A little further on, on the corner of the Campo S. Vio, is the **Palazzo Loredan,** now the **Galleria di Palazzo Cini**. (*Open May to October. 14.00–19.00 weekdays except Mon. Entry L4000.*) Only a small part of the building, on the first floor, is given over to an art gallery but it contains about fifty paintings of the

Tuscan School from the 13th to 16th centuries, including important works by Della Francesca, Filippo Lippi and Botticelli.

The next building of interest on this right bank is white, single-storeyed and strangely reminiscent of a flat-roofed bungalow of the 1920s or 30s, raised on a high platform above canal level. This is the **Palazzo Venier dei Leoni**, so called because of the row of lions' heads near the water. It was intended to be the largest house on the Grand Canal when it was begun in 1749 but only the first storey had been built when building work was stopped. Most probably this halt, which resulted in the alternative name of **Palazzo Non Finito**, was because the owner ran out of money but rumour has it that the Corner family, whose house was opposite, had construction stopped rather than have their view spoiled by a house bigger than their own. It was the home of Peggy Guggenheim from 1949 until her death in 1979 and houses the **Guggenheim Collection** (see page 222).

The Corner house in question is the large *palazzo* on the left bank as the boat comes in towards the landing stage. The **Palazzo Corner del Ca' Grande** (Big House) was built by Sansovino in 1545. The style adopted for this building had a great influence on Longhena who used it as his model for the Ca' Pesaro and Ca' Rezzonico. It is now the **Prefecture**. From the S. Maria del Giglio landing stage a *calle* runs back to the *campo* of that name but the wider outlet to the canal is one block further on in the **Campo Traghetto** where the gondola-ferry is located. Looking down this *campo* one can glimpse a side view of the **Church of Santa Maria del Giglio** (see page 218). The much-restored 15th-century Gothic building on the far side of the *campo* is the **Palazzo Pisani**, now the Gritti Palace Hotel, with a terraced restaurant projecting into the Canal.

We are now approaching the end of the Grand Canal and the right bank is very much dominated by the domes of **Santa Maria della Salute**. Of the group of *palazzi* on the right bank between the Guggenheim Collection and the Salute, the most attractive is the **Palazzo Dario**, a very pretty building erected in 1487, and characterised by its huge Venetian chimneys. The facade is in multi-coloured marble, possibly by Pietro Lombardo. The interesting point about the Palazzo Dario is that it was not the property of one of the patrician families who had a virtual monopoly on the Grand Canal. Instead it was built for Giovanni Dario, a secretary to the Chancery and a member of the middle class. The building with the garish mosaics a little further on is the **Palazzo Salviati**, erected by the Salviati glass company as recently as 1924. The final buildings before the church are the remains of the former **Abbey of St Gregory**. Then the water-bus draws up by the marble pavement in front of the **Church of the Salute** (see page 223). From here a *fondamenta* leads on to the tip of the Canal at **Punta della Dogana** (see page 225).

The water-bus crosses the Grand Canal for the last time. Opposite the Salute landing stage is the 15th-century **Palazzo Contarini-Fasan**, popularly known as 'Desdemona's House' though that is about as realistic as 'Juliet's Balcony' in Verona. There is an interesting patterning of wheels or star-fish on the balconies. Most of the remaining buildings on this left bank are now hotels. There is just the **Palazzo Giustinian** which, since it faces the very tip of the Punta della Dogana, could well be counted as the last *palazzo* of the Canal. A 15th-century building it was Venice's premier hotel in the last century with major figures such as Verdi and Ruskin among its guests. Now it is the headquarters of the Biennale and where you should go for information about either the Art or Film Festivals. Shortly after this the *vaporetto* reaches the S. Marco landing stage at the foot of the Calle Vallaresso, between the Hotel Monaco and Harry's Bar.

Vaporetto Route Number 5 — Circolare Sinistra

The circular route around the historic centre is not as continuously interesting nor as attractive as the route along the Grand Canal, but you do get to visit the neighbouring islands and you penetrate parts of Venice that are otherwise closed to the public. Of the two possible directions taken by these water-buses the anti-clockwise route is described below because this way you enter the Arsenal by means of the main water-gate. But you can take the *circolare destra* or clockwise route and see exactly the same things in reverse order. The time taken for the complete tour comprises about 50 minutes from the Piazzale Roma to Murano and 50 minutes from Murano to the railway station. During the summer months beware that you do not get confused by the smaller *motoscafi* operating the number 5 *barrato* services between Murano and either Tronchetto or S. Zaccaria. The official starting and stopping place for the number 5 is Murano but, as with the journey along the Grand Canal described above, I choose to start at Piazzale Roma.

Through the Commercial Port — Piazzale Roma to Giudecca Canal

At Piazzale Roma the water-bus you want comes in from the railway station to your right. On the *fondamenta* in front of the Piazzale Roma, between the landing stage and the turn into the Santa Chiara Canal, is a group of five buildings. These are the **Magazzini Parisi**, a line of five neo-classical frontages with three windows in the upper storey of each, linked by a single ground floor facade with a doorway flanked by two windows in each building and a portal between each building. Three of these were built around 1850 to house small industries such as a brewery and a manufacturer of imitation pearls. The two matching buildings were added in the early years of the present century by the transport company, *Parisi*. All five act as warehouses and distribution centres for goods brought into Venice.

The water-bus turns left into the S. Chiara Canal under the road bridge carrying traffic into Piazzale Roma. In the last century the left hand bank, along the rear of the Piazzale Roma, was the north-western tip of historic Venice. Everything on the right hand side, apart from the small island of S. Chiara, with its Hospital of the same name, has since been reclaimed from the Lagoon. The canal runs wide and straight under a footbridge, with a dismal industrial landscape on either side. Before a second bridge carrying road and rail over the canal, the Canal di Santa Maria Maggiore bears off to the left: again this was the original shore line of the historic city. For the next 750 metres the land on both sides is reclaimed from the Lagoon and forms the **Stazione Marittima**, the commercial port, built up between the 1860s and the 1920s. The embankment on the right is one of two arms enclosing a deep-water dock 140,000 square metres in extent, where merchant ships and oil tankers berth, although today most of the traffic has moved to Marghera. The embankment on the left, where the water-bus stops at S. Marta, is an area of warehouses and offices, with a motor-road and railway heading for the Maritime Station passenger terminal. It is all fairly monotonous but finally the *vaporetto* emerges into the Lagoon, with the Giudecca Canal opening up to the left.

The water-bus heads out into a Lagoon dotted by a number of low, marshy islands and makes for one island which has been built on reclaimed land only in the present century. This is **Sacco Fissola**. There is nothing of interest to the visitor here; only uninspired modern flats and houses. From here the boat crosses the Giudecca Canal to the Dorsoduro side to stop first at S. Basilio and then at Zattere. This section of the Dorsoduro frontage was the passenger terminal in the great days of ocean liners and cruise ships, when passengers were brought by rail to the Maritime Station. Here also is the large headquarters of the *Adriatica Navigazione* shipping company. You may still see the occasional Yugoslav or Greek passenger or cruise ship alongside the quay near the Maritime Station. However, during this first stretch along the Giudecca Canal your eyes tend to be drawn away from the shipping and towards the huge anomaly which dominates this western end of Giudecca, the **Mulino Stucky**.

Mostly Giudecca: Zattere to San Giorgio Maggiore

Large mills for grinding corn were built by Giovanni Stucky in 1883. In 1895 Stucky wished to expand the business and employed a German architect, Ernst Wullekopf from Hanover, to design the new mill. The result was a design that was totally alien to Italy, let alone to Venice. It looks like nothing so much as the great textile mills of northern England, with a few neo-Gothic, Pugin-like pinnacles to allow the Italians to say it reminds them of the British Houses of Parliament. Stucky was originally refused planning permission to build what the commune felt was an eyesore, but overcame the difficulty by threatening to sack all his workers. Permission was immediately granted and the building was put up in less than a year. Stucky, an immensely wealthy man, was for a short time owner of the Palazzo Grassi on the Grand Canal but he was murdered by one of his employees in 1910 and the mills went into a decline, hastened by industrial developments in Marghera. The building has been empty since 1954 and is falling into ruin, since no one can agree over what to do with it, although plans have been put forward ranging from conversion into housing to the creation of a new cultural centre.

Two three-masted sailing ships flying the red ensign, tied up on Zattere with the church of the Redentore in the background.

Leaving the Zattere landing stage the water-bus practically turns around in its tracks so that it can approach the next landing stage from the right direction. This, the first of three landfalls on the island of Giudecca, is, like the others, directly in front of a church. **Sant'Eufamia** is a small church established here since the 9th century but altered so many times that it has become a mosaic of different styles and periods. The interior is constructed as a basilica without transept, with some columns dating from the 11th century, but decorated in baroque style. The facade is late 16th-century but, apart from that, there is little of interest. In the vicinity is the **Fortuny Factory**, where they still turn out the luxury fabrics designed by Fortuny himself, for sale in the more expensive Venice shops.

The boat moves along Giudecca to the principal monument on the island, the Franciscan **Church of the Redentore**, designed by Palladio to answer the city's pledge that they would build a church in thanks for deliverance from the plague in 1577. The domed church with its classical facade seems to rise directly out of the water and is ideally placed for the annual *Festa del Redentore* when a bridge of boats is built across the Giudecca Canal, leading directly into the doorway of the church. The interior is judged to be Palladio's master-work in applying the architecture of Ancient Rome to the needs of his time. Sadly the interior has been neglected, cluttered up with over-sentimentalised religious statuary and is, in any case, only partially open to the public. Perhaps it is best to reserve your sightseeing to the exterior. The next stop, the last on Giudecca, is in front of another church planned by Palladio, but built after his death, between 1582 and 1586. This is the **Church of Le Zitelle**. The adjacent building was a hostel belonging to a convent in which young girls were taught an extremely fine form of lace-making. To the right of the church is the **Casa de Maria** built in extravagant neo-Gothic style by an artist in 1910. The multi-coloured brick facing is modelled on the facade of the Doge's Palace. Close to Zitelle is the Venice Youth Hostel.

If you have the time to spare, it is worth leaving the boat at Redentore and walking along the *fondamenta* to Zitelle. The views across to Zattere and Dorsoduro are fine and, of course, the nearer you get to Zitelle the more the view of St Mark's Basin opens up to reveal the Molo, Doge's Palace and the sweep of the Riva degli Schiavoni. Closer at hand on the point of Dorsoduro are the domes of the Salute and the golden globe on the Punta della Dogana. The low plain building in front of the Salute, with ten doorways surmounted by ten lunette windows, is the old **Salt Warehouse** which has stood on this site since the 14th century when Venice began to replace the salt produced in the Lagoon with salt imported from Dalmatia.

Giudecca, whatever the season, manages to be relatively free of tourists and day-trippers. One unusual aspect of Giudecca is that, while there is a more or less continuous *fondamenta* along the Giudecca Canal, there is only one public access to the south side of the island and the view over the Lagoon towards the

Lido, which is reached by following the Calle Michelangelo from near Zitelle. To the left, at the eastern end of the island is the most expensive hotel in Venice, the Cipriani. One feature you will notice when wandering about in Giudecca, is the number of gardens on the island, including the largest private garden in Venice, the **Garden of Eden**, not named after the home of Adam and Eve but after an Englishman, Mr Eden, who designed it.

From Zitelle the water-bus makes the short journey to the next small island, **San Giorgio Maggiore**. The *vaporetto* landing stage is on the edge of the pavement before the facade of the church. There has been a monastery on the island since the earliest times and a church dedicated to St George since the 10th century. The present church was begun by Palladio in 1566 and finished, by Sorella, in 1610. The beautiful *ensemble* of white classical facade, low grey dome, green-spired campanile and red-brick buildings combine with the view seen from the Piazzetta to make the church the best-known in Venice after St Mark's.

The facade shows how Palladio reconciled classical design with the high nave and lower aisles pattern of church architecture that had no precedent in classical times. The interior is notable for the rich-white and plain simplicity of its stucco decoration. There are many paintings in the interior from the Tintoretto workshop but the church's prized possession is Tintoretto's finest work, *The Last Supper*. This painting is paired with *Manna from Heaven* as instruction in the meaning of the Eucharist. Both were painted in the last two years of the artist's life. Also worth inspection are the carvings on the choir stalls. From within the church access can be gained to the Campanile, rebuilt in 1791 by Benedetto Buratti on the pattern of the Campanile of St Mark's, after the original S. Giorgio Campanile had fallen down. Today this campanile offers a cheaper and less-crowded alternative to the S. Marco Campanile; with no less spectacular views. (*Open every day 10.00–12.30 and 14.30 to sunset. Entry L2000.*)

The rest of the island is occupied by the former **Benedictine Monastery of S. Giorgio Maggiore**, owned and administered by the **Fondazione Giorgio Cini**. Count Vittorio Cini, who acquired the buildings in 1951, set up the Trust in memory of his son Giorgio who was killed in 1949. There are several schools and academic bodies within the Foundation but they are also responsible for a number of learned and prestigious exhibitions, during which the buildings are open to the public. The most famous episode in the life of the monastery came in 1799–1800 when the Pope had been expelled from Rome by Napoleon and the Cardinals met here in the Conclave that elected Pope Pius VII. Within the buildings the more remarkable features are a cloister and refectory by Palladio and a staircase and library by Longhena. The grounds of the monastery include an open-air theatre, the Teatro Verde, a swimming-pool and a miniature harbour, now a marina.

Through the Arsenal — San Giorgio Maggiore to Celestia

Crossing St Mark's Basin from S. Giorgio Maggiore there is a superb view of the Mint, Doge's Palace and Piazzetta. Then comes the landing stage of S. Zaccaria in front of the **Danieli Hotel**. This De Luxe category hotel has been open since 1822 and has welcomed many famous guests. The main building is the Gothic Palazzo Dandolo and the original courtyard and arcaded staircase are still visible in the hotel's foyer. Long before it became a hotel one of the earliest operas, Monteverdi's *Prosperina Rapita*, had its first performance here. The modern annexe was built in the 1950s and makes one wish that the ban on buildings on this site, which had existed since the 12th century, had continued a little longer.

From S. Zaccaria the water-bus runs east parallel to the **Riva degli Schiavoni**. The word '*schiavoni*' means both 'slaves' and 'Slavs' in Italian because, to the Roman and early Venetian worlds, the Slav peoples of the Balkans provided most of the raw material for the slave markets. The *riva* bearing their name therefore probably began as the quay where slaves were off-loaded. Later it became associated with the Dalmatian coast trade and the area behind the Riva became the Greek and Dalmatian quarter of the city. Along the Riva most of the *palazzi* have long since become hotels, and a number of plaques recall the distinguished visitors who have stayed along this waterfront, beginning with Petrarch in the 14th century. Ruskin was here, as he was everywhere in Venice, and so was Henry James, struggling to finish *The Portrait of a Lady*. Other famous artists commemorated are Wagner, Tchaikovsky, Dickens, Proust and George Sand. Almost out of place among the writers and musicians is a plaque to the physicist Doppler, of the *Doppler Effect*.

What happened to Petrarch's Books?
Just over the bridge next to the Pietà on the Riva degli Schiavoni is a large house (no. 4145) on which a plaque records a stay here between 1362 and 1367 of the poet Petrarch. With his daughter and her family Petrarch was seeking to escape the plague that had broken out in Padua. In return for their hospitality the poet promised the Republic that they could have his library of books. The bargain was struck and Petrarch was given the Palazzo dei Due Torri where he and his family lived for the next five years. Then, in 1367, a group of young Venetians insulted the poet, calling him an illiterate old fool and Petrarch left the city in a huff, never to return.

But what happened to his books? A room was set aside in St Mark's where the books could be kept but, when the Biblioteca Marciana was established a century later no trace could be found of Petrarch's library. Did he withdraw his part of the bargain in a reprisal for the insult offered? Or were the books handed over but then hidden away and forgotten by authorities who did not recognise their value?

On the Riva close to the Zaccaria landing stage stands a massive equestrian statue, built by Ettore Ferrari in 1887 as a monument to the unification of Italy, which makes Victor Emmanuel II look twice as heroic as he ever was. Further along, the white stone facade of **Santa Maria della Visitazione** stands out from the secular buildings along the waterfront. More commonly known as the **La Pietà**, after the orphanage whose church it was, the church has recently been renovated and is used as a concert-hall, particularly for the music of the man inevitably associated with the Pietà, Vivaldi. Vivaldi was violin-master, and later choir-master, to the Orphanage of the Pietà and most of his finest work was written here, either for the orchestra or choir of the orphanage girls. But Vivaldi would not have seen the present church which was rebuilt in 1745 by Massari, while the facade was added in 1906. The interior, only open during concerts, is white and gold baroque, with ceiling paintings by Tiepolo.

At the third *rio* after the Pietà, the *vaporetto* turns into the Rio dell'Arsenale and stops at the Tana landing stage, directly in front of the **Museo Storico Navale** (see page 241). As the boat continues you can see ahead, beyond a cantilevered wooden footbridge, the two brick towers, the **Torri dell'Arsenale**, that guard the water-gate entry to the **Arsenal**.

The word '*Arsenal*' comes from the Arabic '*darsina'a*' or 'workplace', a word that also gives Italian the word '*Darsena*' (a dock or harbour). The **Arsenal** was founded in 1104 around the basin that is now called the **Darsena Vecchia** and, by the end of the century, had a monopoly on the construction of galleys. Over the centuries boat-builders from all over the city were encouraged to move into the area, until the Arsenal covered even more ground than the 32 hectares (80 acres) it occupies today, the whole surrounded by a high, battlemented wall set with towers. The wall was not only to protect the ships but to keep prying eyes away from the methods used by the Arsenal, since the skill and speed of Venetian shipwrights was envied throughout the known world: a prototype of assembly-line and prefabricated production. One famous example of its industry relates to the visit of Henry III of France in the 16th century. Shown the keel of a war-galley laid down in the morning the French king retired to a state banquet with the Doge and Signoria, at the end of which the royal guest returned to the Arsenal to see the finished galley launched.

Although ships have not been built in the Arsenal since 1917 the area still belongs to the Italian Navy and the public are not admitted (although plans are always being announced for new non-military uses for the Arsenal space and buildings). The only way to see within the walls is on the *vaporetto* which moves through the water-gate into the **Darsena Arsenale Vecchia**. First constructed in the 12th century, this was where ships were fitted out for their voyages. Among the buildings that surround the basin the most distinguished is the boathouse for the *Bucintoro* state barge, built by Sanmicheli in 1544. Adjacent, on the right hand side, is the entrance to the immense inner basin, the **Darsena Grande**. Around this dock area, known as the 'New Docks', built in 1450, are the more prestigious buildings, only glimpsed from the boat, such as the rope-works or **Tana**, built by Da Ponte, architect of the Rialto Bridge, and the boatsheds built by Sansovino which have elegant arched colonnades and are known as the **Gaggiandre**.

The water-bus continues under a bridge into the **Canale della Galleazze**, whose quays were constructed in 1569, and then exits through another water-gate into the open spaces of the

Northern Lagoon. Out in the Lagoon can be seen the walled cemetery island of **San Michele** with the spread of **Murano** beyond. Turning west the *vaporetto* makes for the first landing stage on this north side, Celestia. Considering that the name means 'heavenly', there is little to recommend the area around Celestia. There is an old backwater of a canal, narrow washing-hung alleys and even the remains of the old gas-works, all dominated by the menacing wall of the Arsenal. Yet it might be worth breaking your journey here in order to see the otherwise remote church of **San Francesco della Vigna**.

Built on the site of a vineyard (hence the name) this church of the Franciscans also stands on the site where, according to Venetian mythology, St Mark had the vision that told him his bones would be laid to rest in Venice. Site of a church since 1250, the present structure was built by Sansovino in 1534, although the facade in Istrian stone was added by Palladio in 1568, one of the few examples of Palladio's work in Venice proper. The church was paid for by patrician families purchasing private chapels in the church and here you will find chapels for the Contarini, Badoer, Barbaro and Giustiniani families. Sculpture and paintings in the church by Vivarini, Vittoria, the Lombardo family and Veronese are somewhat hard to see in the dim light of the interior. The campanile belonging to the church is modelled on that of St Mark's and is one of the tallest in the city. The cloisters linking the church to the old monastery are a delight.

Out into the Lagoon — S. Michele and Murano

Continuing westwards the *vaporetto* begins to run alongside the **Fondamenta Nuove**, a quayside that runs absolutely straight for the best part of a kilometre, defining the northern edge of the islands where once it had been marshy reed beds. The first stop along this stretch is that for **Ospedale Civile**, the main hospital of Venice, the many buildings of which occupy the entire space between here and the Campo SS. Giovanni e Paolo. The *vaporetto* then moves on to the main landing stage of this north side, Fondamenta Nuove, and, after a short stop, turns north and heads out into the lagoon.

The island of **San Michele** is only 400 metres from the Fondamenta Nuove and is itself little more than 400 by 300 metres in size, a straight-sided rectangle thanks to the high brick wall that virtually surrounds it. It has housed a religious community since the 10th century, although there was a period of about 20 years in the early 19th century when the monastery was suppressed and the island acted as a detention centre for political prisoners. Ever since Napoleon forbade any further burials in Venice proper it has been the principal cemetery for the city.

The *vaporetto* stop, Cimitero, is at the far end of the western side, close to where the wall is breached by the monastery buildings, the church of **S.Michele in Isola** and the tiny **Cappella Emiliana**. The church is a gem of the early Renaissance in Venice, designed by Coducci in 1469 and the first building to have a facade faced with the white Istrian stone that had previously been used solely for damp-courses. It was almost a century before another church had an Istrian stone facade (S. Francesco della Vigna) but Coducci's use of the material set a fashion that led to the majority of later *palazzi* being faced with the stone. The adjacent chapel, in marble, is high Renaissance in contrast. It was designed by Dei Grigi in 1530 and is hexagonal with an onion dome. It is rather attractive but Ruskin thought it looked like a bee-hive. The campanile behind the chapel was built in 1460.

The cemetery can be reached through the cloisters (*open 9.00–16.00*) where you can also obtain a plan of the cemetery. For the average Venetian this is hardly a final resting-place since demand for space ensures that a body remains buried for just ten years, after which the bones are dug up and consigned to an ossuary: the vacant space re-used. The exceptions to this are the graves of the famous. In the protestant section can be found the graves of the composer Wolf Ferrari and the American poet Ezra Pound. In the Orthodox cemetery lies the Russian impressario, Diaghelev. Close at hand is the grave of the cemetery's most famous occupant, the composer who made his name under the patronage of Diaghelev, Igor Stravinsky. The great composer died in New York but was granted the honour of a funeral in SS. Giovanni e Paolo and a resting-place here. His wife is buried beside him. Compare the simplicity of their tombs with that of Diaghelev. Also buried here is that eccentric and idiosyncratic writer, Frederick Rolfe (Baron Corvo).

From S. Michele the water-bus continues a further half kilometre to the island of **Murano**. Murano was settled like the other islands of the Lagoon at the time of the barbarian invasions and, until the year 1000, had an independent existence with its own government. Later the island was used as a sort of summer home for Venetian patricians who wanted more space and gardens than was available as Venice became increasingly built up. As a result there are many *palazzi* on the island, as well as a number of well-endowed churches. In 1292, the glass-blowers of Venice were banished by the fire-conscious Commune of Venice and from that date glass has dominated the economy of Murano. Here you can see glass being made in the workshops, displayed in the museum and sold in the shops.

Murano is not one island but consists of five islets, separated by canals, like Venice itself; it even has its own Grand Canal, the **Canal Grande di Murano**, which divides the main heart-shaped islet from the rest. The *vaporetto* makes a circuit of Murano using this Grand Canal but the first landing stage at the southern tip of the main island is Colonna, adjacent to the Rio dei Vetrai, which runs across the island through the heart of the glass-making district.

If you wish to break your journey to see Murano, you should leave the water-bus at Colonna. This places you at the start of the *fondamenta* alongside the Rio dei Vetrai which, as the name suggests, is lined with glass-makers from end to end.If you like Venetian glass you will have a field day here. (*If, for the moment, you want to carry on with your circular tour but return to Murano later, you are advised to use the* vaporetto *or* motoscafo *services rather than join one of the organised 'Visit the Islands' tours.*) Walking along the Fondamenta dei Vetrai you will find glass-makers and shops on both sides of the canal. There are many specialities involved; glass sculpture, cut glass or crystal, mosaic tesserae, etc. The further away from the tourist traps of the landing stage area that you can get, the more likely you are to find a bargain or nicer small item; so try a few side-alleys. Most of the workshops will admit visitors to see the process of blowing and working the glass. There is no charge for this.

Near the far end of the Fondamenta dei Vetrai you come to the church of **S. Pietro Martire**, a 14th-century building, rebuilt in 1470. It contains a nice painting by Giovanni Bellini and two by Veronese but they are very badly lit. Immediately past the church you come to the Grand Canal and the only bridge across it, the **Ponte Vivarini**. Close to the bridge is a restored *palazzo*, the Gothic **Palazzo Da Mula**. Cross the bridge and turn right along the Fondamenta Cavour, continuing as far as the Museo landing stage and turning up the Canale S. Donato along the Fondamenta Giustinian. In a short distance you come to a former *palazzo* of the Giustiniani family, since 1861 the **Museo Vetrario**. (*The Glass Museum is open every day except Wednesday from 10.00 until 16.00. On public holidays the hours are from 9.00 to 12.30. Entrance L3000, but keep hold of your ticket because there is a second section you are entitled to visit for the same money.*) The museum was re-organised in 1979 and is now beautifully laid out to display examples of glassware from Roman times up to the 19th century. The prize of the collection is the **Coppa Barovier**, a 15th-century cup in blue glass with inset polychrome enamels. In 1984 a second section of the museum was opened to house 20th-century glass, including contemporary submissions by the major workshops. Currently this '**Museo 2**' is housed on the Fondamenta Manin bank of the Rio dei Vetrai.

On leaving the Glass Museum look across the canal to where there is another summer *palazzo*, this being the **Palazzo Trevisan**, claimed to be by Palladio. Continue up the Fondamenta Giustinian to see a building that will repay the trip to Murano even for people not interested in glass. This is the Byzantine church of **Santi Maria e Donato**, founded in the 7th century, although the present building dates from the 12th. See the Veneto-Byzantine apse with its decorated arches supported by twin columns to form an arcade at ground level topped by a first floor loggia. The glory of the church is, however, the 12th-century mosaics covering the floor and beautifully restored in 1977. A guide to the mosaics is available in the church, the proceeds of which go towards further restoration work. The Virgin gained her co-patron to the church in 1125 when the bones of St Donatus were brought back from Cephalonia. Among the good deeds done by Donatus was his ability to kill dragons by spitting on them. And if you do not believe it, the bones of a dragon killed in this way hang over the altar.

Final Stage — Murano to Ferrovia and the Ghetto

Whether you have broken your journey or not, the *vaporetto* now heads back across the Lagoon towards the historic centre, with interesting views of the city as you approach it. The first stop is at the point where we left for our visit to the islands, the Fondamenta Nuove. The route is then resumed westwards, past the end of the Fondamenta, and the large inlet in front of the **Misericordia**, to reach the landing stage in front of the church of **Madonna dell'Orto**, the campanile of which is easily visible as the *vaporetto* returns from Murano, since the church stands at virtually the northernmost point of the historic centre. Built in 1350 it is named after a statue of the Madonna, with miraculous powers, which was discovered in a nearby orchard (*orto*). It was the parish church of Tintoretto, who is buried here, and, not surprisingly, is rich in his paintings. The church was restored quite disastrously in the mid-19th century but rather more successfully, by the British Venice in Peril team, after 1966. If you should happen to break your journey at one of these northern landing stages note that they are unmanned. Be sure that you get a ticket from somewhere before you rejoin the boat or you will otherwise have to pay a L500 surcharge.

This final stretch of the northern shore, as you round the top of the islands and the road and rail causeway come into sight, is fairly bleak. Much of the land at the edge of the Lagoon is reclaimed, with comparatively recent housing on it. These northern districts are residential, largely working-class, areas. Here, the water-bus route bears left into the **Canale Cannaregio**, the second largest canal within the historic centre. Before the road and rail links were built this was the main entrance to the city for traffic from the northern Lagoon and adjacent mainland. To your right as you enter the canal is the **Macello Generale**, the former municipal slaughter-house, set up under the Austrians and built in 1843 by the architect Giuseppe Salvadori, in a simple neo-classical style. There was a movement a few years ago to demolish the buildings and Le Corbusier had designed a modern hospital to be built on the site. But there was an outcry from those who feel that the buildings represent a valuable monument to Venice's industrial past and one of the few examples of good 19th-century architecture in the city. While its fate is being decided the site is used by a rowing club.

The first water-bus stop on the Cannaregio Canal, Ponte Tre Archi, just before the bridge of the same name, commemorates the only multi-span bridge in a city of single-span bridges. Mostly the buildings lining the canal are nondescript but, as you near the junction with the Grand Canal, a few larger *palazzi* appear. On the left, just past the Ponte Tre Archi, is the **Palazzo Surian**, once the French Embassy and scene of the

Venetian adventures of Jean-Jacques Rousseau. Further down on the opposite side is the large 16th-century **Palazzo Savorgnan**. The water-bus stop just short of the **Ponte delle Guglie** gives onto a quayside lined with market stalls selling all kinds of fresh fish. Under the bridge the canal is dominated by the **Palazzo Labia** and **Campanile di S. Geremia** (see page 186). Then, with a loud blast on its horn to warn oncoming traffic, the water-bus swings right into the Grand Canal and makes for the Ferrovia landing stage, having completed its circumnavigation of the historic centre.

You might find it convenient to leave the water-bus at Ponte delle Guglie in order to visit the **Ghetto** by taking the first right turn into the Calle del Ghetto Nuovo.

'Ghetto' comes from the Italian word for a 'foundry', and a foundry was situated on the island now known as the **Ghetto Nuovo** before moving to the Arsenal in the 14th century. In 1516 a new law required all the Jews in Venice, most of whom lived on Giudecca, to move into the area of the Ghetto into which they were confined at night by locking gates. This was a new move for the normally tolerant Venetians and was associated with other regulations such as restrictions on the professions allowed to Jews. Despite this, the Venetians are accounted more tolerant than most other European countries. That remained true down to the present century when no move was made against the Jews in twenty years of fascist government, until the Germans took over in 1943 after the Italian Armistice. At its peak the Jewish population in Venice topped 5,000 and this pressure of population led to the area of the Ghetto being twice extended, to the **Ghetto Vecchio** in 1541 and to the **Ghetto Nuovissimo** in 1633. Nevertheless, the overcrowding gave rise to the unique appearance of the Ghetto today because, thanks to a law forbidding Jewish houses to be above a certain height, the need arose to cram in as many low storeys as possible. The buildings in the Ghetto tend to be the 'high-rise' blocks of their time, with up to seven floors in each house. Another architectural curiosity because of the laws binding the Jews is the appearance of the synagogues. Since no Jew was allowed to be an architect the synagogues had to be designed by Christians and have a most un-Jewish appearance.

The Calle del Ghetto Vecchio leads into the Campiello delle Scuole with two synagogues, the **Scola Spagnola** and the **Scola Levantina**, both re-designed by Longhena. Note in this section incidentally, the marks left by gate hinges from the time when the Ghetto was locked at night, and also the stone inscribed with rules governing the occupants, dating from 1541. Continuing along the Calle del Ghetto Vecchio you come to the bridge over to the island of the Ghetto Nuovo and arrive in the **Campo Ghetto Nuovo**, entirely surrounded by multi-storey houses and with three well-heads. In the top left-hand corner is the monument to the 202 Venetian Jews deported to the death camps in 1943–44, consisting of seven reliefs by Arbit Blatas set into a wall along with an inscribed stone bearing a poem. Facing this, on the longest side of the *campo*, is the **Scola Tedesca**, now also part of the **Museo Ebraica**. (*Open 10.00 to 16.00 every day except Saturdays and Jewish festivals. Guided tour of the Synagogues every hour on the half hour from 10.30 to 14.30.*)

Postscript — an evening excursion

Sunset over the Lagoon

One unforgettable sight in Venice is to see the sun go down over the Lagoon. The huge skies and moisture in the air give a majesty and colour to the spectacle that is seldom seen elsewhere. It is difficult to see from within the city, however, and the spectacle is improved when the domes and campanili of the city are silhouetted against the brightly coloured sky. The view is therefore best from the water. The answer, on a clear evening when the sunset is likely to be particularly fine, is to obtain a place on the ferry between S. Zaccaria and Lido so that you are in transit across the Lagoon at the appropriate time.

Quiet and picturesque alleyways reward the wanderer off the beaten track.

ELEVEN

Two Walks through Venice

If you have followed the routes described in Chapters Nine and Ten you will have a better picture of Venice than 90% of visitors. To cover some of the major sights not so far mentioned, and the land access to some locations previously seen only from the water, as well as describing more fully some locations previously mentioned only in passing, I have chosen two extended walks. It is not suggested that each walk has to be followed in its entirety in one session; each walk can be joined or left at any point along its length. Nevertheless, I have done both walks and can tell you that it is feasible for each walk to be completed in one day.

Walk One — S. Marco to S. Polo, via Accademia and the Frari

Piazza to the Academia Bridge
Leave the Piazza by the Sottoportego dei Preti in the south-western corner, following the signs for Accademia and leading directly into the **Salizzada S. Moisè**, a narrow alley lined with exclusive shops. The first turning on the left is the Calle Vallaresso leading to the Ridotto Theatre and Harry's Bar. The second turning on the left is the Calle del Ridotto where the first state-owned gaming-house in Venice was housed, and which now leads to the Biennale Headquarters in the **Palazzo Giustinian**. As you emerge into the **Campo S. Moisè**, pause on the bridge across the Rio S. Moisè to admire (if that is the word) two of the ugliest buildings in Venice. The modern entrance to the Hotel Bauer Grunwald was so disliked when it was built in the late 1940s that it inspired legislation controlling the erection of modern buildings in the historic centre. But the

facade of the **Church of San Moisè** is so overwhelmingly ugly as to turn ugliness into an art form. The facade is by Heinrich Meyring and, in case you should think that the interior could not possibly be any worse than the exterior, wait until you see the miniature Mount Sinai Meyring constructed for an altarpiece! '*Moisè*' is 'Moses' incidentally and represents the Byzantine tradition of canonising Old Testament figures.

Ruskin Prejudices

Ruskin is widely regarded as the ultimate authority on Venetian architecture. But it is as well to be aware that he had some very blinkered attitudes which he would uphold with all the sonority of High Victorian rhetoric. The major bee in his bonnet was the belief that all Gothic was good while all High Renaissance and Baroque was bad. Here, for example, is what he had to say about five baroque facades, '*San Moisè is the most clumsy, Santa Maria Zobenigo the most impious, San Eustachio the most ridiculous, the Ospedaletto the most monstrous and the head at Santa Maria Formosa the most foul.*'

Across the bridge you enter the **Calle Larga XXII Marzo**. The date commemorates the 22nd March, 1848, when Daniel Manin began his revolution against Austrian rule. The street is one of the most fashionable in central Venice with shops and banks occupying some very fine buildings. A friend of mine once said that if he lived in Venice he would bank with the Banca Commerciale Italiana simply for the pleasure of entering their offices. It is also worth a glance into the Saturnia Hotel to see the Gothic columns and ornamental staircase in the foyer. If you have not yet seen the **Fenice Theatre** it is signposted to the right.

At the end of the Calle Larga XXII Marzo the route bends left, then right, crosses the Rio dell'Albero and emerges in the **Campo Santa Maria del Giglio**. The church is known either as **del Giglio** (of the Lily) or **Zobenigo** (Venetian dialect for the Jubanico family who founded the church). The facade was built by Sardi in 1680, at the cost of the Barbaro family. Five Barbaro brothers are represented on the facade, together with maps of places in the Venetian Empire where members of the family had served. In the latter part of the 18th century the campanile of the church was felt to be unsafe and was reduced to the height of a single-storey building; it is now occupied by a shop. The *campo* at the side of the church is extended to the water's edge of the Grand Canal in the **Campo del Traghetto**, so-called for the gondola-ferry that is based there.

The route to the Accademia continues through bends, up and down steps and over bridges, crossing two *rios*, one of which is flanked by the Ca' Grande, now the Prefecture. The next campo is that of **San Maurizio**, centre of the antiques trade in Venice and venue for an occasional open-air antiques fair. Near the exit to the *campo* towards the Accademia is the former **Scuola degli Albanesi**. Built for the Albanians in 1497, it was closed in 1808. It did possess a cycle of pictures by Carpaccio which was broken up on the closure of the *scuola*: some surviving pictures from the cycle are now in the Ca' d'Oro.

A narrow passageway crosses another *rio* known as the **Rio Santissimo** (very holy canal). Pause on the bridge and look right and you will see that the canal gets its name because it flows directly beneath the altar in the **Church of San Stefano**. Note also from here the amazing degree of tilt on the campanile of the church. A short alleyway follows which includes the sumptuous window displays of the Pasticceria Marchini. Having resisted temptation with difficulty, you emerge onto the beautiful open space known alternatively as the **Campo Francesco Morosini** or the **Campo San Stefano**.

This square is not as wide, but it is longer than the Piazza, and for my money is the most attractive of the city's many *campi*. To the locals and on the street signs it is the Campo S. Stefano but it was renamed some time ago after the man whose family *palazzo* projects into the square to the left of where we have entered it, Francesco Morosini. He was the last great warrior-doge, who revived Venice's fortunes in the late 17th century by recapturing much of Southern Greece from the Turks; there is an entire room devoted to his life in the Correr Museum. He was also, incidentally, the man who blew up the Parthenon on the Acropolis of Athens and broke most of the remaining statues in trying to obtain Athene's chariot and horses as a souvenir.

The upper half of the *campo* is wider than the lower and contains a fine well-head and a statue of Niccolò Tommaseo, a hero of the Risorgimento. The church is at the very top end, by the exit leading towards Rialto, and contains several doge's tombs, including Morosini's of course. But the things to look out for are the magnificent Gothic doorway and the 'ship's keel' timber roof, both from the late 15th century. Opposite the facade of the church, in a narrow alley between the Campo San Stefano and Campo Sant'Angelo, lies the opening known as the **Campiello Novo**. This was the churchyard of S. Stefano and was used as a plague pit during the terrible plague of 1630. So many bodies were buried here that, as can be seen, the pavement of the little square is raised well above the surrounding area.

All the other interesting buildings in the *campo,* the **Palazzo Morosini** and **Palazzo Loredan**, are in the lower half. Behind the Morosini house is the entrance into the Campiello Pisani with the gigantic **Palazzo Pisani**, one of the city's largest buildings. Begun by Monopola in 1614 and continued by Frigimelica in 1728, the intention was obviously to continue to the bank of the Grand Canal but the government intervened, saying the building was far too imposing to be owned by a private citizen and forbidding any further construction. Go into the Campiello Pisani and you may be lucky enough to catch some fine singing or instrumental music drifting from the open windows, because this is now the **Conservatory of Music**. Opposite, below the Palazzo Loredan, is the former church of **S. Vitale** (or **Vidal** in dialect). Now a private gallery housing temporary exhibitions, the church still contains a Carpaccio of *San Vitale* over the altar. The grandiose facade is an attempt to emulate the facade of S. Giorgio Maggiore. The *campo* ends in the garden wall of the Palazzo Franchetti (see page 198), in front of which the flower-sellers usually set up their stalls. Turn right into the **Campo S. Vidal** and you are facing the end of the **Accademia Bridge**.

Accademia to San Trovaso, via Guggenheim, Salute, Punta della Dogana and Zattere

Cross the bridge into the Campo della Carità. Note that rarity in Venice, a public toilet, in the heavy base of the southern end of the bridge. In the centre of the *campo* is a large newspaper kiosk which is not only one of the better sources of foreign language newspapers in the city but has a wider and cheaper range of art books, slides and postcard prints than are to be obtained at the shop inside the gallery.

The **Galleries of the Academy of the Fine Arts** are housed in the former church, convent and *scuola* of Santa Maria della Carità, although the galleries open to the public are confined to the former *scuola*. The **Accademia** was originally founded to provide a nucleus of fine paintings and sculptures for the academic study of art but public interest was such that the picture gallery was opened to the public in 1817. The Gallery claims to possess the finest collection of Venetian art dating from the 14th to the 18th centuries, but only about 25% of the collection is ever displayed. (*The Gallery is open from 9.00 to 14.00 every day except Mondays; but closes at 13.00 on Sundays and public holidays. Entrance L8000.*)

The labelling of exhibits and overall arrangement of the gallery is so good as to make it unnecessary to give an exhaustive listing here. The rooms are largely arranged chronologically so that the 14th-century primitives such as Veneziano are to be found in Room 1. Room 2 is given over to the late 15th and early 16th centuries with significant works by Giovanni Bellini and Carpaccio. Room 5 contains many fine smaller paintings of the Venice school but most notably the Gallery's prize possession, Giorgione's *The Tempest*, an allegorical work which is probably the first painting to make the landscape its main subject. The threat to the painting from the breath and body-heat of the crowds has led to it being one of the few pictures in the gallery to be behind glass. In Room 10 we come to the massive canvases of the High Renaissance and the three giants of the 16th century — Veronese, Titian and Tintoretto. Largest of them all, virtually covering the entire wall, is Veronese's rendition of the Last Supper which got the artist into trouble with the Inquisition by including so much of the seamier side of life in a religious work. The painter merely re-named his painting *Christ in the House of Levi* and got away with it. The works of Tintoretto and Veronese continue into Room 11 but, by the time you get to the other end of the room, the paintings are by Tiepolo and from here on the main rooms, if not all the side rooms, are devoted to the 18th century. Many of the later works, such as those by Guardi and Canaletto are views of Venice and the Veneto, and are more of topographical or historical than artistic interest.

For me the most interesting and charming of paintings are the two cycles exhibited in Rooms 20 and 21. In Room 20 is a series of paintings by various artists who were commissioned by the Scuola Grande di S. Giovanni Evangelista to honour the relic of the True Cross which the *scuola* possessed. Between 1494 and 1501 a number of pictures were painted showing events in Venetian history connected with the relic. Two paintings in the series are particularly well-known. One, (see page 159) is Gentile Bellini's *Procession of the True Cross in the Piazza di San Marco*. Note the way Bellini has moved the Campanile 20 metres to the right so that he can include a view of the Doge's Palace. The other painting is Carpaccio's *Patriarch of Grado Curing a Madman*, which shows us exactly what the wooden Rialto Bridge looked like. Carpaccio also has Room 21 to himself with his fascinating and beautiful *Legend of St. Ursula*, the nine panels of which tell the story of Princess Ursula of Brittany, who agreed to marry the British Prince Hereus if he would convert to Christianity and allow Ursula to make a pilgrimage to Rome in the company of 11,000 virgins. After meeting the Pope in Rome, Ursula and her virgins were on their way home when they encountered Attila outside Cologne and all 11,000 virgins, together with Ursula, were slaughtered by the Huns and achieved martyrdom. Carpaccio's paintings are remarkable not only for the strip-cartoon-like narrative of the sequence but for the wealth of detail as to housing, clothing and living conditions in the late 15th century. You leave the gallery by Room 24 which was the *albergo* of the old Scuola Grande. The painting by Titian and the triptych by Viverini and d'Alemagna are not really exhibits in the gallery but part of the *scuola's* original decoration, hanging where they have always hung, in the place for which they were originally commissioned.

Having left the Accademia, take the Rio Terà A. Foscarini on the eastward side of the Academy buildings and turn left along the Calle S. Agnese, as signposted 'Salute'. At the end of a shop-lined street you come over a bridge into the pretty little **Campo S. Vio**. Just before the bridge you pass the land entrance to the **Palazzo Cini** (see page 198). In the Campo S. Vio is the English **Church of St George**, presented to the English community in 1892. The Calle della Chiesa continues beyond the *campo*, with a number of art and antique shops. When the path divides on either side of a small canal, take the left hand *fondamenta* which turns left at a dead-end and runs up to the concealed gateway which is the entrance to the **Peggy Guggenheim Collection**. (*The Collection is open March to*

December from 11.00 to 18.00. Closed on Tuesdays. Entrance L5000, but there is free admission on Saturday evenings, from 18.00 to 21.00.)

In 1938 the eccentric American, Peggy Guggenheim, whose second husband was Max Ernst, set up an art gallery in London, with the intention of creating the world's greatest exhibition of 20th-century art. The outbreak of war forced her to give that up but, when she exhibited her collection at the 1948 Biennale, she fell in love with Venice, bought the unfinished Ca' Venier dei Leoni and spent the rest of her life in the city; possessing the last privately owned gondola to appear on the Grand Canal. She wanted to leave her collection to the Commune but the intricacies of Italian bureaucracy made that impossible and the collection is now officially the property of the **Guggenheim Foundation** in New York, although a clause in her will prevents any pictures being removed from Venice. Only a selection is exhibited at any one time. Fifty-five works, paintings and sculptures, are exhibited in nine rooms on a thematic basis designed to illustrate the main artistic movements of the 20th century — Cubism, Futurism, Expressionism, Dadaism, Surrealism etc. The great figures such as Picasso, Kandinsky, Mondrian, Braque, Chagall, Ernst and Peggy Guggenheim's protegé, Jackson Pollock, are all present but there is also a policy of encouraging new Italian and American artists. The garden contains further major sculptures by artists such as Paolozzi, Moore and Arp.

Leaving the Guggenheim the *calle* continues between garden walls before emerging over a bridge into the pretty Campiello Barbaro. The next section of the route takes you past several glass work-shops and showrooms and into the Campo S. Gregorio, a very attractive little square with a particularly fine well-head and the Gothic facade of the former church of S. Gregorio. Your route burrows underneath the monastic buildings alongside the church in a short tunnel that leads, by way of a wooden bridge, onto the *fondamenta* in front of the **Salute Church**. After the dark tunnel the white stone face of Longhena's great church seems even more dazzling.

The **Church of Santa Maria della Salute** was begun as a sort of votive offering while the great plague of 1630–31, which killed 25% of the Venetian population, was still raging. The word '*Salute*' significantly has a double meaning; it can mean 'Health' but it can also mean 'Salvation'. The task of building the church was given to Longhena who was just 26 years old at the time. But the church was only completed in 1681, a year before he died. It is an octagonal structure with a large central dome, under which is a central circular aisle instead of a nave, an example of Marian symbolism. The simple lines and beauty of the floor are enhanced when the great doors are opened onto the Grand Canal at the Feast of the Salute and other major occasions. The icon in the centre of the altar is more loot, from Crete in this instance, brought back by Francesco Morosini. The **Sacristy**, which can be opened on payment of a fee to the sacristan, contains the church's main paintings; no fewer than twelve Titians as well as Tintoretto's *The Wedding at Cana.*

Far more important than the interior is the impact of the exterior. The great dome, with a secondary, smaller dome over the altar, situated as it is at the end of Dorsoduro between the Grand Canal and the Giudecca Canal, acts as counterweight to San Giorgio Maggiore in dominating the vista of St Mark's Basin. It is a church made for ceremony with its flight of monumental steps and a pavement stretching from the steps to the water's edge like a massive stage. Add to that the dazzling effect as the white building reflects the water of the Canal. The building is only partially faced with Istrian stone, the rest is brick with a textured surface of powdered marble.

Next door to the Salute is one of the forgotten museums of Venice, the **Patriarchal Seminary**, which houses the **Manfredinian Picture Gallery**, a random collection of pictures left to the Seminary by Marchese Federico Manfredini who lived in Florence, hence the collection is largely from Tuscany or Emilia. Entrance is free at any time as long as you have arranged your visit beforehand (*Tel. 5225 558*). It may not be the greatest picture gallery in the world but it is interestingly different, the authorities usually cannot do too much for you and it is somewhere where you will never suffer from crowds.

Continue along the side of the Grand Canal until you reach the very point where the Grand Canal merges with the Giudecca Canal to form the Basin of St Mark's. Once there was a defensive tower here from which a chain could be stretched across the mouth of the Grand Canal, if enemy ships had ever penetrated this far into the Lagoon. In 1677 the tower was replaced by a triangular Customs House designed by Giuseppe Benoni which has a single storey colonnade, surmounted at the point by the stump of a tower on which twin figures of Atlas in bronze support a large golden ball, on top of which is the figure of Fortune. This is the **Punta della Dogana** which has possibly the finest panoramic view in all of Venice. And yet, despite the wonders of the view, you will often only have to share the Point with a handful of other walkers and one or two fishermen.

Continue around the corner to walk alongside the Giudecca Canal. At first there is a fair amount of commercial activity because the old Salt Warehouses are now mostly boat repair shops. In Biennale years the Salt Warehouses are taken over for exhibition space by the Aperto Exhibits. Once you come to the bridge over the major Rio della Fornace you are on the **Fondamenta Zattere** proper. This walk has all the pleasantness of a seaside promenade, even to the ice-cream parlours and restaurants facing the water. The view out over the water is to Giudecca, with the three main monuments of Zitelle, Redentore and Mulino Stucky plainly visible. Sit for a time on one of the benches under the trees that line the water-front, admire the Giudecca frontage and watch the shipping go by.

There are many interesting buildings along the Zattere, although most are of minor importance. Soon after the Rio della Fornace you come to **Santo Spirito** with a fine Renaissance facade from 1486. Here you are directly opposite the Redentore on Giudecca and have a fine view of the facade as seen from the bridge of boats. The next huge building is the so-called **Incurabili**, once one of the four main hospitals of Venice and designed by that Da Ponte who put up the Rialto Bridge. You now cross the Rio S. Vio, noting on the first building after the bridge a plaque recording that Ruskin lived here for a time in 1877. The most important building on Zattere is the Church of Santa Maria del Rosario, more commonly known as **Gesuati**. This was the first church to be designed by Massari in 1726 with classical restraint. Almost next door is the church of **Santa Maria della Visitazione** with a Lombardesque facade and an interesting wooden roof painted by Umbrian artists in the 16th century. At the side of the facade is one of the surviving *bocca di leone* letter-boxes, not in this instance directed towards the Council of Ten but intended for complaints about health and sanitation. A little further on you pass the Zattere water-bus landing stages and come to a bridge across the Rio S. Trovaso. Take the right turn immediately across the bridge into a *calle* which bends around to cross the Rio Ognissanti into the **Campo S. Trovaso**.

San Trovaso is one of the strange Venetian dialect contractions of two saints into one and represents Saints Gervasio and Protasio. The church is unusual in having two facades, one to the west and one to the south. This is because the church was neutral territory for the two factions that split Venice like the Montagues and Capulets divided Verona. For the benefit of the Nicolotti and Castellani the two facades of S. Trovaso enabled them to attend church without inevitably coming into conflict. The most interesting aspect of the Campo S. Trovaso is, however, to the right of the church. This is the **Squero di San Trovaso**, one of the few boatyards in the city where you can still see gondolas being made according to the traditional pattern.

A typical Venetian well-head in the Campo S. Gregorio, Dorsoduro.

San Trovaso to Rialto via the Frari and San Polo

Continue along the *fondamenta* alongside the Rio S. Trovaso as far as the second bridge where you meet the route coming from the Accademia. Turn left into the Calle della Toletta, a busy thoroughfare with some interesting bars and shops. In a short distance this leads into the **Campo S. Barnaba**. The north side of the *campo* is open to the Rio di S. Barnaba. Turn left along the *fondamenta* here to see one of the more distinctive sights of Venice, a large and well-stocked greengrocer's shop on a barge moored alongside the *fondamenta*. The bridge beyond is the **Ponte dei Pugni** (the Bridge of Fists) so-called because it is one of several bridges in Venice where the young men of the Nicolotti (from S. Polo, S. Croce and Canareggio) would fight their opposite numbers in the Castellani (from Castello, S. Marco and Dorsoduro). These contests would take place between September and Christmas each year and the object was to push all your opponents off the bridge and into the water; the bridges had no side-parapets then. The authorities banned the increasingly violent clashes around 1750 but the bridge at S. Barnaba still has white marble footmarks set into it to mark the starting point of the contests.

If you have not as yet seen the Museum of 18th-century Venetian Life in the Ca' Rezzonico (see page 195), you should cross the *rio* here and turn right along the opposing *fondamenta* towards the Grand Canal. The Ca' Rezzonico is signposted but you could not miss it anyway as the entrance is on this *fondamenta*. If you are interested you could continue your diversion onto the wide thoroughfare that runs across the backs of the Palazzo Giustinian and Ca' Foscari through the heart of the university. You can rejoin the main route beyond the Campo S. Margherita.

If you choose not to take that diversion at this time, continue along the *fondamenta* from the Ponte dei Pugni towards the campanile you can see on the right bank of the canal. Near the second bridge, towards the end of the canal, look for the plaque commemorating the house where the composer Wolf Ferrari was born. Cross the bridge and continue along the side of the church into the **Campo dei Carmini**. The church of **Santa Maria del Carmelo** is a strange mixture of 16th-century facade and 14th-century interior, with fragments remaining of a much earlier Byzantine building. Across from the church is the **Scuola dei Carmini** (*Open from 9.00 to noon and 15.00 until 18.00. Closed Sundays. Entrance L5000.*)

The very long and curving **Campo Santa Margherita** is yet another of the highly attractive open spaces of the city. The square probably seems larger because most of the houses surrounding it — many dating back to the 14th and 15th centuries — are quite low structures. The area is much used by students from the university and by the residents of Dorsoduro, so the shops, eating-houses and bars are rather more economical than elsewhere. At the opposite end a *calle* and bridge lead on over the Rio di Ca' Foscari into the **Campo S. Pantalon**. The church, with an unfinished facade, possesses a unique nave ceiling which is not a painted ceiling as such, but a painting on the ceiling. Executed on sixty panels by the artist Fumiani, it took 24 years to complete, from 1680 to 1704. Unfortunately the artist fell from the scaffolding shortly before completing the work, and was killed. The church is somewhat dark and if you want to see the ceiling you will have to tip the sacristan to light it for you.

Take the exit on the right of the church which leads into the bustling Crosera. Turn left and then right into a *calle* leading over a small canal onto a *fondamenta* behind the Scuola Grande di San Rocco. Make your way round to the front in the Campo S. Rocco but, as you do so, spare a glance for the house on the opposite side of the canal where the balcony and most of the exterior is covered in a complex array of windmills and mobiles, all in primary colours, that twist, turn and spin in each passing breeze. It is an interesting modern manifestation of the Venetian love for embellishing the exteriors of their buildings.

The building housing the **Scuola Grande di S. Rocco** is not a total success. It was begun by Bartolomeo Bon in 1516 but had petered out by 1524 for lack of money. However, an outbreak of plague in 1527 brought offerings pouring in (St Roch is supposed to be particularly efficacious in warding off the bubonic plage) and work resumed in the same year under the direction of Scarpagnino, with another two architects playing a part before it was completed in 1560. A true marriage of styles was not found and the finished building has a disjointed look. However, the people who come to the *scuola* do not come to see the outside, they come for the paintings. (*Open 9.00 until 13.00 every day and also 15.30 to 18.30 on Saturday and Sunday. Entrance L5000.*) When it came to decorating the interior the *scuola* instituted a competition in which many artists participated, including Veronese. The winner was Jacopo Robusti, better known as Tintoretto. For 24 years, between 1564 and 1586, Tintoretto worked on the *scuola* so that the 50 paintings it contains are not only interesting in their own right but for what they can tell us of the man's artistic development over a quarter century. If you are an admirer of Tintoretto this display must be your Mecca; Ruskin claimed that, after the Sistine Chapel, this was the finest building in Italy. If you are indifferent to the artist, pass the building by, it has nothing else to offer.

There are more Tintorettos in the **Church of San Rocco**, the facade of which closes off the *campo* to the left of the *scuola* entrance. The church was built in 1498 by Bartolomeo Bon to house the body of St Roch, brought back from Montpellier where the saint died in 1327, in one of Venice's periodic attempts to corner the market in saints' relics. The church is pleasant enough but it tends to suffer in comparison with the edifice whose churchyard wall lies opposite the *scuola* and whose lofty dimensions and mighty campanile (second only to that of S. Marco in height) dominate the whole area. This is the **Church of Santa Maria Gloriosa dei Frari**. Move down from the area of S. Rocco into the Campo dei Frari where you can begin to see the awe-inspiring proportions of the church.

I Frari (*Open to the public 9.30 to noon and 14.30 to 18.00. Only open, for tourists, in the afternoons on Sundays and church feast-days. Entrance L1000, but free on Sundays and feast-days*) is one of the two great Gothic churches of the Mendicant Orders in Venice. Visitors from Northern Europe, however, may feel alienated by these towering brick walls of aggressive simplicity. The Friars began to build their church in 1250, not long after the death of St Francis, but that first church was scrapped in favour of this more ambitious project, which took from 1330 to 1443 to complete.

The church has a very long nave, with two side aisles, and is built in the form of a *tau* or Egyptian cross. The nave and aisles are separated by massive columns supporting arches. The meeting points of columns and arches are braced by iron tie-beams concealed by timber cross-pieces.The **Monk's Choir** is in the nave and is worth examination, particularly the fine marble screen carved by the Bon brothers and Pietro Lombardo and the wooden choir stalls, carved by Cozzi. The focal point of the entire church is the Sanctuary in the apse containing the High Altar and the altarpiece which is probably Titian's most celebrated work, *The Assumption*. The High Altar is flanked by the tombs of two doges; to the left the pre-Renaissance tomb of Niccolò Tron by Rizzo; on the right the Gothic tomb of the unfortunate Francesco Foscari (see page 195). In the first chapel to the right of the Sanctuary is another work of major interest, the wooden statue of *John the Baptist* by Donatello, commissioned by Florentine merchants in 1438. Recent restoration work has revived its vivid polychromatic appearance. Another major work of art belonging to the church is the altarpiece, *Madonna and Child with Saints Nicholas, Peter, Mark and Benedict*, by Giovanni Bellini. This is in the apse of the Sacristy to the right of the north transept. On the south wall of the nave, just below the choir-screen, is the church's other Titian, his *Madonna di Ca' Pesaro*. In the lower nave one of the first things you will notice is the huge **Tomb of Titian**. 90 years old, Titian died in the plague of 1576 which caused the erection of the Redentore Church and, such was his fame, the artist was the only person who died in that plague year to be granted a church burial rather than be sent to the plague-pit. The tomb is a 19th-century creation erected over where the artist is supposed to have been buried. The tomb opposite is for the sculptor Canova and is supposedly based on his own design for the Titian tomb.

The vast spread of monastic buildings to the north of the church were taken over when the Franciscans were suppressed after the Napoleonic conquest. Here were deposited the **State Archives** of the Venetian Republic which, thanks to the intensive bureaucracy of the Republic, give an exhaustive record of government from the 9th century onwards and fill 300 rooms. It is the most complete documentation of a medieval state in the world and permission to work there is the dream of most students of European history.

From in front of the facade of the Frari, cross the canal and it is a simple matter of successive right and left turns to bring you into the **Campo di San Polo**. This open space, one of the largest in the city, remains fairly deserted, as most people simply pass along the south side of the square, following the route between Frari and Rialto. The square was traditionally used for the Venetian sport of bull-catching; a sport somewhere between bull-fighting, the running of the bulls in Pamplona and bull-baiting. The participants guided the bull by cords attached to its horns while another player had a dog on a long lead. The bull and dog then fought each other. During the contest more and more of the spectators would join in. Today the bulls have given way to small boys playing football.

The **Church of S. Polo** is 15th-century Gothic, heavily

The Ponte S. Cristoforo near the Guggenheim Collection,
Dorsoduro.

restored in the 19th century. The original doorway, by Bartolomeo Bon, has survived. The interior is noted solely for a *Last Supper* by Tintoretto and a fine 'ship's keel' roof. The campanile to the church was built in 1362. At its base there are two lions, carved in Romanesque style in the 12th century. One lion has a human head under its paws, the other a snake.

The eastern side of the square is lined by some fine *palazzi* which seem to break the Venetian rule that the main facade gives onto water. They are not breaking the rule, however, because a canal once ran along this side of the *campo*, although it is long-since filled in. The largest is the **Palazzo Soranzo**, a Gothic structure with a marble facade, which is most notable for having been the home of the Senator who adopted Casanova and introduced him into high society. In the top north-west corner of the square is the **Palazzo Corner Mocenigo**, built in the mid-16th century by Sanmicheli. This is where Frederick Rolfe was living and working when his hosts found that he was writing a book which libelled them and all their friends, whereupon the author was thrown out onto the streets.

Walk Two — Through Castello from San Marco to San Pietro di Castello

Molo to SS. Giovanni e Paolo via S. Zaccaria and Santa Maria Formosa

Begin by crossing the **Ponte della Paglia**, with a sideways glance at the **Bridge of Sighs**, to reach the **Riva degli Schiavoni** (see page 206). Just past the **Prisons** the Calle degli Albanesi leads to the **City Aquarium** (*Open 9.00 to 19.00 every day except Tuesday. Admission L2000, reductions for children.*) which contains fish traditionally found in the Lagoon. Past the Danieli Hotel you cross the Rio del Vin and come onto the busiest part of the Riva with visitors coming and going from the water-bus landing stage and commuters pouring on and off the steamers from the Lido. Take the second turning on the left, under the *sotoportego* into the **Campo S. Zaccaria**.

Zacharias was the father of John the Baptist and at one time it looked as though he would be the patron saint of Venice. Early in the 9th century, the Byzantine Emperor, Leo V, made a good-will gesture to Venice in giving them the body of St Zacharias as a worthy relic for the new city. Contemporary with the building of the first Doge's Palace a church and convent was being built to house the relic, just to the east of the Doge's residence. Then, even as the church was being built, the body of St Mark arrived in Venice and poor Zacharias was cast into the shade. Remains of that first 9th-century church can be seen in the gardens at the entrance to the *campo*. Within the later church the chapels of **Sant'Atanasio** and **S. Tarasio** contain parts of the first church, particularly some fine 9th- to 12th-century floor mosaics. The crypt (always partially flooded) is also part of the old church with tombs of eight early doges. The brick campanile is 13th-century.

The **S. Zaccaria** that we see now was built between 1444 and 1515 and therefore fits into that first flowering of the Renaissance that gave us the re-modelled Piazza and most of the finest buildings on the Grand Canal. It was begun by Gambello in flamboyant Gothic style but, from the first storey up, was completed by Coducci as a Renaissance church in the style of his S. Michele in Isola. The building is one of the most successful marriages of the two styles. In the interior pay special attention to the apse where there are two features that are common enough in Northern Gothic but very rare in Venice: long windows and an ambulatory. This last was probably built for the annual state visit by the Doge at Easter, a ceremony recalling the debt owed to the nuns of S. Zaccaria for the sale of the orchard on the site of which the Piazza was created. The body of St Zacharias is still in the church, under the second altar on the right but the church's greatest treasure now is over the second altar on the left. This is Giovanni Bellini's *Madonna and Four Saints*, painted in 1505 and thought by many to be his finest work. The sculptor Alessandro Vittoria is also buried in the church and his tomb bears a self-portrait bust. He also sculpted the holy water stoups, with images of John the Baptist and his father. Another statue of St Zacharias by Vittoria on the facade has unfortunately lost its head.

Leave by the *calle* facing the church which leads into the Campo S. Provolo and take the first right. When you reach the Rio S. Provolo take the bridge on the left into a narrow alleyway that ultimately becomes the Ruga Giuffa. Along the left hand side keep your eyes open for the narrow Calle Querini (signposted) that leads to the **Palazzo Querini-Stampalia**. (*Open 10.00–12.30 all year round, with afternoon opening from 15.00–18.00 between June and September. Closed Mondays. Entrance L5000.*)

The palace of the Querini family (the second part of their name refers to their feudal rule over the Dodecanese island of Stampalia between 1207 and 1522) was built in 1528. Between 1807 and 1850 the Patriarch lived here but it was opened to the public by the will of Count Giovanni Querini, who died in 1868, and who set up the Querini-Stampalia Foundation. The main care of the Foundation is the Library housed on the first floor which contains over 300,000 books and periodicals and over 1,100 manuscripts as well as prints, maps and *incunabula*. The Count even specified in his will the peculiar opening hours which keep the library open until 23.30. The public is, however, chiefly interested in the Picture Gallery on the second floor, open at the hours shown above. The rooms are laid out entirely with the possessions of the Querini family and therefore present a unique picture of the furnishings and decoration of a patrician family home in the 18th/19th centuries. The gallery is excellently arranged and labelled and the visitor is given a list of exhibits at the door. The art collection ranges from the 14th to 18th century and possesses the work of masters such as Veneziano, Bellini and Palma. But its strengths and weaknesses lie in the collection of scenes of Venice and Venetian life painted by followers of Canaletto, such as Longhi or Bella. Such paintings are not fine art but they have a great intrinsic socio-historic interest. Depending on your own tastes the Gallery will either charm you or leave you indifferent.

Leaving the Querini Palazzo by the bridge over a little *rio* you find yourself at the back of **Santa Maria Formosa**. Work your way round to the front and into the *campo*, which is one of the largest in Castello, and one of the liveliest. There is an excellent open-air market here with stalls selling bric-a-brac as well as fruit and vegetables. All around, on and just off the square, are many *palazzi*, while the house at number 6129 was the home of Sebastiano Venier, the triumphant admiral of Lepanto; there is a plaque to his memory. The red-painted house is, appropriately enough, the headquarters of what was the PCI (Communist Party) before it had its identity crisis.

The **Church of S. Maria Formosa** owes its existence to the

7th-century St Magnus, who had a vision of Mary, not as Virgin or Madonna, but as a full-breasted and beautiful matron, not unlike the painting of *St Barbara* by Palma Vecchia inside the church (*formosa* means 'shapely'). The church is built on the Greek cross plan under a single dome, partly as a result of its Byzantine origins and partly through the Marian symbolism. That original ground plan was maintained by Coducci when he rebuilt the church in 1492. The church was again reconstructed in 1916 after the dome, like the Scalzi Church, had fallen victim to an Austrian bomb in a 1915 air raid. The church is unusual in having two facades, perhaps because it was felt necessary to have an entrance on the *campo*, as the main western facade merely faces a side-canal. The most notable works of art in the church are the *St Barbara* and a triptych by Vivarini. The baroque campanile has a grotesque mask at its base, sufficiently pagan and irreligious as to scandalise Ruskin but with the aim of averting the evil eye.

Cheating on a Statue

In October 1471 the *condottiere* Bartolomeo Colleoni died. In his will he left a vast sum of nearly a million ducats in gold, silver, land and property to the Republic of Venice. In return he asked that an equestrian statue of himself should be raised in the Piazza of St Mark. This presented the *signoria* with a problem. No statue was permitted on the Piazza, not even that of a doge or St Mark himself; while Colleoni was a foreigner and a mere mercenary soldier. On the other hand they desperately needed the money. With the deviousness traditionally credited to the Venetians the government commissioned the magnificent statue by Verrochio but erected it on the Campo di SS Giovanni e Paolo, in front of the Scuola di *S. Marco*.

From midway down the eastern side of the square take the Calle Larga S. M. Formosa, and from there take the left turn into the Calle Trevisan, all the time following the blue hospital signs for SS. Giovanni e Paolo. As directed, this route brings you finally into the **Campo Santi Giovanni e Paolo**. Much photographed, repeatedly painted and drawn by Canaletto, this square is possibly the best known in Venice after the Piazza, probably because it contains not only the huge church itself but also the most beautiful of the *scuole* and the finest equestrian statue, the **Colleoni Monument** (see page 000). The statue was begun by the Florentine sculptor Verrochio in 1481 but was finished after Verrochio's death in 1488 by Leopardi, who also constructed the plinth on which it is mounted. On the far side of the *campo*, between the church and the canal is the **Scuole Grande di San Marco**. The elegant facade was begun by Pietro Lombardo and Giovanni Buora in 1487 but completed by the ubiquitous Coducci in 1495. The *trompe l'oeil* panels on the facade (protected by wire screens) are by Tullio and Antonio Lombardo, while the lunette over the door showing *St Mark* is attributed to Bartolomeo Bon. The front along the canal is by Sansovino. Do not be deceived by the constant stream of people going in and out of the door, they are not art-lovers. Since the suppression of the *scuola* in the 19th century the building has been the main entrance to Venice's civic hospital.

St Dominic and St Francis died within a few years of one another, in 1221 and 1226 respectively. Almost immediately, the great Mendicant Orders were founded in their names and, by 1230, both appeared in Venice looking for a home. Doge Tiepolo granted land in S. Polo to the Franciscans, on which the Frari was built, while the Dominicans acquired a stretch of marshy ground just north of S. Maria Formosa, on which they raised their great **Church of SS. Giovanni e Paolo**, soon shortened by Venetian dialect into **San Zanipolo**. As was the case with the Frari the original church planned for the site was scrapped and a more ambitious project embarked upon in 1333; so ambitious that it was a century later, in 1430, before the church was finally finished and consecrated. Since the Frari change of plan was made in 1338, so soon after the Zanipolo change had been made, we cannot rule out rivalry between the two Orders.

Like its Franciscan counterpart the church is a huge brick structure which, seen from a vantage point like the Campanile, rises over the rooftops like a battleship in a fleet of small boats. The style is pure Gothic in its pointed arch windows and doors but there are transitional Gothic/Renaissance traces on the facade, particularly in the doorway attributed to Bartolomeo Bon. The most complex brickwork is to be seen on the apse. The tombs of three doges are on the outside by the main doorway, including that of Doge Giacomo Tiepolo who granted the land to the Dominicans. The chapel on the southern side of

Near S. Maria del Giglio, narrow secretive canals run down to the open spaces of the Grand Canal.

the church, at the end of the right transept, is the **Capella Sant'Orsola**. Here the Bellinis, Giovanni and Gentile, are buried. It was the *scuola* based here which commissioned the Carpaccio cycle of St Ursula paintings.

The interior is starkly cavernous; over 100 metres long, 45 metres wide and over 30 metres high. The aisles are divided from the nave by graceful columns of Istrian stone, the arches braced with wooden tie-beams. The choir area is very well lit, unusually for Venetian churches. There are the tombs of 25 doges within the church, and the memorials of 21 other major state officials. And, although there is an attractive Veronese ceiling in the **Rosary Chapel** and a superb polyptych by Giovanni Bellini on the right hand side of the nave, there are over-many works of rather lesser importance to clutter the eye. There are indeed too many tombs and pictures to list here and the interested visitor, who wants a full accounting of who and what is where, is advised to get an official guide from the Sacristy (in the left hand aisle of the nave, just before the north transept).

San Zanipolo to the Arsenal via the Scuole San Giorgio degli Schiavoni

The next section of this walk is not straightforward because the route twists and turns, crosses and recrosses canals. But if you get momentarily lost do not worry about it; you will soon find your way back again. And, in the process you will discover that these are some of Venice's most attractive by-ways and prettiest canals.

From the *campo* by the Colleoni Monument return back along the southern side of the church where the *campo* turns into the Salizzada SS. Giov. e Paolo. Opposite the **Ospedaletto Church** turn right into the Calle Ospedale, cross the double bridge over two arms of a canal, with attractive views along both, and then continue along the *fondamenta* of a third canal. Where the way forks bear left over the bridge and follow the twists of the alley until you reach the T-junction. Turn left and keep on until you emerge onto the Fondamenta di San Lorenzo.

On the other side of the canal, across the width of a deep *campo*, is a huge bare-brick wall which is the unfinished facade of the **Church of S. Lorenzo**. The present building comes from a rebuilding in 1592 during the course of which they lost the tomb of Marco Polo who had been buried in the church. The church is now closed but is used for exhibitions, including acting as an overflow for the Biennale. The S. Lorenzo canal is very pretty. The campanile ahead, leaning to an extent where it looks liable to fall at any moment, is that of **San Giorgio dei Greci**.

Leaning Towers

They make a great fuss about the Leaning Tower of Pisa, as if it were unique. As you walk about Venice it rapidly becomes clear that there is hardly a campanile in the city that stands up straight and some, such as S. Giorgio dei Greci and S. Stefano, are so much out of true that they rival Pisa's. If anyone feels tempted to do anything about it, however, they think of the tower of S. Angelo. The church no longer exists although the *campo* of that name does. In the 15th century the Campanile of S. Angelo was leaning so far over that the parishioners became worried. In 1445 they called in an engineer from Bologna who specialised in rendering dangerous buildings safe. He raised his scaffolding and his workmen laboured day and night. Finally the scaffolding was removed and the campanile revealed standing as straight as a die. The dignitaries of the parish organised a banquet at which the engineer was toasted and feted into the early hours and praise was lavished upon him for his great work.

The next morning the whole campanile fell down flat.

Cross the *rio* by way of the bridge into the Calle Lion which leads to a bridge across another canal and thereby to the **Scuola di S. Giorgio degli Schiavoni**. (*Open 10.00–12.30 and 15.30–18.00. Mornings only on Sundays and public holidays. Closed Mondays. Entrance L4000.*) I have to declare a vested interest. The Scuola di San Giorgio is my own favourite place in Venice; at least as far as interiors are concerned. It is very small, only the assembly hall you enter directly from the street has any importance.But it is the paintings that are important and I find it very significant that, if I mention the paintings to anyone who has seen them, a reflective smile crosses their face to indicate a pleasant memory shared. The main work, carried out by Vittore Carpaccio between 1502 and 1508 is a sequence of seven paintings featuring the lives of three Dalmatian saints, St George, St Tryphone and St Jerome. The paintings are, in order, *St George fighting the Dragon, St George Triumphant, St George baptising the Parents of Selene, St Tryphone exorcises the Demon, St Jerome with the Lion, Death of Jerome, St Augustine has a Vision of the Death of Jerome*. The first and last are the most famous but it is the little details in the lesser known pictures that appeal the most; that and Carpaccio's obvious sense of humour. Consider the dragon and how totally woe-begone it looks in the picture of St George's triumph. And the little demon that has just been exorcised from the daughter of the Roman Emperor looks so cocksure and pleased with itself. But, of them all, I love the way in which monks are running in every possible direction in panic at the appearance of the lion. There is an orthodox *Agony in the Garden* and the *Summoning of Matthew* as well, together with an altarpiece by Vittore's son, Benedetto. But it is the sequence of seven pictures that will stick in the mind. Try to see them; they are not only great art, they are fun!

From the *scuola*, take the way south along the canal to the church of Sant'Antonin, the priest of which used to keep pigs, giving rise to the Venetian expression of disbelief, 'And St Anthony loved a pig!' Continue along the Salizzada S. Antonin to the Campo Bandiera e Moro, with the church of **San Giovanni in Bragora** in the bottom south-east corner, the church in which Vivaldi was baptised.

Take the *calle* midway along the eastern side of the *campo* and follow the *Arsenale* signs to the *fondamenta* in front of S. Martino, which extends past the church to reach the ornamental land-gate of the **Arsenal**. Note, in the range of buildings on the Arsenal side of the little *rio*, the Venice headquarters of the *Società Nazionale Dante Alighieri*, established here in memory of the visits Dante paid to the Arsenal in 1306 and 1321, visits which impressed him so much that the Arsenal's heated pitch barrels became one of the torments of Hell in the *Divine Comedy*.

Standing on the Campo Arsenale you can see both the main entrances to the Arsenal. On either side of the canal rise the two towers, the **Torri dell' Arsenale**. To their left is the **Arsenal Gateway**, the land entrance. The triumphal arch in which it is framed was designed by Gambello in 1460 and can claim to be the first structure to be erected in Venice according to Renaissance principles. The gate is surrounded by lions. Note the lion on the 'Greek temple' upper storey of the gateway which is an orthodox Lion of St Mark except that the book is closed on the words of peace. The two large lions flanking the doorway were taken from Piraeus by Morosini in 1687. The graffiti on the left-hand lion are in runes and were carved by Viking members of the Byzantine Emperor's Varangian Guard, sent to Athens in 1040 to put down a rebellion. The other pair of lions probably originate from the Lion Terrace at Delos and were sculpted in the 6th century BC.

You can only enter the Arsenal on water-bus 5 (see page 208). For the moment, cross the wooden footbridge and turn right down the Fondamenta Arsenale to its junction with the Riva in the Campo San Biagio. Here is the **Museo Storico Navale**. (*Open 9.00–13.00 every day, closed public holidays. Entrance L2000. Ticket also admits to the exhibition of boats in the 'Padiglione'. The money is a contribution to the 'Andrea Doria' Fund for the Orphans of Naval Dependents.*)

The museum deals with armaments, uniforms, modern battleships, midget submarines etc., but what captures the imagination and makes a visit to the museum worthwhile, is the display of models. In the Arsenal boats were not built from plans but from perfect scale models and, although many models were lost to Napoleon and now grace the naval museum in Paris, sufficient remain to fascinate model-loving children of all ages. Pride of the collection is a model of the last *Bucintoro*, fully gilded and with 'breakaway' sections to show the sumptuously appointed interior. Back up the *fondamenta* near the Arsenal water-gate are the *Padiglioni* where the full-sized exhibits are kept, including a gondola.

The Eastern Districts — Via Garibaldi, S. Pietro di Castello, Public Gardens

Just a short distance along the Riva from the Naval Museum brings you to the **Via Garibaldi**, a former canal filled in and paved in 1808 to become the widest street in the city. Like parts of Cannaregio this is a working-class and working part of the city. You are far from the tourist traps here and the bars and eating houses are less frantic and intolerant as well as more economical. During the mornings an interesting food market occupies the centre of the street. Beyond the market and the Giardini Garibaldi the old canal appears and the street divides on either side of it. Take the Fondamenta Sant'Anna on the right. Glance down some of the side streets here to see how the

In the Giardini Pubblici one of the army of old ladies who feed and care for Venice's thousands of semi-wild cats.

Venetians hang out their washing on lines strung from one side of the alley to the other.

At the end of the Fondamenta Sant'Anna you cross the Canale di San Pietro onto the island of S. Pietro and turn left into the Fondamenta Quintavalle. Note the Renaissance relief of the *Madonna and Child with St Peter* set into the wall facing you at the end of the *fondamenta*. A right turn brings you into the Calle dietro il Campanile. The buildings on the right were formerly the Patriarch's Palace. Look out for an archway that leads into a pretty little *campo* with well-head and cloisters, the cloisters now occupied with the hulls of boats since the buildings are repair-yards. From behind the dangerously leaning campanile you emerge into the *campo* in front of the **Church of San Pietro in Castello**. Unusually for Venice, this *campo* really is a 'field', unpaved and grass-covered, with trees.

This island was where the refugees in the Lagoon built their first castle in the 8th century. And here they built their first church, dedicated to St Peter. That church became Venice's first cathedral in 775 and remained the cathedral of the city until 1807. If it seems strange that the cathedral of the city was stuck out here on the eastern fringes it was because the Republic feared religious control and papal interference. The Patriarch was kept on the edge of the city and the religious ceremonies associated with state occasions were based in St Mark's which, being the Doge's private chapel, was firmly under government control. It was ten years after the fall of the Republic before the Patriarch could move into the centre and make St Mark's the new cathedral. Yet, despite its long history, the church is a disappointment. One interesting curio in the church is the so-called **Throne of St Peter**, made in the 13th century from stone of Arabic origin, carved with inscriptions from the Koran. The campanile, well separated from the church, challenges S. Stefano and S. Giorgio dei Greci as to which can lean over furthest without falling down.

Retrace your steps to the Via Garibaldi and, halfway down, turn left into the **Giardini Garibaldi** through which you can reach the Riva. From here on, the **Public Gardens** line the Lagoon frontage. The first section contains the **Biennale** site and the gardens are dotted with national pavilions and isolated statuary. Over the canal you come into the Sant' Elena district and the **Parco della Rimembrenza** (Garden of Remembrance). Except in Biennale years this part of Venice is seldom penetrated by tourists and, the combination of greenery and comparative isolation makes for a welcome relief when the press and heat of summer become overwhelming. The view from Sant' Elena back across the whole panorama of the Basin of St Mark's is really worth seeing.

From this spot on the eastern extremity of the city you can choose to saunter back to the centre along the length of the Riva, or you can catch the number 1 water-bus from the Sant' Elena stop.

In the early morning mist an angler at the very tip of the Punta della Dogana makes a catch. In the background the Church of San Giorgio Maggiore.

TWELVE

The Lagoon and Adjacent Mainland

The Northern Islands

To the north of Central Venice lie hundreds of islands, some as large as Venice itself, others little more than sand-banks; some bustling centres of population, others uninhabited or only temporarily occupied by a handful of fishermen. Only a few islands, however, have anything to offer the visitor. Close to Venice are **S. Michele** and **Murano**. Further away towards the northern end of the Lagoon are **Burano**, **Torcello** and **San Francesco del Deserto**.

How to get there

Every travel agent and all the private boat companies along the Molo and Riva degli Schiavoni advertise trips to the islands; by which they usually mean Murano, Burano and Torcello. These trips tend to be expensive, crowded and restrictive on your freedom: the excursion boats complete the round trip in 4 hours, allowing only a few minutes on Torcello and there is a tendency for the recommended glass and lace shops to be those offering the best commission to your guide, rather than being the best choice for quality or price. It is easier, freer and much more economical to use the **Actv** public services.

Route No. 5: (See page 200.) This is the only route that stops at S. Michele. Every 15 minutes from Fondamente Nove. L2,200.

Route No. 5 Barrato: Two *motoscafo* routes for summer only. Tronchetto to Murano via Ferrovia and S. Zaccaria to Murano via S. Elena. Every 30 minutes. L2,200.

Route No. 12/14: *Vaporetto* route. Fondamente Nove-Murano-Mazzorbo-Burano-Torcello-Treporti-Punta Sabioni-Lido, S. Maria Elisabetta-Riva degli Sciavoni. Every 60 minutes. L3,300. Circular route. The stop for Murano is at Faro.

Route No. 13: *Motoscafo* route. Fondamente Nove-Murano-

Vignole-Sant' Erasmo. Every 60 minutes. L3,300. Not really a tourist route.

S. Michele and Murano are described on pp. 209–12.

Lesser islands

Mazzorbo is a largish island with the remnants of long-deserted settlements, some of which are now being restored and some new houses built. At its northernmost tip the island is connected to Burano by a long bridge so it is possible to leave the boat at Mazzorbo and walk on to Burano; making a pleasant country walk in the summer when the built-up streets of Venice begin to pall. **Vignole** and **Sant' Erasmo** are two large islands (Sant' Erasmo is as large as Central Venice), almost a continuation of the Lido towards the north. They are largely uninhabited but are intensely cultivated, acting as market gardens for Venice. There is little to attract the visitor. Between Burano and Sant' Erasmo lies the tiny island of **San Francesco del Deserto**, a Franciscan monastery since the saint himself visited the island in 1220. A handful of monks still live here and welcome visitors between 9.00–11.00 and 15.00–17.00 on weekdays. There are no architectural or artistic works to see here, just the peace of the cloisters, which can be restorative in the height of the Venice season. The island can only be reached by *sandolo* (a form of rowing-boat) from Burano, where fishermen offer their boats for hire on the quayside.

Burano

While Murano is recognisably Venetian, **Burano** is totally unlike anywhere else in the Lagoon. It is a fishing village and the fishermen's cottages are small and low. But whereas elsewhere the stucco is crumbling and there is an air of genteel decay, the cottages of Burano are incredibly neat and all colour-washed in bright primary colours. The *vaporetto* will land you on the northern shore of the island but a short distance into the interior will bring you to the island's main street, the **Via Baldassare Galuppi** which in turn leads into the main square, the **Piazza Baldassare Galuppi**. (Galuppi was an

18th-century composer from Burano, written about by Robert Browning.) The island is still a major fishing community and there are some excellent fish restaurants along the Via Galuppi. But the island's main claim to fame is the activity of the women in lace-making (see page 119).

On the square is the parish church of the island, **S. Martino**, with yet another tilting campanile. Opposite the church is the **Scuola del Merletto**. (*Open every day from 9.00 to 18.00. Sundays and public holidays, 10.00–17.00. Entrance L5000.*) This is known as a 'school' and not a 'museum' because it is exactly that, a place where the traditional skills of Burano lace-making are passed on to a new generation. It was founded in 1872 when it was felt there was a danger of the old skills dying out. In the museum it is possible to see examples of lace-work dating back to the 17th century but the real fascination is seeing lace being made today.It is as well to visit the *scuola* before you think of buying lace at one of the many shops on the island. There is a great deal of inferior, imported lace on sale these days, but a session in the *scuola* will enable you to recognise the real thing.

Torcello

The island of **Torcello** is heavily evocative of the origins of Venice and also a timely reminder of what may happen to Venice if the efforts of the conservationists do not bear fruit. It was virtually the first place to be settled in the Lagoon. In the year 638, Bishop Paul of Altinum, menaced by the Lombards, climbed a small tower (a *torcello*) and was granted a vision of the island to which the people of Altino must retreat for safety. The move was made and the bishop's new cathedral was founded in the following year. Over the next few hundred years the population grew to 20,000 and the island must have seemed a thriving community. But Torcello did not have the deep-water channels with which Venice was blessed and its canals silted up.The population fell away until there are, today, no more than a hundred people on the island. Apart from a few houses, all that is left of a glorious past are a cathedral, a church and mementoes that can be picked up all over the island and which go to stock the museum by the cathedral.

The *vaporetto* leaves you on the opposite side of the island

and it is a 500 metre walk alongside a small canal across the width of the island, to reach the **Piazza di Torcello** where the three main buildings are grouped.

The Cathedral of Santa Maria dell'Assunta. The crypt survives from the first church of 640, as do the foundation walls of the original baptistry. The first renovation was made in the late 9th century and the facade and portico were originally constructed then. Other early features òf the exterior are the windows on the right hand side of the cathedral, which have shutters made of stone slabs. The Campanile is a square, plain structure of the 11th century which is now too fragile to allow anyone to enter. Most of the rest of the exterior was built in the first decades of the 11th century. The interior is aisled, with 18 slender marble columns. Being a Byzantine church it has an *iconostasis* rather than a rood-screen, with paintings of the Virgin and Apostles supported by four carved marble panels. But the glories of the cathedral are its mosaics. The mosaic floor is 11th-century work but there are lift-up wooden panels to reveal the floor of the earlier church. On the west wall is a large *Last Judgment*, created in the 12th century but restored in the 19th (parts of the original are in the Museum). In the semi-dome of the central apse is, however, one of the most famous mosaics of Italy, rivalling those of Ravenna, a *Madonna and Child* on a field of gold. Executed in the 12th century it rises over an 11th-century frieze of the Apostles.

The church of **Santa Fosca** was built in the 11th century to house the body of the saint but has been much restored since then. It is built on a Greek cross plan with an octagonal portico added in the 12th century. The interior is very plain. The central circular drum, supported by marble columns with Byzantine capitals, has a conical wooden roof. On the grass outside the church is **Attila's Chair**, an ancient stone seat which was probably used by the Torcello Magistrate in the early years of the settlement.

The **Museo dell' Estuario** (*Open 10.00–12.30 and 14.00–17.30. Closed Mondays and public holidays. Entrance L2000*) is housed in two *palazzi*, formerly the homes of the Council and Archives of Torcello. They contain relics of Torcello and the other islands of the Lagoon from Roman times until the 16th century. As a result of recent organisation the Roman and archaeological material are housed in the Palazzo dell' Archivio, while medieval and more recent exhibits are magnificently laid out in the Palazzo del Consiglio. Here are fragments from the cathedral, the church and from the other dozen or so churches that existed on Torcello and have now disappeared.

Where to stay in the Northern Islands
These islands are meant to be visited rather than used as bases: there are only two small hotels.
3-star:
Locanda Cipriani, Piazza S. Fosca 29, Torcello. Tel. 730150. Restaurant with just 6 rooms, all with private facilities. Only open in summer and only takes customers on *pensione* terms. From L320,000 per person per night.
1-star:
Raspo de Ua, Piazza Galuppi 560, Burano. Tel. 730095. Restaurant with 6 rooms, none with private facilities. L44,000 for double room. Breakfast L8,000.

Where to eat
Torcello is expensive, Murano is reasonable but very ordinary; the best restaurants in terms of value for money are on Burano.
Murano:
Al Soffiador, Viale Garibaldi. Tourist menu c. L20,000. Closed Sun.
Antica Trattoria Muranese, Fond. Cavour. Tourist menu c. L18,000. Closed Sat. evening and Sun.
Ostaria dalla Mora, Fond. Manin. Menu c. L35,000. Closed Fri.
Burano:
Ai Pescatori, Via Galuppi. A la carte. Closed Mon.
Al Gatto Nero, Fond. Giudecca. Menu c. L22,000. Closed Mon.
Da Romano, Piazza Galuppi. A la carte. Closed Tues. Well recommended (Michelin rosette).
Torcello:
Locanda Cipriani. Luxury food at luxury prices. (Michelin rosetted)
Osteria Villa 600. Fish restaurant. Menu c. L28,000. Closed Wed.

The Southern Islands

The coastline of the Adriatic is broken in three places to form the Lagoon. These three breaches leave two narrow, elongated islands that are little more than substantial sand-bars between sea and Lagoon, the islands being known as the **Littorale di Lido** and the **Littorale di Pellestrina**. Both islands are more than 10 kilometres long but neither is more than 500 metres wide at most and about 250 metres across. On the Venice side of the Lido are a number of small islands previously used as quarantine isolation hospitals or *Lazzaretti*, known together as the **Ospedali Lagunari**. Of these, the only one of interest to the visitor is the Armenian island of **San Lazzaro**.

How to get there
Route No. 1: The continuation of the Grand Canal route, goes to **Lido, S. Maria Elisabetta.** Every 10 minutes. L2,200.

Route No. 2: Express *motoscafo* route from Ferrovia to **Lido, Casino.** Every 10 minutes. L3,300.

Route No. 6: Direct ferry service. Riva degli Schiavoni to **Lido, Santa Maria Elisabetta.** No other stops. Every 20 minutes. L2,200.

Route No. 14/12: Reverse of Circular service 12/14. See page 000.

Route No. 17: Car Ferry from Tronchetto to **Lido, S. Niccolò-**Punta Sabbioni. Every 50 minutes. Rates depend on size of vehicle. Queries to Actv.

Route No. 20: *Vaporetto* service — S. Zaccaria-**San Lazzaro.** Every 60 minutes. L1,500.

Summer Route 34: Express line following same route as No. 1. Every 10 minutes. L2,200.

Summer Route 28: Direct service for **Casino**.

Isola di San Lazzaro

In 1717 an Armenian monk known as Mechitar, driven from his monastery by the reconquest of the Morea by the Turks, came to Venice and set up a monastery on this island which had previously been a leper colony. The monks have been there ever since and have established the most important centre of Armenian culture outside Armenia itself. Since 1789 the monks have specialised in printing (see page 123) and their shop is the best source for prints and maps of old Venice. The **Museo degli Armeni** is open every day between 15.00 and 17.00 but you must be accompanied by one of the monks. The museum is varied in its displays: from an Egyptian Mummy to a Tibetan

Prayer-Wheel, paintings by Tiepolo and the room where Byron studied Armenian. The highlight of the tour is a visit to the print-shops. Entrance is free but you are expected to make a donation or purchase something.

The Lido

The Lido has already been discussed as the location of the Film Festival, the summer base for the Casino and as the only possible place close to Venice to practice certain sports. There is not much more to say about the island in the orthodox sightseeing sense. Most buildings here are 19th- and 20th-century. This is essentially a beach resort rather than a place to visit for its intrinsic interest.

The main terminal for the water-bus services from Venice is the **Piazzale Santa Maria Elisabetta**. This is the bus terminal and taxi stand and visitors fresh from the pedestrianised streets of Venice should remember with caution that the Lido has motor traffic. From the Piazzale a wide shopping street, the **Gran Viale S. Maria Elisabetta** runs 700 metres across the island to the **Piazzale Bucintoro** on the sea-front. From there the **Lungomare Gabriele d'Annunzio** runs north to the free public beach, the Hospital and the airport of S. Nicolò (private planes). On the lagoon side of this rather barren northern section is the **Church of S. Nicolò**, founded in 1044 but now housed in a 16th-century building. Close to the northern channel from sea to Lagoon, this was where the Doge used to greet important visitors coming by sea and where he used to attend mass after the Ascension Day Marriage with the Sea ceremony. Near the S. Nicolò landing stage is the 14th-century Jewish Cemetery.

South from the Piazzale Bucintoro runs the **Lungomare Guglielmo Marconi** with the big hotels on one side and the hotels' private beaches on the other. In gardens just south of the Piazzale is the **Grand Hotel des Bains**, rather reduced in stature since Thomas Mann made it the location of *Death In Venice*. A kilometre along the Lungomare brings us to the **Piazzale del Casino** with the summer home of the **Casino Municipale** and the **Palazzo della Mostra del Cinema**, base for the Film Festival. A canal cuts across the island to a basin behind the Casino so that the special *motoscafo* service from Venice can get to the actual entrance of the Casino. A little further along the *Lungomare* the Lido's major hotel, the **Excelsior** occupies a site on the beach side of the road.

Getting about on the Lido

Actv run three bus services within the island of the Lido.

Service A: San Nicolò-Piazzale S.Maria Elisabetta-Piazzale del Casino. About every 20 minutes.

Service B: Malamocco-Piazzale S. M. Elisabetta-Hospital-Public Beaches. Every 10 minutes.

Service C: Piazzale Santa Maria Elisabetta-Alberoni. Every 20 minutes. This is the bus you must take for the public bathing beaches at the southern end of the island.

Mixed Bus/Ferry Service No. 11 — Lido to Chioggia via Pellestrina

This is probably one of the most interesting excursions that can be made from Venice. You need to catch the Actv bus number 11 from the Piazzale S. Maria Elisabetta. They should leave every 60 minutes but the frequency changes according to the season and not all buses go as far as Chioggia. Check the local timetables. The whole journey takes about an hour and a half and costs in the region of L3,500.

From the Piazzale the bus runs through the pleasant residential part of the Lido known as the **Città Giardino** (Garden City). After about a kilometre of open country the bus then reaches **Malamocco**, capital of the Lagoon federation before 810, although the settlement moved from the sea coast to the Lagoon side of the island after the original town was destroyed by a tidal wave in 1107. More sparsely populated country intervenes before the settlement at the southern end, **Alberoni**. This is where the golf course is located, as well as the less crowded public beaches. The bus is loaded onto a ferry here for the five minute crossing of the **Porto di Malamocco**.

The bus resumes its journey at the settlement of **S. Pietro in Volta** on the island of **Pellestrina**. Pellestrina is even narrower than the Lido and is really little more than a sand-bar. For most of the 10 kilometres of the island the road follows the sea from which it is divided by a stone dyke. The actual village of

Pellestrina is as long and narrow as the island, strung out along 3 kilometres of the road. As with Burano the trades of Pellestrina are fishing for the men and lace-making for the women. The bus terminates at the southern end of the island and passengers transfer to a *vaporetto* (same ticket) for the 25 minute crossing of the **Porto di Chioggia**. Note the **Murazzi**, huge walls of Istrian stone, 4 kilometres long and 14 metres wide, built on either side of the channel in the mid-18th century in a bid to control flooding in the Lagoon.

Chioggia is the second largest settlement on the Lagoon and has sometimes been called a miniature version of Venice. Like Venice it is constructed on a number of islands, with canals running through the centre of the town, linked to the mainland by a bridge. Nearly all the sights of Chioggia are located on the arcaded main street, **Corso del Popolo**. The boat from Pellestrina will put you ashore at the **Piazzetta Vigo** at the end of the Corso. Here there is a Greek marble column surmounted by a lion that is so poor in workmanship that it was renamed by Venetian wits, 'The Cat of St Mark'. To see Chioggia's one great work of art, turn left across the Canale della Vena for the **Church of S. Domenico** which contains Carpaccio's last known work, *St Paul*.

On the Corso del Popolo there are a number of churches which contain little of interest. The most significant building is the **Granaio**, a granary built in 1322 but much restored, the relief on the facade is by Sansovino. Immediately behind is the **Fish Market** which, since Chioggia is one of Italy's busiest fishing ports, is always a sight to be seen (any morning bar Monday). A little further on is the **Duomo**, the cathedral, rebuilt in 1624 and the first major commission given to Longhena. The Campanile is from the earlier cathedral and dates from 1347.

Outside the Duomo is the bus terminal. From here you can go to the mainland section of Chioggia, known as **Sottomarina**, a sort of down-market version of the Lido, with many quite reasonable hotels and camp-sites. From the Duomo it is also possible to catch a bus back to the Piazzale Roma in Venice. But the road route is not very attractive, much the same price as the journey along the islands and not very much quicker. During the peak summer months there is sometimes a direct boat link across the Lagoon from Venice to Chioggia but this is variable and availability should be checked in Venice.

Hotels on the Lido

Some people might prefer to stay on the Lido rather than in the historic centre. It has its attractions but it can be even more expensive than Venice proper and gets more crowded in July–August when the Film Festival takes over. Most hotels are seasonal only. The list which follows is selective, the room cost quoted is for a double room with private facilities, low and high season, where applicable.

5-Star De Luxe:

Excelsior, Lungomare Marconi 41. Tel. 5260 201. Tx. 410023. Fax 5267 276. Rooms L316,000–L546,000. Breakfast L25,000. A luxury hotel since Victorian times, it enjoys international fame and prestige.

4-Star:

Hotel Des Bains, Lungomare Marconi 17. Tel. 5265 921. Tx. 410142. Fax 5260 113. Rooms L214,000–L416,000. Breakfast L22,000. The setting for the book (and film) *Death in Venice*.

Quattro Fontane, Via delle 4 Fontane 16. Tel. 5260 227. Tx. 411006.Fax 5270 726. Rooms L190,000–L300,000. Breakfast L16,500. Open April–September.

Villa Laguna, Via Sandro Gallo 6. Tel. 5260 342. Fax 5268 922. Rooms L152,000–L304,000. Breakfast L18,000.

Villa Mabapa, Riviera S. Nicolò 16. Tel. 5260 590. Tx. 410357. Fax 5269 441. Rooms L120,000–L230,000. Breakfast L15,000.

3-Star:

Belvedere, Via Cerigo 1D. Tel. 5260 115. Fax 5261 486. Rooms L67,000–L135,000. Breakfast L12,500.

Biasutti-Villa Ada, Via Dandolo 24. Tel. 5260 120. Tx. 410666. Fax 5261 259. Rooms L75,000–L140,000. Breakfast L18,000.

Capelli's, Via Perasto 3. Tel. and Fax 5260 140. Tx. 411037. Rooms L91,000–L151,000. Breakfast L14,000.

Centrale & Byron, Via M. Bragadin 30. Tel. and Fax 5260 052. Tx. 410391. Rooms L80,000–L141,000. Breakfast L15,000.

Rigel, Via Dandolo 13. Tel. 5268 810. Tx. 420835. Fax 5204 083. Rooms L85,000–L126,000. Breakfast L13,000.

2-Star:

Cristallo, Gran Viale S. M. Elisabetta 51. Tel. and Fax 5265 293. Tx. 218402. Rooms L50,000–L81,000. Breakfast L12,000.

Rivamare, Lungomare G. Marconi 44. Tel. 5260 352. Rooms L75,000–L81,000. Breakfast L10,000.

Vianello, Via Ca' Rossa 10. Tel. 731072. Rooms L70,000–L81,000. Breakfast L10,000.

Villa Pannonia, Via Doge Michiel 48. Tel. 5260 162. Fax 5265 277. Rooms L54,000–L81,000. Breakfast L15,000.
1-Star:
Giardinetto, Piazzale S. M. Elisabetta 3. Tel. 5260 801. Rooms L60,000–L68,000. Breakfast L4,000.
La Pergola, Via Cipro 15. Tel. 5260 784. Rooms L52,000–L68,500. Breakfast L10,000.

Where to eat in the Southern Lagoon

All the hotels listed above for the Lido have restaurants, even the cheapest. There is a plentiful supply of the type of restaurant you might expect to find in a seaside resort, including many *tavole calde* and fast food places. The restaurants that seem to offer the best value for money are largely outside the centre towards Malamocco:
Al Porticciolo, on Malamocco road. A la Carte. Closed Wed.
Crivellara Bar Tavola Calda, Lungomare G. Marconi 58. About L20,000. Closed Mon.
Da Valentino, Via S. Gallo 81. A la carte. Closed Sun. and Mon.
Hostaria dai Fioi, Malamocco 7. About L30,000. Closed Wed.
Trattoria Da Ciccio, Via S. Gallo 241. About L18,000. Closed Tues.
Trattoria Da Scarso, Piazzale Malamocco 4. About L25,000. Closed Thurs.
On Pellestrina
Da Nane, San Pietro in Volta. A la carte. Closed Mon.

In Chioggia there is an abundance of excellent fish restaurants along the Corso del Popolo, all at very reasonable prices. For the visitor with a budget to watch Chioggia can be the best place in the Lagoon in which to eat. It is pointless to single out any restaurants; they are all within easy walking distance of each other and it is a simple matter to compare menus and prices to make your own selection.

The Brenta

The Brenta, flowing through Padua, is only one of three rivers feeding the Lagoon but, in terms of floods and silting, it has had the most effect on Venice. To control the flow of the Brenta and to check the amount of silt deposited in the channels of the Lagoon, the Venetians have embanked and canalised the banks of the Brenta ever since they gained control of the city of Padua in 1405. In the 1890s a canal was dug from Strà just outside Padua to near Chioggia, effectively diverting the flow from the lower reaches. Before that, the most significant development on the Brenta came in the 16th century when the city centre of Venice was becoming almost totally built up, the former summer retreat of Murano was given over to the glass industry and patrician families were looking for somewhere cool and green to spend the hotter months of the year. The answer was to build a summer retreat, a villa. And the most favoured location was on that stretch of the Brenta between Strà and Fusina. Over a hundred were built, many designed by Palladio. Many of the villas are still standing but only a few are open to the public. Those few include the two largest and finest: the **Villa Foscari (Malcontenta)** and the **Villa Pisani (Nazionale)**.

The **Villa Foscari**, at Malcontenta, 8 kilometres up-river from Fusina, is the nearest to Venice by water. Designed by Palladio in 1559 it set the pattern for those that followed. Raised above the water-meadows on a massive platform the villa has a huge Ionic portico modelled on a Roman temple, while the house itself is based on the plan of Roman public buildings such as the Baths. The Great Hall and most of the rooms off it are open to the public. (*Tuesdays–Saturdays and some Sundays, May to October, 9.00 to noon. Entrance L8000.*) Do not be misled by the alternative name of Villa Malcontenta. It is nothing to do with unhappiness on the part of any of the inhabitants, Malcontenta is simply the name of the place where the villa was built.

The **Villa Nazionale Pisani**, is at Strà, 12 kilometres from Padua. (*Open 9.00 to 13.30. Entrance L6000. Closed on Mondays.*) Thwarted in their plan to build the largest *palazzo* in Venice (see page 220), the Pisani family proceeded to build the largest villa on the Brenta. It was begun in 1735 by Frigimelica, who had completed the Venice *palazzo*, but finished in 1760 by Preti. It was considered suitable for imperial ambitions by Napoleon, who bought the villa in 1807 and, in 1934, it was chosen by Mussolini as the place most likely to impress Hitler at the dictators' first meeting. The exterior is very impressive; as are the grounds, with an ornamental lake, a monumental stable-block, a neo-classical belvedere and a maze. The house itself is rather disappointing, being largely bare of furnishings. Only the ballroom is really worth seeing, with a painted ceiling by Giambattista Tiepolo and frescoes by his son Giandomenico.

Other villas open to the public include the **Villa Widmann-Foscari-Rezzonico** at Mira Porte and the **Villa Querini-Stampalia** at Chitarra. Information about all the villas is available from the **APT Riviera di Brenta**, Via Don Minzoni, Mira Porte. There is also an information office at the **Villa Nazionale** and the APT in Venice should be able to help.

How to get there

Bus & Coach from the Piazzale Roma. There is an hourly **Actv** bus service to the Villa Foscari at Malcontenta. (Cost about L1000.) The coach for Padua is a half-hourly service and goes by way of Oriago, Mira and Strà so that you pass dozens of villas on the way and can be dropped off at the door of the Villa Nazionale. (Cost about L3000.)

The 'Burchiello' is the luxury way to see the Brenta. 'Burchiello' was the name of the barge that plied the Brenta in the 18th century and has now been adopted by the tourist boat which follows the same route from Venice to Padua and vice versa. Leaving the Molo at around 9.00, the journey takes most of the morning and afternoon, arriving in Padua in the early evening. Lunch and entry to several villas, including the Malcontenta, are included in the cost. The boat travels from Venice to Padua on Tuesday, Thursday and Saturday; from Padua to Venice on Wednesday, Friday and Sunday. There are no journeys on Mondays. The cost is L127,000 per person inclusive (L142,000 on Sunday). Bookings can be made at any travel agency in Venice: if you wish to book in advance you should contact **Siamic Express**, Via Trieste 42, 35100 Padova. (Tel. 049 660944) Visitors staying in Venice are recommended to take the boat from Padua to Venice, to avoid the hassle of returning to Venice during the evening rush hour.

Padua (Padova)

Only 37 kilometres from Venice, and Venetian since 1405, Padua tends to be cast into the shade by its neighbour. Yet the city has many claims to the visitor's interest in its own right.

The city has one of the oldest and most respected universities in the world, contains the Basilica of St Anthony of Padua and some of the finest works created by Giotto and Donatello.

The **Basilica del Santo** was built between 1232 and 1307 and started within two years of St Anthony's death. It is a strangely mixed building with Romanesque and Gothic features on the exterior and with Byzantine domes and minarets reminiscent of St Mark's. The finest works of art in the interior are the altar bronzes by Donatello and a series of nine 16th-century carved panels showing the life of the saint and sculpted by Sansovino and Tullio Lombardo among others. Another major work by Donatello is outside the Basilica.This is the **Statue of Gattamelata**, the first large Renaissance bronze statue to be cast in Italy. It is a forerunner of the Colleoni Statue in Venice and the two are often considered to be rivals for the title of 'finest equestrian statue'.

In the **Scrovegni Chapel** are the paintings that draw most visitors to Padua, a cycle of frescoes showing the *Life of Christ and the Virgin*, painted by Giotto between 1303 and 1313. The paintings are arranged on three tiers with a background of blue. They should be read in sequence. A warning: the chapel is always crowded and a time limit is sometimes applied to visitors.

The **University** was founded in 1221 and is therefore the oldest university in Italy excepting Bologna. There are four guided tours each day (apply to the Direzione Amministrativo), on which you can see the first-ever Anatomy Theatre (1594) where William Harvey, who discovered the circulation of the blood, took his degree and did his research.You can also see the lectern used by Galileo when he taught physics here and the statue of Elena Corner Piscopia, the first woman ever to obtain a university degree.

Although much of the city was rebuilt after the last war and the outskirts are dreary modern industrial there are still attractive medieval houses and streets around the three linked market squares in the city centre. The Venetian administration was based in 15th- and 16th-century buildings around the **Piazza dei Signori** and they still exist, including a clock tower even older than that of Venice.

How to get there: There is a half-hourly coach service between Venice and Padua, (see above) but by far the easiest, quickest and most economical way to travel is by rail. There is a train every half hour from Venice to Padua and in the reverse direction. The journey takes 30 minutes. Make sure that you get on the local train. All the main international trains out of Venice stop at Padua but you have to pay a surcharge to use them.

Where to stay: Despite an increasing tendency to escape the crowds of Venice by staying outside the city, Padua was not well served by hotels until recently. Most available accommodation tended to be in 1- or 2-star hotels chiefly catering for students, pilgrims or businessmen. In the last few years the situation has improved, with several new hotels having been built and several others modernised and up-graded. Room-finding services are provided by the APT office at the railway station. Two hotels that are quite well spoken of for their pleasant location near the Basilica are:

4-star:
Hotel Donatello, Via del Santo 102–4. Tel. (049) 8750634. Modernised and utilitarian. Good restaurant on square facing the Basilica.

2-star:
Casa del Pellegrino, Via Cesarotti 21. Tel. (049) 8752100. Formerly a hostel for pilgrims it has recently doubled in size and been up-graded from a single star. Basic restaurant and bar.

Where to eat: Better served by restaurants than hotels, the best place to look is around the three squares: the Piazza della Frutta, Piazza delle Erbe and Piazza dei Signori. The squares themselves and surrounding streets are lined with restaurants, trattorie, pizzerie, cafés and bars. By simply walking around the area for a few minutes you should find somewhere to suit your taste and purse.

Treviso

Situated 30 kilometres due north of Venice and the first city on the mainland to come under Venetian rule in 1389, Treviso is now best known for being the airport for charter flights to Venice. Yet the city is attractive in its own right and, for those visiting Venice, as easy to get to and from as Padua. At the height of the season it is worth considering as a base away from the crowds.

Although much damaged in the Second World War the Old City has been rebuilt with arcaded streets and canals vaguely reminiscent of Venice. The main square, the **Piazza dei Signori**, is particularly fine and stages open-air concerts during the summer. Peculiar to Treviso is the practice of painting frescoes on the facades of buildings rather than dressing them with stone. Best examples of this are along the main street, the **Calmaggiore**. The finest works of art in Treviso are the paintings of Tomaso da Modena, a follower of Giotto who dominated Italian art in the mid-14th century. There are many of his works in the **Church of S. Nicolò** but his masterpiece is a cycle of frescoes telling the story of St Ursula. Unfortunately, it is almost impossible to see these works since they are housed in the **Church of S. Caterina** which is always locked. To get the key you must apply at the Civic Museum, a kilometre away! For an excellent guide to all the sights and works of art in Treviso, as well as hotels and restaurants, ask for the *Carnet del Turista* at the **EPT** information office in the Via Toniolo.

How to get there: As with Padua there are coach connections with the Piazzale Roma but the most convenient and economical way to get there is by rail. Trains run from Venice about every half hour and take 30 minutes.

Where to stay: There is a useful number of hotels to choose from if you think it worthwhile staying here: consult the hotel lists available from the EPT (Palazzo Scotti, Via Toniolo 41, 31100 Treviso. (Tel. (0422 547632) Possibly the best value among the hotels is the **Becchiere** (2-star), Piazza Ancillotto. Tel. (0422) 540871).

Where to eat: Treviso is more renowned for good food than Venice. One restaurant with an excellent reputation, as well as a Michelin rosette, is the **Alfredo — Ei Toulà**, Via Collalto 26. You are likely to pay heavily for the privilege of eating here, but not as much as a similar meal would cost in Venice. For good food at much more reasonable prices, try the **Becchiere** (as above). A full list of restaurants is again available from the EPT.

Language

English is widely spoken in Venice by all those in regular contact with tourists — hotel, restaurant, shop and information office staff. You might have trouble off the beaten track and with ordinary Venetians but otherwise the non-linguist should have few difficulties. It is, however, not only useful but simple politeness towards your hosts to know something of their language, and a simple course in Basic Italian such as those produced by the BBC is recommended. Unlike the British the Italians do not behave as though a foreigner speaking their language is hilariously funny. An Italian will suffer your attempts with great courtesy and will probably compliment you on your ability, even if you only manage three words. Do not feel too shy to make the effort.

What follows is not a long list of 'useful phrases' because the chances are you would not understand the reply even if you managed to ask the question. I merely list some of the basic words you need to exchange the courtesies of life and some of the words you are likely to need to understand street signs or the information found on notices. Many of the terms you will need in ordering food or drink will be found in Chapter Five.

Greetings and everyday words:
Good morning: **Buon giorno**. Good afternoon/evening: **Buona sera**.
Good night: **Buono notte**.
(Note that the greeting **ciao** is only used between friends and should not be used with strangers.)
Yes: **si**. No: **no**.
Thank you: **Grazie**. Note that the Italians do not often use the word 'please'. It is either indicated by tone of voice or by making a request conditional, as in **Vorrei . . .** — 'I should like . . .' If you wish to be extra polite, two terms you can use for 'Please' are **Per favore** or **Per piacere**.
You're welcome/Don't mention it: **Prego**.
Sorry/excuse me: **Mi scusi**.
Do you speak English? **Parla inglese?**
I'm sorry, I don't speak Italian: **Mi scusi ma non parlo italiano**.
I do not understand: **Non capisco**.

Sir: **Signore**. Madam: **Signora**. Miss: **Signorina**.
Where is . . .? **Dov'è . . .?** How much? **Quanto?** How much
does it cost? **Quanto costa?**
If you want something in a shop or bar you can point at it and
say, **Uno di questi** . . . One of these, or **Uno di quelli** . . . One
of those. The grammar will probably be wrong but the assistant
will know what you mean.

If you want to ask if something is allowed; such as sitting at
someone else's table, or you want to get past someone. Smile
and ask, **Permesso?**

Signs and notices:

Aperto — open. **Chiuso** — closed. **Libero** — free. **Occupato** —
occupied/engaged.
Ascensore — lift. **Parcheggio** — parking.
Destra — right. **Sinistra** — left.
Divieto — forbidden, prohibited, as in **Divieto di sosta** — no
waiting.
**Domenica, Lunedi, Martedi, Mercoledi, Giovedi, Venerdi,
Samedi** — days of the week.
Entrata or **Ingresso** — entrance. **Uscita** — exit.
Orario — Timetable or hours of opening. **Feriale** — daily.
Festive — public holidays.
Oggi — today. **Domani** — tomorrow. **Stasera** — this evening.
Senso unico — one way.
Solda/solde — sale/sales. **Sconto** — discount.
Suonare — ring for attention. **Spingere** — push. **Tirare** — pull.
Traghetto — ferry.
Vietato — forbidden, prohibited, as in **Vietato fumare** — no
smoking.

Abbreviations and acronyms:

ACI — Automobile Club.
Actv — Venice public transport system.
APT — Tourist information office (municipal): **EPT** —
Information office (provincial).
DOC — Guarantee of origin of wine, like French *appellation
contrôlée*.
FS — State Railways.
IVA — V.A.T.
PT — Post Office (Post and telecommunications).
RAI — State Radio and TV.
SIP — State telephone service.

SS — When followed by number — State Highway. When followed by names — Saints.
TCI — Touring Club.

Pronouncing Italian:

All letters are pronounced in Italian, even in double vowels. Most consonants are straightforward but note that before **e** or **i** the letter **C** is soft and pronounced *ch*, the letter **G** is pronounced *j* and the letters **SC** are pronounced *sh*. In double **c** or **g** before **e** or **i** the first letter is hard and the second soft, as in *kch* or *gj*. The combination **gn** is pronounced rather like *ny*, **gl** like *ly*.

In Italian the stress is normally on the penultimate syllable as in 'occu*pa*to' or 'do*ma*ni' but there are many exceptions to this. Where the stress is on the last syllable it is normal to put an accent over the letter e.g. città, Moisè. However, many placenames put the emphasis on the first syllable without indicating this with an accent e.g. *Pad*ova, *Mod*ena. An example where mistakes are often made is in Veneto which is not V*en*eto but *Ven*eto.

Some other words appear to follow no rules, usually when they are adopted from another language. The example of this that gives most trouble in Venice is *Accademia* which some people insist on pronouncing as though it were spelt in English 'AcadeMEya', where it is in fact pronounced as though it were spelt 'AcaDAMEya'.

Venetian Dialect

The Venetian dialect is, to all intents and purposes, another language. Mostly the visitor will not meet it in everyday conversation but it can cause confusion on two levels. Firstly the question of names which can appear in either their Italian or Venetian version on street signs, it can be confusing to see signs saying *San Zulian* when you are looking for *San Giuliano*. And secondly the specifically Venetian terms for streets, canals and other places in the city: what is the difference between a *ramo* and a *ruga*? And what are they anyway?

Names:

Venetian family names sound most un-Italian because it is the practice to drop the final vowel. If you come across an Italian name ending in -**ton** or -**son**, as, for example, in **Benetton**, you can assume that the family comes from the Veneto. To complicate matters, some families use both the Italian and Venetian forms of their names as with **Corner/Cornaro** or **Dolfin/Delfino**. As far as Christian names are concerned, particularly when used as the names of churches, the use of contractions often leave the Venetian word very different to the Italian. This is most noticeable where two saints names are merged into one, as in **San Zanipolo**. One rule that helps you understand the meaning of some of these Venetian names is that the soft 'c' or 'g' is replaced in Venetian by 'z'.

Alvise — Luigi (Louis)	**Polo** — Paolo
Anzolo — Angelo	**Salvador** — Salvatore
Bortolomio — Bartolomeo	**Stae** — Eustachio
Domenego — Domenico	**Zan** or **Zani** — Giovanni [Gianni]
Isepo — Giuseppe	**Zorzi** — Giorgio
Piero — Pietro	**Zulian** — Giuliano

Topographical Terms

Ca' — short for *Casa* or House. Used in the same sense as 'Chatsworth House', in other words the house of a noble family. Later replaced by the word *palazzo*.

Calle — street. **Calle Larga** — wide street.

Campo — square. **Campiello** — small square.

Corte, Cortile — courtyard.

Darsena — dock, body of water in the Arsenal.

Fondaco (Fontego in dialect) — warehouse belonging to foreign merchants.

Fondamenta — pavement alongside canal. **Riva** — a wide *fondamenta*.

Merceria (Marzaria in dialect) — shopping street.

Piscina — pool that has been filled in to become *calle* or *campiello*.

Ramo — side street **Ruga** — shopping street.

Rio — canal **Rio Terra (Terà** in dialect) — canal filled in to form street.

Sacca — body of water into which canals empty.

Salizzada (Salizada in dialect) — usually followed by name of saint because it is the main thoroughfare of a parish.

Sottoportico (Sotoportego in dialect) — alley running beneath building, either as tunnel or arcade.

Squero — boat-building yard (especially gondolas).

Leading Figures in the Art and Architecture of Venice

Bellini, Gentile (1429–1507). Specialist in narrative painting. His two best-known were contributions for the *Relic of the Cross*, now in the Accademia.

Bellini, Giovanni (1430–1516). Younger brother of Gentile. Best known for his *Madonnas* for a variety of churches, most of which are now in the Accademia.

Bon, Bartolomeo (1422–1464) Sculptor and architect. One of a number of brothers who were active in the city. Work on the Ca' d'Oro and the Porta della Carta accredited to him.

Bon, Bartolomeo the Younger (active 1504–1529) Architect. Suffers from coming between two giants in Coducci and Sansovino. He completed the Procuratie Vecchie and began the Scuola di San Rocco. He also topped out the Campanile above the bell-chamber.

Canaletto (Antonio Canal) (1697–1768). Greatest of the *vedutisti* he developed the current fashion for painting views of Venice as background to great events, mixed it with the Dutch school of townscape painting and created the most detailed pictures of 18th-century Venice. His career coincided with the popularity of the Grand Tour among the sons of the British aristocracy. That, combined with the patronage of Joseph Smith, led to almost all his output being sold abroad. His diploma piece is in the Accademia and two of his views in the Ca' Rezzonico, but that is all that remains in Venice.

Canova, Antonio (1757–1822). The last great sculptor produced by Venice. A few examples of his early work are in the Correr Museum but his major output came while working in Paris or Rome. The tomb he designed for Titian in the Frari serves as his own tomb.

Carpaccio, Vittore (1465–1525). One of the great Venetian painters, he specialised in the narrative cycle of paintings, notable for their detail, narrative strength and insight into the dress, architecture and customs of Venetian life. In the Accademia is his cycle of the *Life of St Ursula* and his contribution to the *Relic of the Cross* sequence, while his *SS. George, Tryphone and Jerome* are in the Scuola di S. Giorgio degli Schiavoni.

Coducci, Mauro [can also be spelt **Codussi**] (active 1469–1504). A giant figure in the architecture of Venice, his first work, the church of S. Michele in Isola, is regarded as the first Renaissance church in the city, and his Palazzo Vendramin as the finest early Renaissance domestic building. His principal monument is however the north side of the Piazza, with the Torre dell' Orologio and the Procuratie Vecchie.

Gambello, Antonio (active 1460–1481). A strangely transitional architect. His classical triumphal arch entrance for the Arsenal in 1460 is acknowledged to be the first Renaissance structure in Venice, while his plan for S. Zaccaria is pure Gothic, although very much closer to the Gothic of Northern Europe than that of Italy or Venice.

Giorgione (Giorgio da Castelfranco) (1475–1510). The most enigmatic of Venetian painters, an enigma aided by the small number of accredited works (6) that still exist and his early death. His famous and mysterious painting, *La Tempesta,* is the most prized possession of the Accademia.

Guardi, Francesco (1712–1793). The most famous of the *vedutisti* after Canaletto, his is a much freer and less literal technique. He is more attracted to the water and the Lagoon than to the buildings and a scene frequently reproduced is S. Giorgio Maggiore across the Basin of St Mark's. Like Canaletto, most of his work is to be found abroad.

Leopardi, Alessandro de' (1482–1523) Responsible for casting the Colleoni Monument after the death of Verrocchio had left it unfinished. He also designed the base of the monument and the bronze bases to the flag-poles in the Piazza.

Lombardo Family. The family name was Solari but Pietro moved to Venice from Lombardy in 1467 and took the name of his place of origin. Together with his sons Tullio and Antonio, he set up a workshop of sculpture and stonemasonry that imposed the Lombardesque style on early Renaissance architecture in the city. One of the finest examples of their work is the Palazzo Dario.

Longhena, Baldassare (active 1624–1682). Longhena was to the 17th century what Coducci had been to the late 15th and Sansovino to the 16th. Like the other two he was *Proto* (chief architect) and is largely responsible for introducing the baroque into Venice, although his brand of baroque is fairly restrained. His main work is, without doubt, Santa Maria della Salute but his secular buildings are also notable, particularly the

Procuratie Nuove, Ca' Pesaro and Ca' Rezzonico.

Palladio (Andrea di Pietro della Gondola) (1508–1580). A native of Padua, Palladio moved to Vicenza in 1532 and made his name designing villas for the local families. The leading Italian architect of the 16th century, he did precious little in Venice itself, despite submitting designs for a new Doge's Palace and the Rialto Bridge. His *Four Books of Architecture,* published in Venice in 1571, were translated into English in the early 18th century and influenced European architecture for the rest of that century.

Ponte, Antonio da (active 1570–1600). Winner of the competition to build the Rialto Bridge in 1588. He also designed the Arsenal Ropeworks, part of the Doge's Palace after the 1577 fire and the Prisons. His nephew Antonio Contino designed the Bridge of Sighs.

Rizzo, Antonio (active 1467–1499). Chiefly known for his rebuilding of the eastern side of the Doge's Palace after a fire of 1483, including the Scala d'Oro and the Scala dei Giganti.

Sanmichele, Michele (also spelt **Sanmicheli**). The only one of Sansovino's contemporaries to make a mark on Venice, although he was primarily a military architect whose main work was the Fortezza di Sant'Angelo which guards the Lido entrance to the Lagoon.

Sansovino (Jacopo Tatti) (1486–1570). A Florentine sculptor and architect who had learnt the techniques of the High Renaissance in Tuscany and Rome. Forced to leave Rome after the Sack of 1527, he, like many other Roman refugees, took refuge in Venice bringing the ideas of the Renaissance. He was appointed Proto on the death of Bartolomeo Bon the Younger in 1529 and from then on dominated the architectural scene in Venice. His work on the Zecca, Libreria Marciana, Loggetta, the completion of the Procuratie Vecchie and the original plan for the Procuratie Nuove show how this one man transformed the area of the Piazza and Piazzetta.

Tiepolo, Giovanni Battista (1696–1770). Inspired by Titian, Tintoretto and others of the 16th century to create a second 'Golden Age' in Venice. Noted for his altarpieces and frescoed ceilings, his masterpiece is the ceiling of the ballroom in the Palazzo Labia.

Tintoretto (Jacopo Robusti) (1518–1594). One of a trio of great Venetian painters in the 16th century, together with Titian and Veronese, he was the most Venetian of the three, only once leaving the city in his whole life and that for just a day. Also unlike the other two, the majority of his work is in Venice. Much of his best work is in his own parish church of Madonna dell'Orto where he is buried but his master-work is undoubtedly the Scuola di San Rocco.

Titian (Tiziano Vecellio) (c.1488–1576). No one knows exactly when Titian was born, only that he was about 90 when the plague killed him in 1576. He was certainly the greatest artist of the mid-16th century and was probably as influential in the development of art as his contemporary Palladio was in architecture. He combined colour with energy and a classical inspiration, together with a strong personal vision. His works are to be found all over the world but his greatest work in Venice is probably *The Assumption* altarpiece in the Frari, where he is buried.

Veneziano, Paolo (Paul the Venetian) (c.1290–c.1360) The first Venetian painter of any note he is still very much within the Byzantine iconographic tradition of flat images against a plain or gilded ground, but his work nevertheless shows signs of Gothic influence so that his style can be called Veneto-Byzantine rather than pure Byzantine. His greatest work surviving in Venice is a polyptych in the Accademia.

Veronese (Paolo Calieri) (1528–1588). Born in Verona as his nickname suggests he moved to Venice in his early twenties. His speciality is the use of colour and dramatically posed figures against a background of Palladian classical architecture. There is a great amount of Veronese's work in Venice but much of the best was looted by the French or bought cheaply by the Austrians during their occupations.

Vittoria, Alessandro (1535–1608). A pupil of Sansovino Vittoria became the leading sculptor in the latter years of the century and made a speciality of moulded stucco such as that on the Scala d'Oro and the stairs of the Libreria Marciana. His main effort as architect was the Palazzo Balbi with its proto-Baroque facade.

INDEX

272 Index